THE ART OF
EVERYDAY
ECSTASY

ALSO BY MARGOT ANAND

THE ART OF SEXUAL ECSTASY:
THE PATH OF SACRED SEXUALITY
FOR WESTERN LOVERS

THE ART OF SEXUAL MAGIC:
CULTIVATING SEXUAL ENERGY TO
TRANSFORM YOUR LIFE

You may all have diff. ideas about this program — it's about being sucessful in your vision. It's not just about making goals + ckng them off — I want to take you to kind of a sub-structure that leads you to your goals that leads to your success

your success
Set realistic action
Goal setting + plan to
Decision clarity
Choices
? Thoughts feelings attitude vision dreams

THE ART OF
EVERYDAY
ECSTASY

THE SEVEN TANTRIC KEYS
FOR BRINGING PASSION, SPIRIT,
AND JOY INTO EVERY PART
OF YOUR LIFE

MARGOT ANAND

BROADWAY BOOKS ❧ NEW YORK

"Tantric keys to ecstasy" to include — not in catalog

BROADWAY

THE ART OF EVERYDAY ECSTASY. Copyright © 1998 by Margot Anand. All rights reserved. Printed in the United States of America. No part of this book may be reproduced or transmitted in any form or by any means, electronic or mechanical, including photocopying, recording, or by any information storage and retrieval system, without written permission from the publisher. For information, address Broadway Books, a division of Bantam Doubleday Dell Publishing Group, Inc., 1540 Broadway, New York, NY 10036.

Broadway Books titles may be purchased for business or promotional use or for special sales. For information, please write to: Special Markets Department, Bantam Doubleday Dell Publishing Group, Inc., 1540 Broadway, New York, NY 10036.

BROADWAY BOOKS and its logo, a letter B bisected on the diagonal, are trademarks of Broadway Books, a division of Bantam Doubleday Dell Publishing Group, Inc.

Library of Congress Cataloging-in-Publication Data
Anand, Margot.
    The art of everyday ecstasy: the seven tantric keys for bringing passion, spirit, and joy into every part of your life / Margot Anand.—1st ed.
        p.   cm.
    Includes bibliographical references and index.
    ISBN 0-7679-0164-9 (hardcover)
    1. Ecstasy.   2. Sex—Religious aspects—Tantrism.   I. Title.
BL626.A53   1998
294.5'514—dc21   98-4872
                                                                      CIP

FIRST EDITION

Designed by Laurie Jewell

98 99 00 01 02 10 9 8 7 6 5 4 3 2 1

To Osho my gratitude
for showing us so
profoundly that

Life is wild
Love is wild
God is absolutely wild

To Vinit my beloved wildman
who takes me there

To all those who dare to
walk the path of ecstasy

Class Intro:

- want us all to "wake up"
- many opportunities
- I will challenge, & share &
  learn much more from you
- interactive
- fast-paced & will take plenty of time also
  - will take the space to
    deal w/ whatever comes up
- experiential

- on the spot coaching
- give specific "how to's"
- stretch your creativity & share since my own
- unique ideas for furthering your
  creative & traditional knowledge

- about creativity; it's like a muscle
  that needs to be exercised continually –
  you don't walk in, exercise on
  use your math skills... you get
  rusty in that dept... so let's use
  some Brillo n SOS pads or
  even some DW40 on the
  stuck n squeaky
  mental joints

- learn how to
  cultivate some stellar
  re-ignite some forgotten ones

bring SOS pads? notes?
WD40 Hose? clean "dumb" part tape?
rather these our whittle?
which foods are edible? first?

Intro: What holds you back?

Contents

ACKNOWLEDGMENTS

I am grateful to all the people who have contributed in a myriad of ways to a deeper understanding and integration of the ecstatic experience in daily life.

On the spiritual level, my gratitude goes to Osho, the Great Master of Crazy Wisdom, with whom I trained in India (the rituals and meditations for the Throat *Chakra* and the Empty Sky Meditation are inspired by his book *Meditations: The First and Last Freedom*); Ma Prem Kaveesha, Founder and Director of Osho Academy, for her heartfelt friendship, inspiration, and wise counsel; Lynda Guber for her joyful spirit, her encouraging friendship, and her courageous choice to follow the path of the ecstatic heart; Shaykh Sidi Muhammad, leader of the Sufi Council of Jerusalem, for his initiation into a new vision of Sufism as the Sacred Marriage between Allah and Laila; Master Adi Da Samraj for his powerful inspiration into Tantric devotional practice and artistic accomplishments; Dr. Gary Burstein for his masterful guidance in the ways in which modern psychology, psychoanalysis, Tibetan Buddhism, and Dzogchen can complete one another as skillful means on the path to awakening; Paul Lowe for his unwavering dedication to a new vision of awakening; and Jon Marc Hammer for his masterful expression of Jeshua, the spirit of Christ. I have been most challenged and enriched by my collaboration with Dr. Deepak Chopra, at the Chopra Center for Well Being.

All my gratitude to those without whom this book could not have been complete: Lauren Marino at Broadway Books for her unwavering trust and encouragement; Doug Childers, writer and samurai of the pen, for his amazing editorial skills;

Naomi Lucks for her contribution to the architectural design of the book as well as her editorial skills; Sandra Dijkstra, my agent, who has been a great advisor and support to my career as a writer.

I also thank my many friends and colleagues who contributed their personal stories, life experiences, and insights for this book: Kosha Pati, longtime partner and international leader of the SkyDancing Tantra Training, Vinit Allen, my beloved ecstatic coach, Ariel and Ama Kalma, Ron and Sousan Heifetz, Robert Gass, Michael Harrison, Anne Chandler, Terumi and Leonard Leinow, Steve Sisgold, Paul Ramana Das and Marilena Silbey, Pennel Rock, Achintya Vasey, Aman Schroeter, Raz and Lisa Engrassi, Chuck Stormon, Shabda Khan, Harold Dull, Jill Eikenberry, Michael Tucker, Shea O'Neil, Leila Gass, Shana Stanberry, Don Campbell, Anne Chandler, creator of the Chakra Rock power chants, David Gershon, Duncan Campbell, Clarice and Dent Goodyear, and the Omega Institute.

As ever, all my thanks to my ecstatic tribes of SkyDancers around the world: Jocelyn Olivier, Kay Thompson, Nital Brinkley, Aman Schroeter, Achintya Vasey, Yatro Werner, Renee Koopmans, Robert and Liliane Baillod, John Hawken, Armin Heining, Joan Lakin, and Robert Marantz.

I am particularly grateful to the graduates of the SkyDancing Tantra Teachers Training of 1997 who gracefully contributed their personal stories, experiences, and responses to the practices given in this book.

Last but not least, all this work would not have been possible without the unwavering friendship, support, and availability of my two patient assistants, Sohini Genevieve and Agnes Liebhardt

— Margot Anand

WHAT IS ECSTASY? AN INVITATION

The *Art of EveryDay Ecstasy* is about waking up and finding that you are in love with life. As we stand on the threshold of a new millennium, more and more of us now long for healing, for conscious lives infused with Spirit. We long for our vocations to fulfill us spiritually as well as materially, for our homes to be filled with the grace of the sacred, for our love to be unconditional. We seek a life that is authentic, expanded, and joyful.

Bringing healing, balance, and joy to our daily life in a world that is in the grip of what I term "the anti-ecstatic conspiracy" isn't easy. This book is a calling to understand the nature of this conspiracy, its effect on our psyche and in our lives. It invites us to confront and transform the old anti-ecstatic model into a more wholesome and holistic partnership model. Above all, it offers a vision—magical, mystical, and practical—of what your life can be when you allow the spirit and sparkle of ecstasy to permeate your being.

(handwritten annotations:)

The WAKE UP LIST!

Top Ten "Wake-Ups"
- what that's do you
- which ones come up every day with/wd up.

- what loads stimulate you?
- what topics of convers
- when do you feel like you're in perfect harmony w/ life?
- what expands you?
- what makes you cry?
- what are you doing when you feel like you're in love w/ life?

- When you are "lost" in something for a long time & the hrs. have flown by, what are you effortlessly doing?

(left margin, vertical:) "myonjeful" dream statements; tweak (and participants to help... next week again. a few samples of "wake-ups" from us... way to/use about (succeed people notes) (they belief) Def: succeed clarify use good, leeateoupenyy

(bottom handwritten:) Add these to your vision — synthesize... patterns next week I would like @ to clearly state their ideal, very good dream — in less than one minute; myonjeful.

#3 - taking good care
Scon it my Sabble day - strictly for family;
caught up w/ sons & grandsons & watching of kids,
unless
something very special only happen that Sunday

SEVEN TANTRIC KEYS OF AWAKENING

The practices and rituals you will find here are doorways that
reveal the inherent beauty and meaning of our ordinary moments.

- Say yes to life in all its erotic passion.
- Go with the flow of the life force within and all
  around you.
- Trust yourself, and allow your personal power to
  manifest in life.
- Open your heart in loving compassion to the self
  and others.
- Authentically express your creativity and your
  truth.
- Look within to achieve clarity and insight in your
  life.
- Surrender to your Source and know gratitude, spiritual peace, and a new capacity to live at your maximum
  potential in every moment.

These seven Tantric keys can open us up to our essential selves
and unleash in us that abundant, joyous energy—EveryDay Ecstasy—that allows us to be all that we can be as human beings
with our partners and our children and in our work, our community, and the world. In the process, we discover the meaning
of *elegance,* the art of achieving maximum results with minimum
effort. Elegant people are in love with life. And their love calls
them to make contributions beyond the call of mere duty, to
participate fully, to share their joys, pains, gifts, and truths with
others. And, by their example, they remind us that beyond our
apparent differences, we are connected in Spirit, We are One.

My own spiritual journey, which led me to the path of
EveryDay Ecstasy, began in Paris, when I was eighteen years
old. I was wildly in love with my boyfriend; and the first time
we made love, at the peak of orgasm, my consciousness expanded until, suddenly, unexpectedly, nothing was left but the
absolute certainty that I was utterly and totally free and that this

absolute freedom was, for me, the secret of life. This realization set the course of my life.

This may seem like an unusual beginning to many people. Yet most of us have enjoyed one unforgettable peak moment that leaves us with a yearning for that sense of ecstasy, wholeness, or exquisite peace. Unfortunately, our culture does not teach us the value of such experiences or the skills to cultivate them. But after this first ecstatic moment, I knew I wanted to discover how to integrate spirituality with sexuality in my daily life.

My studies and degrees in psychology and philosophy at the Sorbonne in Paris did not bring any answers to my quest. Later, my practice as a therapist failed to satisfy my hunger for experiential wisdom. I turned to the study of bodywork therapies and self-development groups: bioenergetics, encounter groups, rolfing, Gestalt, Arica, integral yoga. And still I found no direct answers that explained the connection between sexuality and spirituality. I set out on a journey to explore the traditions of sacred sexuality around the world. I soon was introduced to the ancient Eastern science of Tantra; like yoga, Zen, and Sufism, Tantra is a spiritual path to enlightenment. But unlike most mystical paths, Tantra includes sexuality as a doorway to ecstasy and enlightenment. The essence of the Tantric teachings can be summarized as this: Choose with awareness what gives you joy, ✧ you and it will lead you to Spirit. A particularly attractive approach, will I thought, for us Westerners so deeply influenced by the puri- create tanical Judeo-Christian tradition, which conceives of pleasure your not as a door to heaven but rather as a shortcut to hell! own

Although this book is not about sexuality, as my other success books have been, the Tantric perspective has greatly influenced my work.

WHAT IS TANTRA?

Many people today mistakenly believe that Tantra is a spiritual bastardization of sexual therapy, an excuse to indulge in sensual games, an addiction to hours of sexual orgasms. Nothing could be farther from the truth. The Tantric path teaches us to embrace and unify the ordinary, the erotic, and the sacred dimensions of life, which all have their roots in Spirit.

The beauty and wisdom of Tantra is that it embraces sexuality as a doorway to the "ecstatic mind of great bliss." Truly, at the peak of orgasm, we pierce through the illusion of fragmentation and separation, and glimpse the unity and interconnectedness of all beings. And through the other—our partner—we fall in love with life.

Because sex holds this great potential for opening our being to the experience of ecstasy, Tantra has for millennia taught the cultivation of sexual love as an art, as a skillful spiritual practice. Then, as now, Tantra challenges the belief promoted by most spiritual and religious paths that we must suppress or transcend our sexuality to practice meditation or awaken our Spirit. Tantra arose in rebellion against these ascetical and life-negating creeds. It acknowledges that sex is at the root of life and that to make human sexuality and erotic union a form of worship and meditation is to practice reverence for life, leading us directly through the pleasure of the senses to spiritual liberation.

Tantra teaches that we master desires not by avoiding them but by immersing ourself in them. Once known and experienced deeply, they can be transcended. In fact, Tantra teaches that *nothing* is to be excluded from our understanding of reality. We need not suffer by sacrificing pleasures. We can cultivate them as opportunities for awakening. Tantra teaches us to embrace every moment in our totality, to respond bodily, feel from the heart, perceive with clarity, and be fully present to others and to life. In this book, we will explore ways to bring such energy, passion, and awareness to all our seemingly ordinary, and extraordinary, moments and to make our everyday life a journey of awakening.

Tantra is a Sanskrit word derived from the root *tan,* "to expand." In the process of my study and practice of the Tantric arts, I developed this definition: Tantra is the art of weaving the often contradictory aspects of our self or personality into a unified whole, for the purpose of expanding our consciousness. Scholar Ajit Mookerjee defines Tantra as "knowledge of a systematic, scientific, and experimental method which offers the possibility of expanding man's consciousness and faculties, a process through which the individual's inherent spiritual powers can be realized."

WHAT IS ECSTASY? AN INVITATION

Tantra originated more than three thousand years ago in India from several sources. One of the original sources of Tantra is the ancient Shivaite Hindu tradition of Shakta worship, the worship of the Great Mother. Tantra, still alive in India today, has preserved the wonderful myth of Shiva and Shakti, whose loving union created the universe.

THE STORY OF SHIVA AND SHAKTI

Thousands of years ago, there dwelled a great god in the jungles of India. An ascetic and a yogi, he lived in distant hermitages, reposing in yogic postures for hours on end. Immobile, his consciousness removed from the world, uninterested in human affairs, he had transcended all passions and worldliness and dwelled in unending meditation on the divine void, contemplating the reality of his true nature: That which is never born and never dies.

Like the wild ascetics of the remote Indian jungles, he cared not about his looks or about ordinary human conventions. His hair was uncombed and wild, his body was naked but for a scant animal skin wrapped around his loins. His skin was of a bluish gray hue, for it was covered with the sacrificial ashes he used during his sacred practices. Silent, eternal, he was the Lord who dwelled beyond time and beyond death, in the eternal now.

Sometimes as this renunciate sat in meditation under his favorite tree, he would get an erection and feel the throbbing power of his *vajra;* yet he was not concerned. As his consciousness expanded and traveled to merge with the vastness of the whole universe, he simply observed the workings of his human form; and his precious *vajra* arose to meditate with him as the ultimate manifestation of virility: a contained yet all-encompassing male power at rest in its potency.

Through his advanced yogic practices, he became the ruler of all the worlds, the strongest of all the gods. And his elusive presence was felt and honored by all as the symbol of transcendence and detachment. His very name was revered: Shiva, Lord of Transcendence.

Meanwhile, the great Goddess Devi, Mother of Creation, decided the time had come to bring the powers of this great god-man back from the vast expanses of the universe to the earth to test his strength and to reveal to him advanced teachings he had never even imagined. It was time for Shiva to transcend his own detachment and bring his Spirit back into his body, to be immersed in the world through his body and his senses, and to draw his Spirit more deeply into the here and now.

The Great Goddess manifested in the form of an exquisite beauty whose name was Sati. She was radiant and joyful, her body exquisitely shaped. Her dark hair was long and shiny, and her eyes large, like those of a deer.

One day, as he wandered through a village, Shiva saw Sati, and his heart was touched beyond control. All his yogic powers were of no avail. In one sweeping moment, his heart became the ruler of his soul . . . not to mention the ruler of his *vajra!* Shiva's consciousness merged with his heart, and his body suddenly longed for human contact and presence. This was exactly what the great goddess Devi had intended.

Eventually, Sati and Shiva fell in love, and married. They lived in blissful union for many years in a hermitage on the sacred Mount Kailash. Countless adventures followed. And at last Sati died. Shiva was inconsolable. He wandered about the land, mad with sorrow, for he had loved Sati as he loved himself, as an inseparable aspect of his own divine nature. But he needed this very human sorrow, for through it he tasted the humble descent of the lover into the dark night of the soul. And he knew that love and union could no longer be separate from meditation and contemplation.

The other gods, seeing his misery, decided to help. Sati was reborn, reincarnated in the person of an even more exquisite young woman, Parvati, later known and honored throughout India as Shakti. As soon as they met, they were reunited as husband and wife.

Shakti was a great yogini, devoted to Shiva, yet matching his powers in her own feminine way. She was the embodiment of pure energy, the mother and matrix of all manifestation. The source of her great power resided in her *yoni:* her sacred garden, her sex, the matrix of creation. Shakti's name comes from the Hindu root *shak,* meaning "ability" or "power." Shakti represents the power that weaves the universe and manifests in all forms, the *prima mater,* the first mother. But until Shiva and Shakti met, their respective qualities had remained barren, devoid of dynamic creativity. Each was waiting for the missing energy that would awaken his or her enlightened completion and allow them both to realize their ultimate mission: to become the creators, the father and mother of the world.

As they perfected their yogic practices, Shakti accepted Shiva as her guru, her teacher; and he taught her the ways of transcendence to guide her to her ultimate liberation. And Shiva accepted Shakti as his guru; and she initiated him into his ultimate liberation through the fusion of the transcendental, or pure consciousness and Spirit, with the immanence of manifestation in and through the body and the senses. They became spiritual partners, co-creators of their ecstasy. And Shakti taught Shiva to temporarily relinquish asceticism to integrate the art of love and sexual union into his spiritual practice. Thus from the path of yoga was born the path of Tantra, the yoga of love.

Shiva and Shakti, in their blissful practices, discovered new ways to channel their orgasmic powers through spinning vortexes of their energy centers, or *chakras,* and developed the great path of Tantra. This science encompassed the knowledge and skills of music, astrology, massage, painting, dance, poetry, visualization, ecstatic ritual, meditation, and teachings for the "householders" (lay practitioners). These teachings were imparted through numerous scriptures called Tantras. They were presented, in their original form, as a dialogue and a teaching shared between Shiva and Shakti, and the Tantric scriptures note that each man and each woman carries within himself or herself the power of Shiva and Shakti. If we know how to honor and worship each other skillfully, we can re-enact, in the moment of our union, the primordial and blissful union of the God and Goddess; and through that union give birth to enlightened realization.

MY TRAVELS CONTINUE

I traveled throughout Asia, India, Europe, and America studying the traditions and teachings of sacred sexuality. On the way, I met extraordinary men and women, including a variety of Tantric adepts, spiritual masters and mistresses, from whom I received personal guidance. I also worked with cutting-edge researchers in transpersonal psychology, humanistic psychology, sexology, and other interrelated fields. These teachings removed veils from my psyche—veils made of fixed beliefs, fears, the longing for security, and the many attachments that prevent the seeker from being authentic and free.

Many of my spiritual guides—among them the great mystic Osho—belonged to the "crazy wisdom" tradition of shocking the disciple into awakening through wild and unpredictable actions. In their company, life too became wild and unpredictable, a passionate adventure full of surprises, revelations, mysteries, initiations, and ecstasy but also difficult confrontations, seemingly insurmountable challenges, risky journeys, difficult missions, and blind alleys. Yet the common thread was always this: *Go back home to your daily life and find ways to integrate what you discovered.*

HOW I DEVELOPED SKYDANCING TANTRA

Gradually, all that I had discovered coalesced within me into a new shape and meaning. I called the body of knowledge and the ritual practices I had developed over many years "SkyDancing Tantra: The Path to Bliss." This path came to me as a revelation rather than as a tradition; yet, the path of the SkyDancer is indeed one that goes back to eighth-century Tibet, when Yeshe Sogyel, the consort of Buddha Padma Sambhava, was called the SkyDancer. Together they developed Tantric Buddhism.

Originally, the SkyDancers were wild, free ecstatic "dakinis," also called feminine buddhas or female awakeners. The word *dakini* means "woman who dances in space" or "woman who revels in the freedom of emptiness." SkyDancers were, and are, women of passion who were profoundly devoted to spiritual awakening. The path of the SkyDancer is a path of spiritual partnership that teaches the complete reciprocity of male and female practitioners as they learn the art of integrating ecstatic states and ecstatic practices in their daily life. It reintroduces in our world the understanding that to heal the world, we need to rediscover and respect the fact that women can be and are awakeners and initiators and enlightened teachers.

SkyDancing Tantra is a unique path that weaves together my studies in humanistic and transpersonal psychology, bodywork

WHAT IS ECSTASY? AN INVITATION

therapies, sexology, yoga, music, and metaphysics with my work with human energy systems through the use of light, music, movement, visualization, and particularly (and primarily) the energy map of the *chakras*. The Tantric *chakra* system offers a perfect map for the transformation of energy and consciousness from raw sexual lust to love, to visionary power, and to awakening.

SkyDancing Tantra: The Path to Bliss, teaches us that when we learn to approach life with a relaxed body, an open heart, a peaceful mind, we can access ecstatic states and learn to weave them into the daily fabric of our lives.

SEXUALITY AS A METAPHOR FOR LIFE

I have had the good fortune to work as a guide on the Sky-Dancing path with thousands of men and women around the world—the youngest was twelve and the oldest, seventy-four. Mostly, we worked together, building an ecstatic community in the context of the Love and Ecstasy Trainings taught worldwide through the agency of the SkyDancing Institutes. Over the years, we have discovered that all people—regardless of creed, sex, race, religion, and age—have an amazing propensity for ecstasy. We all receive great joy and healing in our lives when we access ecstatic states.

In this book you will have the opportunity to discover many methods, rituals, dances, and meditations that people of all ages—from teenagers to the elderly—have practiced successfully to move beyond pain and doubt to the expression of their highest potential. In my experience as a teacher, everyone who learns these rituals can feel the deeply healing nature of ecstasy. I have seen ecstatic experiences remedy acute cases of low self-esteem, anorexia, stress disorders, eating disorders, addictions, ailing marriages, timidity, drug dependency, and depression. I have witnessed countless relationships between estranged spouses blossom again into new love affairs with open, heart-to-heart communication; new joy and creativity in life; renewed sexual intimacy; and the discovery of an underlying spiritual connection that is joyful, creative, and profoundly fulfilling.

Through the practices presented in this book, I have seen many people experience reduced work stress; increased creativity, abundance, and success; greater inspiration, self-trust, and power; enhanced leadership abilities; and expanded commitment to the service of others and the world.

This book emerged from the realization that the way we live our sexuality is a metaphor for the way we live our life. Originally, the Love and Ecstasy Training focused on sexual ecstasy, on developing the skills to become a great lover and expanding orgasmic potency all the way to ecstasy. But I soon realized that it is possible to bring the skills of a lover into every area of life.

My long journey around the world, which began with my awakening to Spirit through sexuality, led me to understand that the skills cultivated through Tantric sex—intimacy, opening the heart, visualizing, focusing, letting go of the mind, being fully present, loving self and others, moving beyond fears—were in fact the *essential skills of life*. I realized that life was not about having more and better orgasms, but about *being orgasmic in every moment*.

The Love and Ecstasy Training that inspired this book has been studied at several universities in Europe, where formal psychiatric, psychological, and medical research examined its effects. A statistical analysis conducted at the University of Munich studied a sample group of fifty participants for a year and a half; the group experienced "greater powers of concentration, a more direct and honest communication, an expansion of creative abilities, and the capacity to take initiatives." Since then, a special training for doctors and other helping professions has been designed and is now offered in Europe.

As a therapist, I knew that the process of healing emotional wounds by focusing on the past to find their source was limited. Although it can bring about healing, it all too often promotes a fascination with the problematic. Furthermore, when we focus obsessively on our problems and pains, the ecstatic potential in most of life's moments goes unrecognized and unacknowledged, and our lives are emptied of a sacred and joyous dimension. Life appears problematic rather than ecstatic, more a puzzle to be solved than a pleasure to be cultivated. I realized that existential or psychological pain was actually the *absence of ecstasy*. It was the outcome of being cut off from the source of one's being, the source of life. On the other hand, cultivating ecstatic states of consciousness and learning how to integrate them into our lives can have profoundly healing effects. I have come to believe that our sickness and suffering have their roots in the loss of ecstasy and that reclaiming our natural ecstasy holds the key to our healing and our liberation.

WE CAN BE ORGASMIC IN OUR DAILY LIFE

Being erotic means thoroughly enjoying our five senses. When our senses are awake, pleasure is available in everyday moments. The natural ecstasy of life's simple moments comes pouring in. You can be orgasmic by choosing to surround yourself with what you value as beautiful and sacred; by wearing clothes (or not wearing clothes!) that add to your beauty; by cooking and eating with erotic awareness; by allowing music to flow through your ears and vibrate in your entire body; by speaking and reading and writing words that are poetic, powerful, and inspiring to your soul; by singing your joy.

In this book I make a distinction between what I call Ecstatic Awakenings and EveryDay Ecstasy, or the Ecstasy of Flow. Ecstatic Awakenings are transcendental occurrences that come now and then but are not meant to become permanent in this world. If they did, we would be unable to function. They are moments of opening, spiritual fireworks, like a cork pulled out of a champagne bottle. They are dramatic divine encounters meant to remind us, often in moments of hopelessness or despair, that ecstasy is the essence of our nature and of existence itself. EveryDay Ecstasy is that steady stream of joyful aliveness that connects us to our Source, that can become our true and permanent state when we have fallen in love with life, embracing it like the lover it is.

A BOOK OF MANY VOICES

To write this book I met and spoke with hundreds of people who have discovered ways of weaving together the various strands of their creative, family, business, spiritual, and above all, ordinary lives in a way that is joyful and ecstatic. Among these were my current students, graduates of my trainings, psychologists, doctors, people I met in the streets, artists, writers, musicians, philosophers, teachers, celebrities, spiritual leaders, therapists.

The participants in my trainings practiced many of the meditations and rituals included in this book, and I recorded their experiences and feedback.

While writing this book, I also had the good fortune to meet many eminent spiritual teachers, with whom I discussed essential questions about ecstatic states, spiritual practices, enlightenment, love, and the state of the world. These teachers belong to many different traditions: Sufism, Islam, Christianity, Tantra, Buddhism, Judaism. Others belong to none, believe in none, and declare that ecstasy and enlightenment exist beyond and apart from all paths and methods. Many of the pearls of wisdom I received have also found their way into this book.

USE THIS BOOK AS YOUR TREASURE CHEST

Here is a summary of what this book will offer to you. First, the exercises and information in this book can help you achieve your full potential as a human being. You will explore the skills of love and learn how to apply them beyond the bedroom. You will learn to cultivate balance by harmonizing your "inner man" (your active, assertive masculine qualities) with your "inner woman" (your receptive nurturing, feminine qualities). You will explore and learn to create sacred space in your home and life. You will learn the elements of ritual and how you can weave these elements into your own creative expression to make special moments sacred. You will explore the anatomy of ecstasy using the maps of the seven *chakras* and learn how to release blocks, allowing you to access more energy and to create a blueprint for an ecstatic lifestyle that nurtures creativity, accomplishment, insight, love, healing, and empowerment. You will explore a different vision of spirituality, one based on reverence for male-female partnerships and the embracing of your sexuality as a door to higher states of consciousness.

By following the path of EveryDay Ecstasy outlined here, you may experience greater success and health in life, deeper and more meaningful relationships, fuller connections to your community and planet, and a more profound realization of your essential nature as a human being. This book is a vehicle for the ecstatic expression of life in the world.

A NOTE: In this book I have chosen to use the terms *yoni* for the female genitals, and *vajra* for the male genitals. *Yoni* is a Sanskrit word that means "cosmic matrix, womb of creation." In the Tibetan tradition, *vajra* means "thunderbolt, powerful scepter" and symbolizes pure energy and power that carries light. I use these reverent terms to avoid the typically uninspiring connotations that our common language attaches to these parts of our bodies. When partners honor each other in this way, joy and a sense of fun and pride emerge.

PART I

WAKING UP TO ECSTASY: BRINGING SPIRIT BACK INTO YOUR LIFE

[handwritten annotations across top of page:] intense contentment" complete happiness fulfillment lost in thought or a when you are specific action, you feel alive 24/7 you feel like you want to thought that ecstatic, what are you doing? describe how it the action felt.

CHAPTER ONE

BRINGING ECSTASY TO LIFE:
A GREAT ADVENTURE

Friend, hope for the Guest while you are alive.
Jump into experience while you are alive!

          ❧ Rumi

Have you ever, in moments of deep silence, heard the song of your soul? Can you recall a time when the beauty, the sweetness of life, welled up in you by surprise? One day, perhaps, you fell in love. Or for one blinding instant, lovemaking called you back to an ecstatic relationship with life. Perhaps it happened for you with the birth of a child. Suddenly you were filled with an over-whelming, all-encompassing love such as you had never experi-enced. Perhaps you glimpsed ecstasy in the spaciousness of meditation; during a five-mile run; or while contemplating a clear mountain stream, listening to a symphony, walking in a thunderstorm, or dancing and singing through the night. Per-haps you were propelled beyond your mind and body into a transcendent moment when life, which had seemed ordinary, became suddenly mysterious, poignant, and filled with grace, and time seemed to stop as you stepped into eternity.

Such luminous moments offer glimpses into the dimension of the sacred. They remind us of our true nature. They are a promise of the joy that can fill our life. They are insights into ecstasy. In these moments, we know it is possible to live life fully, to be creative and free of confinement.

WHAT IS ECSTASY?

During the 1950s, psychologist Abraham Maslow did years of research on what I call "ecstatic states" and that he called "peak experiences." His findings may surprise you: "Almost all people have or can have peak experiences." And psychologist Stella Resnick, in her book *The Pleasure Zone,* comments: "Peak experiences are intensely pleasurable times that can last for just a minute or for several weeks or more. They are periods of complete happiness and fulfillment . . ." Maslow found that certain individuals—people he called "self-actualized"—enjoyed a much higher frequency of peak experiences than did individuals in the general population: "They felt fulfilled in their lives, motivated not by need, but by the desire to grow."

We seek comfort, pleasure, and ecstasy from the moment we are born. Comfort is a natural state of well-being in the absence of pain. Pleasure comes from the gratification of our physical needs and emotional desires. Ecstasy is an experience of intense contentment, inner joy. It is, in most cases, a discontinuous state. It happens, it peaks, then it is gone. And we are left with the intuitive insight of an expanded potential for wholeness. At this juncture, we are drawn to the patient inner work that is needed to recognize and transform the behavior patterns that sabotage our ability to be joyful, contented, and self-actualized. As we become increasingly aware of this potential, we gradually discover ecstasy as an intense state of stabilized contentment that helps us choose what is pleasing to ourself and others. Such states are uniquely personal and hence difficult to define.

One dictionary defines *ecstasy* as "a state of exalted delight surpassing normal understanding" and "a state of emotion so intense that rational thought and self-control are obliterated." The word *ecstasy* comes from the Greek *ex stasis,* to "move beyond stasis," beyond the seemingly solid and fixed, into movement, or life. It is liberation from the known. Its Latin root *ex stare* means "to stand outside yourself," as in transcendence (which means "to climb, to go beyond"). Fundamentally, *ecstasy* means to transcend yourself, to go outside and beyond what you think, know, and believe is possible. An ecstatic state is a glimpse into the infinite.

We experience such states through music, love, religion, sex. Still, our ecstatic potential goes mostly unfulfilled. Most people are not educated (or trained) to value and recognize life's sacred dimension. And because they are often too busy to notice or value the simple joys of daily life, ecstasy eludes them. They do not recognize that *every moment is pregnant with ecstasy*. For ecstatic states are not separate or opposed to ordinary life. Ecstatic states happen spontaneously. They are as natural as sleeping and breathing. Ecstasy was programmed into us the moment the sperm met the egg in our mother's womb. It exists inside us right now as a potentiality. And it is possible to create joy within, to live a life cut like a precious jewel that reflects who we truly are, that radiates an energy that is healing and enchanting. And every step we take carries the possibility of such an awakening.

OUR ECSTATIC ANATOMY

Perhaps the most common experience of ecstasy is the feeling of joy, relief, and exhilaration that comes with the sudden release from a difficult situation, when a crisis is successfully resolved or averted.

Another common experience of ecstasy comes during love-making. With its moment of intense pleasure and blessed release, orgasm may seem the most reliable form of ecstasy available to us in our busy lives. But it is just a taste of what is possible: *Ecstasy transcends sex*. We can learn to cultivate the quality of a great lover in the way we live our daily life. Ecstatic moments can be cultivated on a daily basis when we enter into a love affair with life.

The natural rhythm of life is ours: heartbeats, pulsing blood, firing brain synapses, inhalation-exhalation, expansion-contraction. The human body is a rhythm orchestra, a vibrant totality singing and dancing to the beat of life. In their essence, life and creation are ecstatic activities.

Human beings are born to enjoy, love, and create beauty. And Ecstasy is a skill that we can learn. As we achieve mastery in living, we are able more and more to integrate and experience ecstatic moments in our daily lives.

Ecstasy is both our true nature and a state to be realized through self-mastery. Christian mystics call it Christ consciousness. Buddhists call it our Buddha nature. It is our essence, our eternal nature, untouched by all that is impermanent, changing, appearing, and vanishing. And whether we or others notice it or not, it is always shining through.

It is what I call the "Sky Mind," the awareness of our essential nature. It is not something we acquire or develop. It is that within us which was never born and will never die. And when the veils of our illusions, our beliefs, our confusion, and our wounds are lifted, our Sky Mind is revealed, like the blue sky itself when the clouds pass away.

THE BEST-KEPT SECRET OF OUR TIME

While researching this book, I realized—to my amazement— the best-kept secret of our time: Many of the most successful people today cultivate ecstatic states. They have learned how to make ecstasy a part of the fabric of their everyday lives. I believe that there is a direct link between their openness to exploring and incorporating unconventional insights and experiences in their lives and their original contributions to the world. And though they have their own ways of experiencing ecstasy, they must remain private, even undercover, to avoid the damaging label of *oddball* or *mystic,* which might diminish their credibility in the public eye.

Even spiritual leaders risk being discredited. Jean Houston, author and co-founder of the Foundation for Mind Research, and Marianne Williamson, popular author and spiritual teacher, were erroneously accused in the press of holding a seance in the White House. And this, simply for daring to consult with leaders and explore political issues from a more spiritual rather than conventional point of view.

Nonetheless, the quest for deeper meaning is growing and touching more people. As Houston says, "We're not on the fringe; we're on the frontier." It's not just famous, successful people who are exploring the timeless frontier of higher consciousness. Researcher Paul Ray has studied more than a hundred thousand Americans and has identified a distinct new subculture of about *forty-four million people* that he calls "cultural creatives" and that I call "ecstatics." These people are looking for authentic experience and authentic relationships. Instead of being side-tracked by the anti-ecstatic mind-set of our culture, they are pioneering new frontiers, going on journeys of spiritual self-discovery, seeking public service in addition to or in place of their everyday jobs, practicing voluntary simplicity instead of spending mindlessly, working for ecological sustainability rather than consuming irreplaceable resources. According to Paul Ray in an article he wrote for *Utne Reader:*

> Cultural creatives demand that all the pieces of their lives fit together to create an authentic whole. In his view, we are at "a tipping point in civilization, a great divide" in history. If the ranks of cultural creatives harness their collective energies and carry them into public arenas, we can forge a new kind of "integral" culture: one that merges the best of modernism and traditionalism, embraces both East and West, and ushers in a new form of Renaissance.

Although ecstatic practices have traditionally been accepted and cultivated in Eastern cultures, our society is extremely suspicious of ecstasy. And to admit one's own experience of it is almost like coming out of the closet. Yet ecstasy can open a door to great healing and awakening.

Ecstasy Can Transform Your Life

There's a great momentum in spirituality as we
come up to the millennium. The last time we had
an industrial revolution. This time we're having
a consciousness revolution.

                             ❧ Lynne Franks

I have spoken to men and women of all ages and from all walks of life: from business people, financial planners, and attorneys to artists, writers, and musicians to contractors, salespeople, and gardeners to full-time parents and teachers. As I explored the meaning of ecstasy in daily life, people I met shared their experiences with me—many opening up for the first time. Their stories were unique in details but similar in essence: each had had an experience of ecstasy that profoundly transformed his or her life.

I would like to share one powerful story of a peak experience that changed the life of my friend Tom, a successful businessman who manages his own multimillion-dollar software company.

"Sharon and I fell madly in love seven years ago," Tom told me. "We had two children, a successful business, and a wonderful home. But somehow, within a few years, we fell out of love." He explained:

We were often angry at each other and only communicated around the kids. When I discovered Sharon was having an affair, my whole world fell apart. I didn't tell her I knew. I was so angry I couldn't sleep. I'd lie awake at night staring at the ceiling, clenching my fists, trying to calm down. Finally, I'd go outside and run through the woods. Sometimes I'd scream or pick up big branches and hit them against trees until I started crying.

One morning I was walking in the woods and thinking "I've been coming here all these weeks and I never noticed how beautiful it is." I sat down under a tree. A deep peace filled my heart. Then I saw this little fern growing out of the ground. The sun was shining on it. It was silvery around the edges, its tiny leaves were curled, ready to open. It was the most beautiful thing I had ever seen. Just a little fern, but it was so alive and vibrant.

I stared at it for a long time. And the peaceful feeling started increasing. I fell in love with this little fern. Then I looked up and saw the whole forest that way; the fingers of sunlight streaming through the leaves, creating a patchwork of light and shadow all around me. I felt overwhelming gratitude for the beauty of this place. I took a deep breath, and it felt as if my head opened at the top and somebody was pouring liquid love into me, until my whole body had filled up and I was overflowing. I felt total rapture, joy, and gratitude. And I started praying, "Thank you God." I knew that I loved my wife, and she loved me, and the walls between us were made of fear, but they weren't real.

I walked out of the woods and back to the house. I was radiating love. I went up to Sharon and embraced her. I felt myself flowing into her, and her flowing into me. I could feel us melting together into one being, one heart. And I thought, Now we are truly married. She didn't know what had happened to me, but she felt my unconditional love. She started sobbing, and we embraced for a long time. We still had emotional work to do, but on a very, very deep level we had forgiven each other.

Ecstatic Awakening comes by surprise, often in moments of great stress and pain, opening us to a sacred dimension. And it is very much like the EveryDay Ecstasy we knew, and lost, as children, when life was touched with wonder and each moment was an adventure, a plunge into the unknown.

Remember the passion of shouting loud and jumping high and spinning until you drop, the unbearably sweet smell of newly mown grass, the thrill of colors in the crayon box, your joy at hearing a favorite bedtime story, the wonder of raindrops on a spiderweb, the mystery of a shadow on the wall?

To grow up, we build an ego that sets boundaries between the self inside and the world outside. And society initiates us into a world ruled by laws, structure, obedience, and duty, gradually replacing the ecstatic mind of childhood with the more rigid and conventional mind of adulthood. As this ego takes on a life and personality of its own, it controls and directs our attention, limiting our vision to matters of fear, hope, and survival, and cutting us off from the freedom and joy we knew as children. Its constant chatter, judgments, and interpretations filter out much that is essential to our wholeness, separating us from ourselves and the world of others in which we live.

After a while, every spontaneous impulse, every natural urge to express a feeling or an emotion, must struggle through a labyrinth of socially conditioned responses. We become "educated," but in the process we lose our true self, our "original face." We fix our awareness in the "everyday world" and lose touch with a deeper dimension of life.

The brilliant philosopher and author Aldous Huxley described this selective awareness as "eliminative": it screens out vast quantities of information that bombard us moment to moment, retaining the small amount of information useful for survival. Huxley says, "That which, in the language of religion, is called 'this world' is the universe of reduced awareness, expressed, and, as it were, petrified by language. The various 'other worlds' with which human beings erratically make contact are so many elements in the totality of the awareness belonging to 'Mind at Large.' "

Our society calls this reduced awareness *reality*. Clearly, if we lived in a constant state of full-blown ecstasy, we might die of starvation or be run over by the next passing car. Yet most of us have learned a bit too well this narrowing of attention to the mundane. Our mind at large is capable of perceiving dimensions and worlds beyond this one visible realm of our present perceptions. Yet we live like castaways on a desert island who have forgotten where we came from.

We reduce an infinite ocean of apparent chaos to a tiny trickle of seeming order. And we reinforce our contracted view by becoming specialists who know more and more about less and less. But we are cut off from our potential, from our Source, from the universe of infinite mysteries and possibilities, from our own ecstasy.

After years of learning to fit in, we forget how to open to the wonder and complexity of life. The energy of love, the affirmative life force, is our original innocence that contains within itself an unconditional yes to life, and it becomes distorted and suffused with repression, shame, guilt.

We live in an anti-ecstatic society based on the conceived separation between flesh and spirit. We are encouraged and taught to repress our sexual nature, to doubt our mystical and spiritual nature, and to fear whatever does not conform to conventional behavior. But when we ignore the sacredness of life and the possibility of living life ecstatically, we risk losing our self—our soul—in the process.

The Dark Side of Ecstasy

*It is the great tragedy of our Western society that we
have virtually lost the ability to experience the
transformative power of ecstasy and joy. Ecstasy was
once considered the favor of the gods, a divine gift
that could lift us out of our ordinary reality into the
realm of the immortal soul.*

           ❧ Robert Johnson

Ecstasy is the language of the soul. But in today's world it is a
foreign language. We discount ecstatic experience by equating it
with delusion or drug abuse. We think of those who do it as
oddball mystics or self-indulgent hedonists who pop it in the
form of a pill. Drugs and alcohol may offer a taste of ecstasy,
which is why they have been used for millennia. But while
drug-induced states may offer glimpses of the possibility of
transformation, they cannot, of themselves, transform us. The
states they bring are only temporary.

Some people fear ecstasy thinking it means losing their
mind. Some say the experience of ecstasy is a pathological break
in consciousness. But this has been proven false. Psychologist
Carl Fischer has studied the relationship between ecstasy and
schizophrenia. He found that while certain psychotic episodes
appear similar to ecstatic states, they are not the same. Mental illness is a shattering event. But ecstasy has the power to heal and
transform by drawing together the parts of ourselves that have
been alienated, opening heart and mind and allowing us to feel
our connection to all that is.

As the daily assault of modern life wears us down, more and
more of us long for healing, for new ways to connect with our
Spirit, to feel joy in our lives. There is a burgeoning interest in
the esoteric, in the spiritual practices of the world's traditions,
such as Tantra, Zen, Shamanism, Sufism, Buddhism, Christianity,
Judaism, and Yoga.

At the same time a new attitude of healthy skepticism toward church dogmas seems to be emerging. Even theologians are increasingly questioning the idea of heaven as a far-off place where you stand on clouds wearing wings, strumming a harp, singing hymns, and waiting for God to pass by on his fiery chariot.

Jeffrey Burton Russell, a Catholic theologian, writes in *History of Heaven:* "Heaven is not dull, not static. It is an endless dynamic of joy in which one is ever more oneself as one was meant to be; it is reality itself." Rosemary Altea, author and healer, writes: "Heaven is not a place, it's a state of awareness." Annemarie Schimmel, Western scholar of Islam, writes, "Once the journey to God is finished, the infinite journey in God begins."

Heaven is presented in various scriptures as a garden, a city, a kingdom, a temple, a womb, a fire, a luminous vision of light, the promised land, the abode of ecstasy. These images have also been used by ancient mystics and modern men and women to describe the ecstatic experience.

To me, heaven is the ecstatic, which can be lived here and now. It is where we are when we wake up and experience our connection with the Source of creation. Whether we call it the Father, the Mother, the Source, the God or Goddess, or All That Is, this awakening happens through the inner marriage of energy and consciousness, of life and Spirit, of body and soul. It is within us now, always possible, always available. Theologians of today confirm it: Ecstasy is in.

The essence of ecstasy is the experience of light, whether it be visions of light; the metaphorical light of wisdom, understanding, and revelation; or the ecstatic bliss of the light of divine love. Paul was "blinded by the light," Buddha was "en*light*ened," Christ was baptized by light in the form of a white dove. William Blake and Rumi turned their blissful visions into ecstatic poetry. Such peak experiences are the defining moments of individual human lives, of whole cultures, and of human history itself. The experience of light is at the core of the spiritual transformation of saints, shamans, mystics, and avatars, as well as of countless lovers, artists, and so-called ordinary people. You and me.

Ecstatic states are accessible. And you do not have to spend years meditating on mountaintops or alone in dark caves and you do not need to study the holy books to experience ecstasy and harness its vibrant energy.

Somewhere along our journey of awakening, with all its struggles, joys, and disappointments, ecstasy will be revealed, as a confirmation, a blessing, a message from the Source. Then all that remains is to live with joy, love, and laughter.

INTO THE HEART OF ECSTASY

Ecstasy is the final stage of intimacy with yourself. . . . It is a shift in perception in which direct contact with spirit is made.

          Deepak Chopra

Ecstasy is at once universal and uniquely personal, an experience of deep connection with self and with life as a whole. People describe their ecstatic experiences in contradictory terms: transitory, timeless, infinite, familiar, peaceful, thrilling, joyous, complex, intense, calm, inspired, temporary madness, absolute clarity. Here are just a few descriptions I have heard:

   Experiencing light and color: "Everything was bathed in light." "I saw the colors of things as they really are."

   Experiencing energy: "I actually saw vibrations of energy radiating from the flowers." "I felt the life force streaming through every cell in my body." "I had the deep understanding that everything on earth was alive, intelligent."

   Unusual physical sensations: "I felt as if I had been lifted up about six inches." "I felt like I was flying, I was so light." "I felt heat energy rise up my spine and blast through the top of my head." "I felt as if light was being poured into me." "I couldn't stop vibrating."

   Receiving mystical knowledge and understanding: "I understood that the secret of life was simplicity and connection." "I saw that everything on earth and in the universe was connected in a pattern that was very simple yet infinitely complex, and it made perfect sense."

   Time loses meaning: "I have no idea how long

it went on." "Time stood still." "It could have been a minute or an hour, I have no idea." "It was eternity." ☙ *Deep feelings:* "Inexpressible joy poured through me." "Everything was overwhelmingly beautiful, even the cracked sidewalk." "I felt peace permeating every cell in my body, like I was floating in liquid tranquility."

The following are stories by men and women—old, young, married, single, straight, gay, on spiritual paths or secular paths—who share a common experience of deep insight into a new dimension of their being.

ROBERTA'S ECSTASY: DANCING

I came to the first session of the Love and Ecstasy Training feeling tense, insecure about myself. Margot invited us to dance. Great music was playing, and she said, "Let your breath carry you into the dance!" We danced for twenty minutes, until I was lost in the dance. Then Margot shouted, "Stop! Stay still, watch what is going on in your body." As I relaxed into the stillness, I started feeling as if my body were dancing on its own from within. It was amazing. Heat, breath, sweat, all mingled in this feeling of vibrations coursing through my body, like little streaming currents of electricity.

The more I relaxed, the more the streaming sensations started to expand, moving up my legs and through my spine up through my neck. Then the energy rushed through my head and expanded beyond the boundaries of my skin, as if I had wings. In my being there was a great yes—to me, to my body. I felt so grateful for the gift of being alive. I could actually feel this physically, feel the dance of life like a pulsation in every cell in my body. Grace, a blessing. I felt like flying. So aware. I could hear every sound around me crystal clear. I felt light, liberated, ecstatic.

KIP'S ECSTASY: SWIMMING
WITH THE DOLPHINS

I was on a trip to Maui to swim with the dolphins for my birthday. I took a charter boat along the coast with some friends. The wind was coming over the waves pretty strongly, there was a heavy chop, and the boat was bouncing up and down. As we rounded the point on Lanai, we saw hundreds of dolphins swimming in the same direction. We slowly cruised in with them and they began bow riding with the boat. You could reach in the water and touch them if you wanted to.

We dropped anchor and got in the water, but the dolphins swam away. I was disappointed.

So I just floated in the water, closed my eyes and breathed deeply through my snorkel. I did this for about five minutes. When I opened my eyes there were three dolphins less than four feet from me, looking into my mask, like they were smiling. I was so happy it felt like my whole body was humming. I could hear the dolphins singing. It felt as if I were being totally supported by the dolphins. They were inviting me to just be open to the joy that was with them all around me. And the next thing I knew there were dolphins everywhere, swimming below me, beside me, and I was going beneath the waves with them. I felt like I was a dolphin myself.

This lasted for about an hour and a half, but I felt like there was no passage of time. I felt like a dolphin, completely safe, with no fear at all. My heart was beating wildly, but at the same time I felt extremely calm. I felt very aware of my body. My consciousness was sharp. My forehead was vibrant and throbbing. In this experience it seemed like my consciousness actually expanded beyond my body. It was as if all the blocks that keep me from feeling everything there is to feel, all the joyful feelings, had dissolved. I was able to feel and experience life on a much deeper level. Ever since that day, I have felt more playful and relaxed.

LAURA'S ECSTASY: CHILDBIRTH

Ecstasy took me by surprise when I had my baby. After more than nine months of worrying and waiting, feeling like a beached whale, I was ready to get that baby out! Labor had to be induced. I was hooked up to a heart monitor and a fetal monitor and a blood pressure monitor. The contractions were incredibly painful. It was just a joke to think you could breathe and make them go away. I couldn't believe women had to go through such pain to continue the human race, and I couldn't imagine why I had thought having a baby was going to be a good idea.

But then, suddenly, my baby girl was born. And when I held her and looked into her eyes such a deep feeling of euphoria washed over me. I was transported out of the delivery room, away from the pain, and the machines, and the doctors. I felt connected with the earth, and with every woman who had ever given birth. I could *see* a current of love flowing between us, me and my baby, and I felt merged not only with her but with the entire human race, down through the millennia.

MARTIN'S ECSTASY:
WALKING DOWN THE STREET

I had just graduated from college, I was working at my first job, and trying to figure out the meaning of life. I was just walking down a residential street in the suburbs one evening when I heard a sudden *snap!* And my consciousness seemed to rise up to about six inches above the top of my head. My entire awareness seemed to expand without limits, just *whoosh*.

I knew, absolutely, that everything—people, plants, animals, stars, air, water, even the sidewalk I was on, I mean *everything*—was connected in an intricate but elegantly simple pattern of energy and consciousness. The whole universe seemed to be smiling. I got the message that everything is perfect, just the way it is, and that by worrying so much about what my path should be, I was actually getting *off* my path. It lasted for a few minutes perhaps. But I was euphoric for hours afterward. That experience changed the way I look at everything. I'm exceedingly grateful for this mysterious gift.

It was my wedding day, in San Diego, in May, which is mostly overcast and cloudy. So we told our friend James that his job was to create sunshine. James put a talisman, a piece of metal with holes in it in the sand. We danced, and started singing "Sunshine on Your Shoulders." As we sang the clouds parted and a golden ray of sunshine came down striking the metal talisman. I looked at this diamond-like brightness and suddenly I was in a state of bliss, a state of grace, beyond time and space. . . . the ecstasy was so great! The sun stayed ten minutes, shining brightly over everyone. You never know when grace will happen.

Bringing Ecstasy to Life

I found God in myself and I loved her. I loved her fiercely.

     Ntozake Shange

I estimate that about 80 percent of the thousands of people I have worked with in the Love and Ecstasy Trainings have redis-covered their ecstatic selves in the process. It is much easier, of course, when we are gathered with others for this purpose, in supportive environments, removed from the common stresses of our daily lives. But what about the rest of the time?

Consider this: To make a garden grow, you cultivate and fer-tilize the soil and water the plants. To deepen your love in a re-lationship, you create emotional intimacy by communicating, embracing physically, by making tender love, and by sharing simple moments. To raise your children, you feed them with your attention and your love, play with them, teach them, and provide for all their needs. And what about your Spirit? What helps the Spirit grow?

All relationships, even our relationship to our own Spirit, require attention, presence, and love. The care for body, heart, and soul are required for our fullest well-being. And when we open ourselves to the guidance of Spirit, our invisible Source, we create the conditions in which ecstasy may become a part of our daily life.

~~~~~~

EVERYDAY ECSTASY

PURPOSE

~ To remember an ecstatic moment, anchor it in your body and access it whenever you need it.

PREPARATION

~ You can do this meditation alone, with a partner, or in a group.

~ Set aside half an hour, during which you will not be disturbed.

~ Wear loose, comfortable clothes.

~ Create a sacred space.

PRACTICE

~ Sit comfortably in a chair or lie down. Let yourself breathe deeply and gently.

~ Now we will go on a journey. You may experience what is about to happen through feelings, images, visions, and/or thoughts. Allow yourself to accept whatever comes up. Even if no visual images come forth immediately, they will eventually, perhaps when you repeat the experience.

~ Imagine that you are sitting in a movie house, watching a blank screen. Allow images to appear on the screen.

~ Call forth memories, visions, images, and sensations of the most delightful, joyous, or even ecstatic moments in your life. These may be childhood moments—playing in a field, jumping in the arms of a loved one, climbing a tree—or they may be adult moments—a meaningful conversation with someone inspiring; an intimate moment when you felt cared for and recognized in all your dimensions as lover, poet, wise one, God/Goddess, magician, muse, nurturing mother. Perhaps you were playing music, singing, or dancing. Just let the images or sensations of such moments appear on the screen of your consciousness without censoring them.

∾ After a few minutes, select one particularly strong recollection that feels delightful and ecstatic.

∾ When you feel it, see it, sense it, see yourself getting up from your chair in the movie house, walking slowly toward the screen, and entering into the picture.

∾ Now you are in this scene in the movie and you are living this moment again. As you breathe deeply and gently, let the visual impressions be strong and clear for you. See all the colors, the details of the landscape around you, the surroundings, the light.

∾ Now feel all the sensations again: the touch of a hand on your skin, the warmth of a breath, the streaming of the energy through your limbs, the quickening of your heartbeat, the rush of your blood, the inner peace, the feeling of joy or release . . . whatever you feel, be with it. Feel the resonance of that vibration in your body, in your heart.

∾ Keep breathing deeply and go on to the auditory experience. Listen: what do you hear? The wind, the music of nature, the voice of your beloved, your own voice? Immerse yourself totally in the sounds.

∾ Continue this journey with the smells: flowers, perfume, the smell of your lover's body . . . smell it again now. Deeply. Breathing, inhaling. Exhaling. Smelling.

∾ And now recall even more intensely the touch and the tastes, and taste this ecstatic moment again. Were you eating? Drinking? Kissing? Licking? And now let yourself expand to encompass all your sensory perceptions of this ecstasy: taste the smells, see the feelings, touch the colors.

∾ As you inhale, gently lay your hand on your body—your cheek, your arm, your chest, anywhere you like—and let your hand rest there. As you touch yourself, breathe deeply and feel that you are anchoring this wonderful experience in your neurologic memory. You are creating a "recall focus," creating a place for this experience of ecstasy to reside in you. A place from which it can be recalled.

∾ Breathing deeply, let that experience sink into your body through the touch of your hand.

∾ After a few minutes, let your hand return to your side. Take a deep breath, gently stretch your body, open your eyes, slowly come back into the room, and sit up.

∾ From now on, every day, take a few moments to relax and touch yourself exactly on the same spot and recall that ecstatic moment. In this simple way, you will begin to cultivate ecstatic recall: the natural ability to remember and access ecstatic states any moment in your life.

∾ Communicate what happened with your partner or write it in your journal.

POINTERS

∾ When you sit up, ask yourself what quality made this moment so special? When I do this exercise in seminars, people usually offer the following categories of response. *Presence:* "I was totally there, 100 percent focused." *Trust:* "My heart was completely open." *Excitement:* "I was breathing deeply and feeling totally." *Acceptance:* "I felt loved and taken care of." *Grace:* "I was overwhelmed by the beauty around me; I felt the presence of God."

∾ When you sit up, ask yourself what event triggered this ecstatic moment? Possible triggers are nature; a beloved person; unusual weather (lightning and thunder or a brilliantly clear day); a line of poetry; music; a particular taste, smell, dance, or movement; and meditation. The possibilities are nearly infinite.

∾ If nothing happens at first or if you fall asleep, don't give up. Explore this meditation with a friend guiding you, and it will grow on you!

In the next chapter, we examine what I call the anti-ecstatic conspiracy in a culture that has lost a sense of the sacred by separating flesh from Spirit.

This deep suppression of ecstasy has brought us to a collective "dark night of the soul." Before we or our culture can weave ecstasy into the fabric of our lives, we must understand the context in which we live. But first, we must go through the darkness consciously and understand its origins.

CHAPTER TWO

LIFE TODAY: CONFRONTING THE ANTI-ECSTATIC CONSPIRACY

Looking down on Los Angeles from an airliner,
I never fail to notice that it is like looking at a
printed circuit: all those curved driveways. . . .
As long as the Reader's Digest *stays subscribed*
to and the TV stays on, these modules are all
interchangeable parts within a very large machine.
This is the nightmarish reality: the creation of a
public herd. The public has no history and no
future, the public lives in a golden moment created
by a credit system which binds them ineluctably to
a web of illusions that is never critiqued.

❧ Terence McKenna

Too often the way we live and love is a facade behind which we hide our pain; the pain of neglect and manipulation; the anguish of our aloneness, of not knowing who we are; the grief of broken relationships that mirror our unfinished business with our parents; our sexual fears and frustrations; and the sorrow of a life that seems to lack ultimate meaning. Gold, once the alchemical symbol of transformation, is now just the color of money, itself an empty symbol for which it seems we must sacrifice our wholeness and work until we die, the life squeezed out of us day by day.

The American Dream has become a workaholic nightmare. The news of our dark excesses fills the collective mind with images of scandal, horror, and madness. The gorier, the better. A man rapes his wife, she cuts off his penis, and he becomes a celebrity. Priests molest young boys. Children as young as ten are arrested for murder. The media of our popular culture distracts our minds with lurid and degrading "facts" while ignoring the truths that might set us free. On daytime TV, ordinary people expose their most intimate sufferings and shameful secrets for our titillation. People who suffer publicly become celebrities.

An anti-ecstatic conspiracy that today dominates our world has boxed in our soul. *Conspiracy,* from the root *conspirare,* means "to breathe together and against," to plot for one's own group's interests regardless of the consequences to others. While we did not personally initiate this conspiracy, we have inherited it. And we sustain it by our daily participation. By our meek submission to its rule, we conspire against our own freedom. And by unwittingly speaking the language of anti-ecstasy, we separate ourselves from pleasure, from love, and from each other.

We do it in work: "Only the strong survive." "Keep your shoulder to the wheel and your nose to the grindstone." We do it in play: "No pain, no gain." "Winner takes all." We tame the wild innocence of youth by incarcerating our children in assembly-line schools. We squander the wisdom of the elderly by consigning them to nursing homes. Meanwhile, we spend our days in great office buildings, warehoused like livestock in tiny cubicles, working under artificial lights, breathing recycled air.

Why do we create nightmares when we so long for joy and meaning? If ecstasy is our true nature, why do we think we have to die to go heaven? If life is a celebration, why is it taking so long to get to the party? Yet to awaken to the light, we must be willing to travel consciously into the heart of darkness. Every spiritual and mystical tradition speaks of a dark night of the soul, when we must face our inner demons and choose truth over illusion. Only then can our spiritual rebirth occur, can our consciousness realize its ecstatic nature.

Albert Einstein said wisely, "No problem can be solved from

the same consciousness that created it." As apathetic co-conspirators and obedient conformists, we cannot break free. But as ecstatic beings, we can do anything. Our wild selves know the truths that our conventional egos cannot contain.

WHERE WE ARE NOW

The mind goes insane without the guidance of
the heart.

           Marianne Williamson

For thousands of years we took the survival of our species for granted. Apocalypse seemed unimaginable. Now, for the first time in history, human survival and ultimate apocalypse seem two sides of a coin spinning in the air, about to fall. The nuclear threat of planetary annihilation (in my opinion the ultimate premature ejaculation!) is only one dark possibility facing our species. There is also global warming, ecological destruction, cataclysmic weather changes, holes in the ozone layer, species extinction, drought, famine, environmental disasters, genocide, political corruption, religious fanaticism, and killer viruses.

On June 24, 1997, U.N. General Assembly president Razali Ismail opened Earth Summit+5 with these chilling words: "We continue to consume resources, pollute, spread, and entrench poverty as though we are the last generation on Earth. We as a species, as a planet, are teetering on the edge, living unsustainably, and may soon pass the point of no return."

Yet the anti-ecstatic mind poisons not only our planet but also our human relationships. By internalizing its values, we lose our faith, our sense of life's meaning, our connection to Spirit. And our view of the world takes on a gray, hopeless cast. Feeling guilty about our responsibility for the course we have charted, we feel powerless to change it. We bury our heads in the sand or become apathetic, hoping to avoid the knowledge of our complicity, the experience of our own pain. Or we grow numb with despair. As one teenager said to me, "What's so special about human beings anyway? They just keep killing each other!"

We armor ourselves so we don't feel grief. Yet when we repress our pain, we numb our capacity to feel and care. We love less intensely. Our joys diminish. Our breath is shallow. We lose our vital energy, and our bodies grow insensitive to pleasure. When pleasure is gone, we may throw ourselves into work, as if making money and being successful were tangible things we could build on. In *Tantra, The Supreme Understanding,* the great mystic Osho said, "Activity is an escape from yourself—it is a drug. In activity you forget yourself, and when you forget yourself there are no worries, no anguish, no anxiety. That's why you need to be continuously active, doing something or other."

But we cannot escape, by any fearful strategy, the psychological and emotional effects of the anti-ecstatic conspiracy. Not by changing jobs, having sex, pursuing pleasure, taking vacations, wild partying, shopping sprees, or abusing drugs. Joanna Macy, the author of *Despair and Personal Power in the Nuclear Age,* says of such futile strategies, "The frantic quality of it all does not suggest a healthy lust for life . . . but rather a sense of impending loss." The truth is that there is no escape. There is only transcendence or deterioration.

WHAT DOES THE ANTI-ECSTATIC CONSPIRACY WANT?

We have a vested interest in keeping the game going. Your industrial-military complex understands this very well. That is why it opposes mightily any attempt to install a war-no-more government anywhere.

Your religious community also holds this clarity. That is why it attacks uniformly any definition of God which does not include fear, judgment, and retribution, and any definition of self which does not include their own idea of the only path to God.

                                        ❧ Neale Donald Walsch

In an era of alienation and cynicism, chronic misery and stress become normal. When money and possessions are the measure of bliss, greed and consumerism become inevitable. Yet I have found in cultures not as driven by money, such as India and Bali, people laugh more, play more, relax more. Ecstasy is understood as part of a healthy life. But in the West we step over ecstasy in our race for the dollar.

Consequently, by our late twenties, many of us have mortgaged our futures to the system for college loans, cars, houses, credit card bills, and more. A job, perhaps begun out of real interest, becomes something we cling to for survival, a way to keep the creditors off our backs. We put aside our big dreams. Meanwhile, the hours get longer, the grind gets harder, and our relationships suffer as we grow more and more tired and drift farther apart.

Why do we join the conspiracy? We are born into it. Our souls are put to sleep through years of indoctrination. The corporate, political, and religious institutions of the anti-ecstatic conspiracy have a vested interest in keeping us asleep. That is the point of the conspiracy: *to keep people from waking up.* Our ecstasy is dangerous to those who would control us. For when we awaken, we refuse to continue as expendable parts in the soulless machine. When our eyes open to the truth, we realize our freedom is more important than money, that love is greater than power. Then our desperate search for happiness no longer lures us down dark or glittering avenues of consumerism. And we no longer give our power to hierarchies and institutions that feed on our hopes and dreams. Our ecstasy frees us, make us unexploitable—drunk with God.

In *The End of Patriarchy,* Claudio Naranjo says, "Just as the ant has no awareness of its limited freedom, neither does robotocized humankind have an awareness of enslavement; but . . . when one acquires the capacity to be more aware and to take responsibility for one's experience in the here and now, a thousand new things can happen."

The Murder of Ecstasy

*Without the Goddess we're cut off from both the
full power of motherhood and the power of
creativity in the larger sense—because all of us have
the capacity to birth something. . . . Christianity is
. . . a religion that needs a lot of healing and a lot
of waking up—to the lost Feminine side of God, to
its fear of sensuality, to its anti-Semitism, and to its
own lost mystical tradition.*

           ❧ Matthew Fox

The anti-ecstatic conspiracy is rooted in the very beginnings of
Judeo-Christian civilization: in the triumph of the vengeful
God Yahweh (Jehovah) over the ecstatic partnership of God and
Goddess honored as a spiritual truth all over the world, and be-
gun as early as 25,000 B.C.

For many centuries most of the world—including those
countries that today worship the patriarchal God of Judaism,
Christianity, and Islam—were ecstatic cultures established on
what Riane Eisler calls the partnership model, a model of equal-
ity between men and women. All activities—spirituality, family
needs, art, love, commerce—had their place in the celebration of
life.

Women held great power in this earth-centered culture.
Their natural life cycles, in rhythm with the waxing and
waning moon, helped set the lunar calendar. The original holy
trinity—Maiden, Mother, and Crone—paralleled the earth's
cycles: spring's renewal, summer's fertility, and winter's barren
fire.

The Goddess myths at the foundations of society were not
judgmental or wrathful but erotic and ecstatic. In the beginning,
it was said, Gaia bestowed on humankind a sacred fig tree called
Astore, or Astoria. In every religious rite at her temple, people
ate a fruit of this sacred tree. Eating the ripe, juicy fig, with its
numberless seeds embedded in moist, pink flesh, symbolized

eating the flesh and drinking the nectar of the Goddess. And to let her juices flow in the sacred act of sexual communion connected one to the very source of life. Yet this ecstatic rite has echoed down to us in a very different form as the story of Adam and Eve, the snake, and the apple.

How did we lose our reverence for Gaia, for her wonderful sensuality and her graceful fertility? How did we lose the sense of pride in our own sexuality, the knowledge of our bodies as holy and of sexuality as the sacred foundation of life itself? How did we get from the bliss of eros, of Aphrodite and Adonis, to the notion of original sin and the expulsion of Adam and Eve from the Garden? And how did we arrive at the unholy and anti-ecstatic trinity of guilt, shame, and judgment that has held us in bondage for millennia? In other words, how did we murder ecstasy?

WHEN GOD BECAME A MAN WITHOUT A WOMAN

Between 1000 and 1800 B.C., the male priesthood of a little-known nomadic people called the Hebrews brought monotheism into the Near East with their vengeful and jealous male god, Yahweh.

When they arrived in Canaan, "the Land of Milk and Honey," they found the Canaanites worshiping the Great Goddess. They made war on and finally overthrew the tribes who worshiped the Goddess, imposing their religion and their patriarchal sexual morality on those they conquered. And the Levite priests replaced the ecstatic myth of the fig tree with their own tragic myth of Adam and Eve's original sin.

Now, instead of eating the original fruit of the divine fig tree as an ecstatic sacrament, the serpent tricked primordial man and woman into tasting forbidden fruit, thus violating the law of God. The serpent, symbol of the liberating power of eros, now became a symbol of evil, initiator of lawless rebels into forbidden knowledge. Knowledge itself, the truth that once set us free in ecstasy, became a crime against God for which humankind was expelled from paradise. And by the logic of this myth, we humans were condemned to wander the earth, guilt-ridden, suffering, alienated from God, ashamed of our bodies, and our lovemaking called a sin.

Doubtless, the era of the Goddess was not a paradise. But its overthrow undeniably fostered an age of violence, desecration of feminine values, and grim submission to male authority.

The aftershocks of the patriarchy's assault on Goddess worship, and ultimately on femininity and sensuality, are a matter of historical record. In the Middle Ages, the Crusades and the Inquisition spread torture, death, and destruction throughout Europe. Even in the Renaissance, witch hunts killed untold numbers of women and men. The Church's consistent linking of sex with the devil and its horrible torture and execution of millions over the centuries, in the name of God, effectively eroticized domination and violence under the guise of spirituality.

Ultimately, the subjugation of women by men wounded both, cutting them off from inner access to that wholeness of Spirit which is born of the union of male and female. And this wound, this split in the psyche, is at the core of the anti-ecstatic conspiracy. We have strayed far from the sacred eroticism of our forebears.

Our culture has lost the understanding that sexual energy is the physical expression of our spiritual power. When we hold sexual union in reverence, we call this power forth. When we deprive sexual union of its sacred dimension, sex remains a purely physical, instinctual drive, disconnected from heart and Spirit. As a result it is often misused, repressed, and directed against life itself.

THE MARRIAGE OF SEX AND VIOLENCE

How can we hope to heal the planet, save the rain forests, establish peace among nations and religions, when the universal symbol and activity of human love is poisoned in our individual minds? How can love flourish when our religions tell us sex is sinful, and that our flesh is the enemy of our spirit? I agree with Havelock Ellis, who said: "Sex lies at the root of life, and we can never learn reverence for life until we learn reverence for sex." The damage caused by the condemnation of sex, to human beings and to civilization, is incalculable. We see the results all around us: violence, rape, numerous psychological and emotional afflictions, perhaps even war itself.

And then there is the war at home: rape, domestic violence,

sexual harassment, child abuse, incest. The statistics speak volumes:

> ❧ In the United States, 1.3 women are raped every minute.
> ❧ The United States has the world's highest rape statistics of the countries that publish such statistics—twenty times higher than Japan.
> ❧ In a study of college men, 35 percent indicated some likelihood that he would commit a violent rape of a woman who had fended off an advance—if he could be sure of getting away with it.

In her 1995 speech to the United Nations Fourth Annual Conference on Women in Beijing, First Lady Hillary Rodham Clinton chose to address this worldwide problem:

> It is a violation of human rights when babies are denied food, or drowned, or suffocated, or their spines broken, simply because they are born girls . . . when women and girls are sold into the slavery of prostitution . . . when women are doused with gasoline, set on fire, and burned to death because their marriage dowries are deemed too small . . . when individual women are raped in their own communities and when thousands of women are subjected to rape as a tactic or prize of war . . . when a leading cause of death worldwide among women ages fourteen to forty-four is the violence they are subjected to in their own homes. . . .
>
> Human rights are women's rights—and women's rights are human rights. . . . As long as . . . girls and women are valued less, fed less, fed last, overworked, underpaid, not schooled, and subjected to violence in and out of their homes, the potential of the human family to create a peaceful, prosperous world will not be realized.

Eroticized violence is destructive to men and women alike. The abuse of women in the world is the abuse of the Goddess, the universal feminine principal, which exists within every one of us, male or female. When we deny half of ourselves, we are no longer whole. And everyone suffers.

THE WAR BETWEEN MEN AND WOMEN

The demeaning of the feminine harms women and men. For women, the devaluing of her inner woman causes low self-esteem. And without a strong inner man, she has no inner support. We hear much of such women who can't seem to leave abusive relationships, who fear leaving their houses alone.

Girls have a particularly difficult transition around puberty. Even today, menstruation is often associated with shame. Sex, forbidden and attractive, cheapened by advertising, and condemned by conventional religion, is still too controversial for simple education to be provided in schools and often at home. False images of womanhood—air-brushed supermodels and centerfolds—do untold damage, visible in the disturbing proliferation of eating disorders and self-mutilation by young women in their teens and twenties.

Leila, the daughter of a friend of mine, now her early twenties, lamented her confusion during puberty:

> I did not understand the body changes that were happening to me, from about the time I was fifteen and 115 pounds to the time I was lost, confused, and depressed in college when I had gained 30 pounds. I was so out of touch with my body. I wish I had been more comfortable with my nakedness and my body as it went through the transitions of puberty.

For men, the loss of the inner feminine is also damaging. Life seems to give boys two choices: to be a sissy and face daily torment or to be masculine and fit in. Steven Sisgold, a therapist and early leader of the men's movement, explained to me the tremendous stress this puts on boys and men:

> You can't cry, you can't show feelings. Many of us envied the girls because they did not have to worry about the army, how they were going to make money. It was

okay for them to have emotions, to cry. But we had this constant pressure on us to live up to a certain image of what a man was. We had to provide, to perform, to keep up our image. We lived in a very secretive world. Among ourselves, we weren't able to talk about anything except for the boxing score, who hit what that year, who beat up whom.

Without strong inner models, both women and men have difficulty being authentically "themselves," and often opt for roles chosen from popular culture. Women in past decades chose from extremes: a madonna or a whore, a good girl or a bad girl, a wife and mother or a slut. Today, the choice is somewhat different. In light of feminism, the sexual revolution, and an increasing necessity to earn a living and survive, women challenge men more directly. They often must eschew their femininity to be successful in a "man's" world.

Boys, once groomed to be tough, now grow up to face new problems in a world of shifting gender lines; like dealing with women who want them to show their "feminine side." Sisgold remembers, "I was totally confused. When I came on strong, my girlfriends would say, 'That's too much, you are too male, you are just a pig, you are just like all the other guys.' So I turned around and tried to be the sensitive New Age guy. I would be awfully quiet, sensitive, trying to listen, and I was told 'You are not enough sexually. You are too weak. I'm tired of weak men. I want a strong man!' I couldn't seem to do anything right—I was either too much or not enough."

The effect of this gender confusion on intimate relationships is devastating.

SEEKING A BALANCE

The distortions that divide men and women in the world flow from the split between the inner man and woman in each of us, a split that goes back to the mythic subjugation of the Goddess by a jealous and warlike deity. And that inner split between feminine and masculine, sex and Spirit, body and soul, energy and consciousness, separates us from the healing power of ecstasy, both in ourselves and in our culture.

We must not seek to replace the male deity with a female, but to restore the divine feminine to the world. And especially her reunion with the divine masculine, who in his wrathful appearance as God the patriarch is wounded by her absence just as we, their children, have suffered unbearably from their separation.

Says Boston-area therapist Greta Bro, "Living under the image of 'God the Father,' a woman never has her identity affirmed as a reflection of the divine. . . . To reclaim a sense of entitlement and wholeness, a woman must realize that divinity has a female aspect as well." I would add that men living under the image of God the Father also suffer a spiritual lack. Women's experiences of the body, of sensuality, of intuition, of the creative experience of birth and nurturing have value for both sexes. The world can only benefit from women's passion and power to awaken and initiate change.

First, the world knew the divine as Mother, the matriarchal model of Gaia, the earth goddess, whose qualities are fertility, nurturing, healing, receptiveness, ecstasy. Then, the pendulum swung in the opposite direction and the world honored the divine as the Father, Yahweh, Jehovah, the god of thunder, judgment, creation, war. Now for millennia, humanity has honored God in his male aspect. But many of us are now struggling to go beyond these old models and realize a Divine at the center of the universe, within and without, a god who transcends gender distinctions by uniting them into one Whole.

Author Zia Budapest, devotee of the Goddess and a pioneer of women's spirituality, has said, "All of this questing for higher things, these are male ideas. [Men] need quests. . . . They are happier that way because then there's achievement. And then they sell it to women as well. . . . It's a linear thing to go higher up, it sets up duality, it sets up hierarchy. There is no such thing. We are here. This is it."

We cannot realize a divinity that transcends gender or establish a culture that honors and integrates both genders until we realize within ourselves the union between our inner God and Goddess. Shiva and Shakti must stand united in our hearts, the female and male within each of us joined in the *hieros gamos,* the sacred marriage. This alone will make us whole. For we can only realize a god who is whole by becoming whole ourselves. And from our wholeness, the New Woman and the New Man of the second millennium will be born. And they will defeat the anti-ecstatic conspiracy not by fighting it or by seizing power but by living as spiritual partners.

CHAPTER THREE

ECSTATIC PARTNERSHIP: INVITING ECSTASY

When opposites no longer damage each other,
Both are benefited through the attainment of Tao . . .
Therefore, the wise identifies opposites as one,
And sets an example for the world.

                           ☙ Tao Te Ching

The modern world is full of dualities, of opposite forces and moods in apparent conflict; female and male, receptive and aggressive, loving and hating, winning and losing. All these polarities exist simultaneously and endlessly strive within our own natures, creating pressure. Our wholeness and our ecstasy come when we find our balance amid life's tensions, in the ever-shifting flow of forces within and around us. And this state, symbolized as the sacred marriage of self and Spirit, of the God and Goddess within us, enables us to create ecstatic partnerships with others.

It is hard to accept that one state, one action, one feeling, coexists with *its opposite;* that when you love, hate might arise; that when you give, you also receive. The Beauty and the Beast live within us. And we try to reject the one and accept only the other, to match an ideal of how we *should* be.

Sooner or later, those committed to their growth understand that unity is a potential contained in diversity and separation. In the Tantric path, we confront life as it is, not as we wish it were, and so find our balance. Ordinary life teaches us to become more aware of responses, beliefs, interpretations, motivations, and goals. So why not embrace yourself as you are and life as it is and learn to integrate the seemingly contradictory aspects of your nature with compassion and wisdom? Not hating what is difficult and only loving what is beautiful, but accepting all that is just as it comes. In the process, we integrate and balance our inner feminine and masculine natures, which is the key to life beyond struggle and partnership beyond strife.

The choice for wholeness makes life a challenging adventure, both for individuals and whole cultures. And we are now in an era of transition from the old anti-ecstatic patriarchal model to a new, more sacred and balanced partnership model. Worldwide, authoritarian governments and structures are being challenged, overthrown, and changed. And the roles between the sexes are also shifting. Men are raising children at home while their wives build careers. Women are gaining access to echelons of power previously denied them. Women's voices, unique gifts, and powers are being acknowledged and valued as never before; women are emerging dynamically in the world at large.

At every level, men and women are working together, integrating their skills and energies, and cooperating in larger numbers than at any time in history. As a result, millions of individuals and entire cultures are being forced to confront and resolve the traditional tensions and conflicts between feminine and masculine. A marriage of yin and yang, which can be disturbing but is ultimately a healing integration of opposites, is occurring globally at every level.

At the same time, this marriage of opposites is taking place as a spiritual process within men and women who are seeking to balance their female and male polarities. And all these interrelated phenomena are visibly changing our religions, our politics, our psychologies, our professions, and our laws. Whatever the final result may be is a matter for speculation. But the evidence of this profound human shift, occurring at individual and collective levels, is undeniable.

Healing the Mother and Father Within

Even in the best of circumstances, we are all just
learning. No parents are fully enlightened. Children
will unconsciously absorb their parents' fears and
biases and later in life will, one hopes, learn to
become conscious of these conditioned attitudes and
find ways to release them. This is normal; this is
the work we all have to do.

                                         ▸ Richard Moss

We first learn what it means to be female or male by observing our parents. All children desire the archetypal family: the child at the center, protected, nurtured, and loved by a mother and father joined together harmoniously. This is the child's intuitive vision of the family as a womb in the world. But as Richard Moss points out, our reality often falls short of this vision. The "partnership model" our parents might have taught us more often resembles an uneasy truce. And we grow up and enter the world wounded and disappointed, still trying to bring together and heal—in our own hearts, bodies, and psyches—the relationship between our father and mother, whom we internalize as our own inner man and woman.

Intuitively, we long for the sacred marriage in the same way that as children we longed for the womb. The longing for union is programmed in our genes and epitomized in the very moment of conception. The original fusion of sperm and egg that sparked us to life contained the innate intelligence of all creation; the coding of our entire species; and even the archetypal image of our future wholeness, the union of our inner female and male. In that moment of passionate merging, we were given our very DNA and our life blueprint was oriented toward our return, consciously, to an ecstatic awakening as life itself.

The paradox of life, of being and nonbeing, was somehow mysteriously resolved at this zero point, when life as pure energy, driven by the forces of love and biological desire, drew us into matter. And the longing of life within us—the forces of consciousness, love, and desire—draw us still toward new conceptions, new births, new awakenings.

Yet as adults, we carry the unhealed wounds that we received as children. We often live and love inauthentically, our consciousness bound by or in reaction to our emotional pain, our grief over broken or shallow relationships, our loneliness and alienation, our fear of the future, our resentment of the past, and the fundamental inner division of our male and female natures. Our inner same-sex self-image is often damaged by an imbalanced relationship to our parent of the same sex. And our inner self-image of the opposite sex is as often the most problematic wound to our wholeness.

In the West, men are taught to reject their feminine qualities to acquire masculine power, to earn respect and a place of honor in the "tribe." Psychologically, for a boy to gain his independence and his manhood, he must reject his mother's rule. He must shake loose of the woman's grip on him. This rejection of his mother's rule plays out in his future relationships with women. Yet to be whole, he must learn to accept his own nurturing, receptive, and intuitive feminine nature. This delicate task requires wisdom-based rituals and initiations that are sadly lacking in our culture. Many fathers are absent (emotionally and often physically) or negatively present as passive or aggressive models of imbalanced manhood. And most boys leave childhood in conflict with, or possessed by, their inner feminine, while their masculine side is equally wounded and unbalanced. And they are driven by this wound to seek in outer partners what is lost and unhealed within themselves.

The girl in our society begins to lose her inner male model as her father becomes more distant during her adolescence. Made uncomfortable by their daughters' blossoming sexuality, many fathers withdraw from them, emotionally and physically. In some cases they respond inappropriately, from their own wounds, with aggression and even abuse. And many mothers, wounded in their own femininity, in conflict with their sexuality, frustrated by cultural barriers erected against their freedom and power, inflict their dilemmas, fears, and resentment or impose their unfulfilled dreams onto their daughters. Thus the girl enters adulthood, like the boy, fragmented, wounded in her femininity, separated from or possessed by her masculine side, and seeking her lost inner wholeness through outer relationships.

For an outer relationship to succeed, both partners must perform heroic inner work. Women and men must heal their inner male and female components. And our relationships are mirrors that inevitably reflect what is undeveloped in ourselves.

Our lovers inevitably reflect this internal image of the opposite sex that we carry in our psyches. This inner image drives us in often painful ways that we can neither prevent nor control. We are drawn to those whose wounds fit our own. And the ensuing drama will either teach us what we need to do to become whole or, if we refuse to learn, drive us deeper into fragmentation. Then, to varying degrees, all our relationships will be theaters of suffering. And this will remain the case until we consciously balance and unite our inner male and female.

A TANTRIC PERSPECTIVE ON THE MYTH OF ADAM AND EVE

Every time a man and woman make love, they reenact the myth of Shiva and Shakti who, by their Tantric union, conceive and give birth to the universes. Since we are children of the West, I would like to present a positive, ecstatic version of the myth that plagued us with original sin. To do this we have to go straight to the root of the problem: our sexuality. In your mind, imagine Adam and Eve in Paradise, sitting naked under the Tree of Knowledge, kissing . . .

Adam and Eve are becoming aroused, and Adam wants to make love. Eve hesitates. She says to Adam, "I'd like to be different, more spiritual this time." Adam is confused. "I'm not sure I know how."

Eve says, "Me neither. Let's ask God to help us." She calls God in a prayer: "Dear God, be with us in our joining and bring us your blessings that we may experience your divine light and become one with you. Thank you for giving us Paradise."

Now there is a great Sssweeesh! in the leaves of the tree above their heads. And a great big sexy slinky boa constrictor slowly slides down to them holding a shiny red apple between his fangs. Eve gently stretches her hands out to receive the apple, and thanks him. Holding the juicy sweet apple in her right hand, she settles her naked body on Adam's lap, nestling his erection against her round, smooth belly. They begin to sway their pelvises against each other, kissing passionately. Adam slides his tongue into Eve's mouth. She sucks his tongue, licks his lips, and pulls away to take a bite of the apple. Then she slides the juicy bite into his mouth and they suck and chew on it together while his *Vajra* gently penetrates her *Yoni*. A shudder of delight ripples through her spine as she takes another bite, shares it. Then another and another, while they make love.

The juice of God's apple oozes from their mouths onto their bodies, as the juice of her *Yoni* drenches his *Vajra*. Their excitement rises with every bite until they can hold it no longer and she cries, "Now, oh yes, Adam, come, oh dear God . . ." And at that very moment God comes in the form of a great white light, filling their mind, their third eye, their entire body with bliss. And they hear this whisper: "I am the Holy Spirit. And ye are my children, in whom I am well pleased. Be you blessed, for the Father and Mother have united in you and through you they will now bring forth healing to the Earth, that She may always be honored as our Mother."

And from the moment Adam and Eve ate the apple, they knew that God had listened to Eve's prayer and that they must use wisely the revelations that would pour down to them through the fruits of the Tree of Knowledge, and give back to Gaia, the Earth, in loving kindness, the beauty that she bestowed upon them.

Adam and Eve exist within each of us as the original man and woman, father and mother. Through them we need to acknowledge our inner male and female components, as archetypes of the God and Goddess, images of our dual nature fulfilled in the creative and spiritual dimensions. In every relationship and act of love, women and men are seeking the union of their inner male and female selves, their own divine wholeness. Yet we achieve union not through an outer lover, but by uniting these inner male and female archetypes in our own psyches. Ultimately, the key to ecstasy, inner peace, tribal peace, and world peace is our own individual wholeness.

My Journey to Rediscover My Inner Woman

Touching each part of your body, I also touch my
body and I realize we are One.

           From the Sri Chakra

           Yantra ceremony

Several years ago, in the midst of a successful and dynamic career, I separated from my beloved Tantric partner of many years. To my dismay, I suddenly felt I had lost the ground under my feet and my sense of self-worth. Almost as if I had lost myself. I had studied enough psychology to know that I was projecting my inner man onto my outer partner and seeking my own projected masculine self in my lover's persona. Yet knowing this did not help. I felt as if I needed to have him in my life to be validated as a woman.

It was especially disturbing and frustrating because I had thought my many years of spiritual study and inner work had taken me beyond this place. Many times, in deep meditation, I had experienced profoundly my innate wholeness, the truth that I was complete as I was: I did not need a father, a lover, a husband, a guru, or any outer male figure to be whole as a woman. Yet in this relationship, I seemed to have forgotten what I knew.

I had lost my inner balance, the harmonious interplay between my inner male and female. I seemed to act either from one or the other, yet in a chaotic and confusing fashion. First, I would throw myself into a career in the marketplace driven by the longing for success and accomplishments. Eventually, fed up with performing and producing, I would flee to the world of meditation, to India, where I could sit, receptive, in the simple enjoyment of being. But I could not remain at peace for long in either state. And I found myself running back and forth between them, dissatisfied with each. On retreat I would berate myself for not being responsible, active, and productive; for not serving and contributing to the world. And in the world I felt that the busy hustle and bustle of professional accomplishments were empty dreams. And I would long for a simple life of silence and meditation.

Even more upsetting, my connection to the Goddess archetype within my own psyche was very vague. I was not truly at peace with my own feminine nature. I was looking outside for a solution I could only find within. I knew that for my own healing, I must bring into balance my inner male and female independently from an outer partner. But first I must find and realize the living Goddess within myself.

AN INVITATION FROM THE GODDESS

In that moment of aching realization, as I was yearning to reconnect with the Goddess, I received an invitation from a student in my training to visit her Tantric master, Guruji, at his ashram in south India.

Guruji is a most unusual man, a remarkable combination of scientist and mystic. His chosen name is made up of three syllables: *Gu* means "ignorance," *ru* means "removal," and *ji* is a title of respect. Guruji thus means "respected one who removes ignorance." A physicist, Guruji worked for the Indian government for many years. But when his work turned toward defense and armament, he felt uncomfortable. He wanted to work toward world peace, not serve the cause of war. One day as he was praying in the temple, a powerful apparition of the Goddess Devi showed herself to him. She told him she would protect him and take care of him if he would start a new life in service to Her. The presence of the Goddess is potent in India, where the feminine aspect of the divine is deeply revered. Guruji took his vision seriously.

He prepared himself for years and at last returned to the village where he was born. There, by the grace of the Goddess, people stepped forward with money. He was given four acres of land. There he built a temple to the Goddess. *Devipuram,* "abode of the Devi," is an amazing three-story temple based on the form of the *chakras,* our subtle energy centers, and filled with 108 statues of the Devi in her manifestations as different goddesses. But it is more than a temple filled with statues. It is a place of education at many levels, where women are worshiped as embodiments of the Goddess. Devipuram is devoted not only to the exploration of the sacred but also to programs of social activism, such as opening banks specifically for women and training teachers to go out and educate the community.

Guruji's words cut to the heart of the anti-ecstatic conspiracy. He says, very simply and clearly:

> The world is full of richness and variety. The old religion is in fact the oldest religion there is. It is the religion of love. When separation entered religion, it caused alienation among nations. Alienation creates boundaries. Cooperation is the real key—two heads are better than one, ten sticks together are stronger than one stick. Cooperation. Resonance with nature and environment. Harmony. Peace. These are human values approaching divinity. Competition, struggle for success, fear of failure, loss of face, frustration, anger, violence— these are neurotic subhuman values. They disrupt peace, stability, harmony, environment.

THE GIFT OF THE DEVI

I arrived on February 14, which has always been an auspicious day for me. It is the day of my initiation into Tantra in 1977, when I received my name Ma Anand Margot, "the path to bliss," from Osho in India. It is also Valentine's Day, a day celebrating the love between man and woman and the day of the New Moon of the Goddess, according to the Indian lunar calendar. On this day, Indians hold the Sri Yantra ceremony, a profound adoration of the Goddess that is based on one of the most ancient *yantras* (symbols) in the Tantric tradition.

The Sri Yantra mandala is a design made up of nine interlocking triangles—four pointing upward and five pointing downward. This potent image, at least five thousand years old, symbolizes the entire universe, all of creation: from microcosm to macrocosm, from the smallest atom to the largest galaxy. It also represents the body, the emotions, the natural world, the five senses, the love between man and woman, all powers and forces, life, death, and nature.

The eight triangles pointing downward symbolize the energy of the feminine. The eight triangles pointing upward represent the energy of the masculine. The center where they intersect is the *bindhu* point of creation, symbolizing the joyous union of Shiva and Shakti, Spirit and matter, consciousness and energy, and the infinite possibilities of creation through the ecstatic union of male and female polarities within each human being.

THE SRI YANTRA CEREMONY

Hundreds of people came from all over India on this day to participate in the Sri Yantra ceremony. To prepare the temple, devotees went to a sacred lake several miles from the ashram and brought back one thousand fresh lotus flowers, in fragrant, billowing armfuls, and arranged them around the Goddess.

Then they undressed the statue of the Devi on the top floor of the temple. Carved of gleaming black granite, she sits in the half-lotus position, one leg folded, one leg hanging down, relaxed yet powerful. I watched as they began washing her with milk, honey, and ghee (melted and clarified butter), symbols of fundamental nourishment. As they washed the Devi, they made many invocations and *mudras* (sacred hand gestures) to her: to her crown, to her breast, to her *Yoni,* praising all her qualities and asking for her protection and blessing.

As I watched this ancient, sacred ceremony, I imagined that it was my own Goddess self being worshiped in this way. I felt empowered as a woman, embraced in my feminine nature. As I joined the chant of the Devi mantra, praising the transcendent integration of male and female energies, an all-encompassing clear consciousness rose in my being. I felt the presence of the Goddess growing within me.

CREATING THE INNER PARTNERSHIP

> *What is the psyche's way of effecting the renewal*
> *process? The interplay of opposites reversing one*
> *into the other, and union. . . . One has the*
> *experience of being brought into a hieros gamos,*
> *or sacred and heavenly marriage.*
>
>   ✍ John Weir Perry

The inner man and woman are psychological, emotional, and spiritual realities alive within us. They appear in our dreams and sometimes even in visions as archetypes. Swiss psychiatrist Carl Jung called them *anima* and *animus,* and he wrote extensively on their expression in our lives. Jung, and later psychologists, also noticed common themes and archetypes appearing in the dreams and visions of patients undergoing certain life passages. For instance, patients in periods of crisis and change often dream of death, cataclysms of nature, the mass destruction of war. And when they enter the phase of healing and renewal they often dream or have visions of the inner fusion of male and female archetypes.

Jung realized that these archetypal images of death and rebirth have meaning on a collective as well as a personal level. He knew that we, as individuals, carry in our own psyches the burdens of our wounded cultures; and that by resolving the clashing of opposites within we solve a piece of the collective problem. Our culture becomes freer through us, and our ecstasy becomes a healing force as we move beyond our fears to live a new vision into the world.

THE ROLES OF THE INNER MAN AND INNER WOMAN IN OUR PSYCHE

How can we become aware of our inner man and woman? By observing and understanding their influence and effects on our inner experience and our outer behavior. Here are some general examples of the positive and negative behavior of these inner figures. Of course, they vary according to the individual.

&. *Your inner woman.* Allows you to meet experiences openly: not goal oriented but trusting, intuitive, receptive. You follow the flow of energy, connected by your feeling, guided by intuitive wisdom, present to what is. Your emotions are deep, your love and presence are healing to others.

&. *Your inner man.* Allows you to meet experience directly, confidently, act with power and natural authority and speak your truth. Your will, guided by clarity and wisdom, cuts through obstacles as you follow your destiny. Your energy and clarity are a light and inspiration to those around you.

&. *Imbalanced inner woman.* You tend to be overwhelmed by problems. You lose yourself in a person or idea, surrender your identity to others. You see many sides, yet lacking an anchoring perspective, lose sight of the essence or goal. Paralyzed by confusion, you have difficulty making decisions and choices. Your sensitivity makes you vulnerable emotionally, to situations, people, and your own chaotic states.

๛ *Imbalanced inner man.* You rely on will and exclude the heart. You try to dominate people and situations. You focus on progress and results in life. You ignore subtle qualities and feelings that make life pleasant or painful and signs that warn you may be off track. Too sure of yourself, you become angry, rigid, and judgmental when your infallibility is questioned. You avoid responsibility and demands for fear of making mistakes and avoid long-term commitments for fear of losing your freedom.

DISCOVERING YOUR INNER WOMAN AND INNER MAN

PURPOSE
๛ To better understand how your inner man and inner woman behave and respond and to balance them, thereby gaining strength and clarity of choice in life.

PREPARATION
๛ Set aside thirty minutes to one hour when you will not be interrupted.
๛ Have your journal or a notebook and pen handy.
๛ Create a simple sacred space.

PRACTICE
๛ Begin with a Heart Salutation (page 75)
๛ Sit for five minutes with your journal and pen. Relax and take a few deep breaths. Close your eyes and relax your neck and shoulders, let go, be soft inside. Ask yourself, "Who am I in my receptive, feminine side? How do I act and respond?"

≈ Now list the answers as they come (for instance, patient, tolerant, open hearted, caring, seductive, timid, insecure . . . whatever comes to you).

≈ After five minutes, close your eyes again, and ask yourself, "Who am I when I am in my active, masculine side? How do I respond?"

≈ Now list the answers as they come (for instance, taking initiative, expressing my needs, asking for what I want, wanting things my way, too goal oriented . . . whatever comes to you).

≈ Now have fun evaluating how you respond in each life situation: Is it your male side or your female side that is dominant at work? At home? In your relationships? At parties? With your children? When you are making love? Evaluate the proportion of male to female responses in each situation (for instance, work: 70 percent male, active; 30 percent female, receptive).

Situation	Female/Listening (Percent)	Male/Taking Initiative (Percent)
At home		
At work		
With your partner		
With your children		
Making love		
Totals		

POINTERS

≈ Remember, both genders are both receptive and active, so both men and women can do this exercise. An ideal score for everyone would be close to 50 percent male and 50 percent female overall.

≈ Both men and women may find they have very imbalanced scores, such as 90 percent male and 10 percent female, or 70 percent female and 30 percent male.

≈ Whatever your final tally, the results may surprise you. From them, learn how to create more balance in your life in the way you respond to situations. For example, if you are imbalanced toward the male, you may want to practice more receptive behavior, such as patience, empathy, and trust. If you are imbalanced toward the female, you may want to practice more active behavior, such as jumping in, exercising authority, and taking initiative and responsibility.

❧ This is a great exercise to share with your partner. Do not talk while you write. Avoid sharing information about your scores during the exercise. Wait until you have finished, then share and have fun!

Balanced and integrated, our inner man and woman guide us through life with clarity and intuition and generate a wellspring of vital, creative, and loving emotional energy. The result of the inner marriage of male and female is wholeness, inner peace, and power. It does not make us neutered androgynes, as if our dual qualities, once joined, canceled each other out. In truth, we become a dynamic whole, a shifting interplay of yin and yang, qualities harmonized in complementary partnership. No longer at war, they form a unified whole greater than a sum of parts, which we might call the *integrated self*. Through this inner union we become impregnated with the conception of an endless creativity and joy in life.

Such a balanced man acts dynamically, with calm clarity, trusting his own nature, his life. He is gentle, yet strong. He willingly accepts responsibility, out of deep commitment to his vision. He does what is required with integrity, holding back nothing. By spending himself fully, his flow of energy increases. The secret of his power is his connection with his inner feminine, which enables him to love deeply, and this gives him faith in life. He finds his ecstasy through service and accomplishment.

A balanced woman is patient. She has a deep, intuitive sense of how life works and what is required of her. She is loving and clear. Her emotional strength nurtures those around her and draws others into her sphere as co-creators. Connected to spirit and life at an intuitive level, she is a natural healer and a source of inspiration. The secret of her depth is in her heart. Her connection to her inner masculine gives her power and clarity. And she finds her ecstasy by nurturing and empowering others and in acts of creation.

These are descriptions of our inner man and woman in balance, on whose energies and qualities we can call for strength and guidance. Establish a relationship with these inner figures. Visualize them. Feel their qualities. Engage them in inner dialogue. Notice them in dreams. Access them in daily life. Consciously draw on and manifest their strengths and virtues. Make this a practice, even a discipline. In this way, you will come to know and learn from these inner teachers. (A dream journal is an invaluable tool for conscious work with these inner figures. Your dreams chart the course of their development and your own.)

Also, observe yourself when you are out of balance, and notice the qualities of your inner man and woman in their imbalanced or negative states. Which is dominant? The inner man or inner woman? Feel what they, and you, are like in these states. At times it may feel disturbing and unpleasant. But as you become sensitive to yourself you will begin to catch yourself when you are influenced by your inner man or woman in their negative forms, and bring yourself back into balance and move into harmony with yourself, others, and life. You enjoy your own company more. And so do others.

EXPRESSING YOUR INNER MAN AND WOMAN

PURPOSE
To spontaneously express the male (active) and female (receptive) sides of your nature, have fun acting them out, and know yourself better through this.

PREPARATION
Wear loose clothing in which you feel comfortable moving and stretching.
Have a sound system available, and two types of music:

(1) gentle music you associate with the feminine and (2) dynamic music you associate with the masculine.

❧ Prepare to dance for ten or fifteen minutes expressing each side (male and female) of your nature.

PRACTICE

❧ Begin with the Heart Salutation (page 75).

❧ Create a nice space, free of clutter, where you can move around and dance in privacy.

Expressing Your Inner Woman

❧ Begin to play your favorite feminine music.

❧ Stand with your eyes closed, relax your body, and pay attention to your breathing as it goes deeper.

❧ Begin to sway to the music, enjoying the movement, letting your breath connect you and carry you into the movement. Now, imagine, see, think, feel (whichever way works for you) that it is the woman inside you who is moving.

❧ As you dance, allow yourself to see yourself as a woman or imagine her behind your closed eyes. Your inner woman is now appearing to you, dancing. See her from within. How does she feel? Comfortable, light, heavy, happy?

❧ If the image or feeling is blurred, stop for a moment, be still, and really call forth an image of her, a feeling of her inside yourself.

❧ Now, once again, grow into the feeling of her. Dance her; act out this inner feminine. Exaggerate if necessary—you are expressing a polarity, an aspect of yourself. Move as a woman, let your hips sway, breathe as a woman. Really feel and visualize your beautiful, female self. Appreciate and love her and have fun letting her express herself.

❧ When you have a complete image and feeling of your inner woman alive within you, close your eyes, come back to yourself. Put your hands on your heart, slow down, relax, and feel the quality of your energy.

❧ Listen to your inner woman's message, right now. She is telling you how she feels to be inside you. What does she say?

❧ Thank her for her message and let her go.

ᔕ Now change to the more masculine music. Again, close your eyes and relax.

ᔕ Follow the same steps as above, imaging your inner man dancing within you.

ᔕ Grow into the feeling of him, dance him, act out this inner masculine. Move as a man, let your hips sway, breathe as a man would. Really feel and visualize your strong, male self. Again, exaggerate—you are expressing a polarity. Improvise a fun caricature that shows this side of yourself. How does he move his shoulders? His hips? How does he hold his chin? Appreciate and love him, and have fun letting him express himself. Try making the sounds he would make, parody his voice. Study him in detail until you are familiar with every aspect.

ᔕ Listen to your inner man's message, right now. He is telling you how it feels for him to be inside you. What does he say?

ᔕ Thank him for his message and let him go.

ᔕ After relaxing for a few minutes, ask yourself: How would I like to end this exchange with my inner polarities?

ᔕ If that feels appropriate, you may focus on the space behind your closed eyes and visualize, imagine, think, or feel (however it comes to you) your inner man and your inner woman meeting, hugging, dancing, conversing, and making friends with each other. Enjoy their relationship.

ᔕ Turn off the music.

ᔕ When you are ready, open your eyes and come back into the room. Feel your inner man and woman strong and live inside you.

ᔕ Decide, if you wish, that from now on, you will let them be with you, speak to you and advise you in every moment of your life: Should I wait? Should I say it? Should I ask for it now? Ask them, inside, and you may enjoy a new level of clarity.

POINTERS

ᔕ If you are a woman, you may be more comfortable experiencing the inner woman first. If you are a man, you may be more comfortable connecting with your inner man first. Go with what feels right to you.

ᔕ Even if you are not used to dancing on your own, try it anyway, as a meditation in movement and awareness. You will be surprised, after a few times, how clear you will be in your everyday life's moves and decisions.

꙳ If you are doing this with your partner, it's fun to play the opposite polarity at the same time—if you are a woman, act the man while he acts the woman. Let them interact with each other.

EVOKING THE INNER GOD AND GODDESS

Not long after my journey to Devipuram, I went to Australia to participate in an unusual experiment. Several friends and I did a retreat. We fasted in isolation, silence, and nondoing—no reading, writing, or even meditating, just being—for twenty-one days.

For days and days, I went through layer after layer of resistance followed by letting go. I moved through states of confusion followed by new insights. It seemed as though I were dying to myself. I saw how much of life is based in addiction—to certain foods, emotions, and situations and to love, comfort, and sex. All this started to fade away. Yet I had nothing to replace it with. The urge to do something was at times unbearable. I became acutely aware of the tension between the masculine urge to act and the feminine desire to rest within myself.

One afternoon, about two weeks into the process, I sat under a tree, breathing, gazing at the sky, feeling the tree against my back. I closed my eyes. And I had a powerful internal vision. I saw myself in my male form sitting in the lotus position under the tree. Simultaneously, I saw myself as a woman sitting in the lap of the man. I was two distinct individuals, yet joined as one—body, heart, and soul—in blissful union. And I experienced in my body rushes of energy, waves of bliss. There I/they/we were, entwined, joined, Margot-male and Margot-female, making love, breathing together, exchanging energy, sharing love—me as man, short haired and strong, with me as woman, long haired and soft, merged in ecstasy. I closed my eyes and felt as if this man Margot were on one side of my body and this woman Margot were on the other, God and Goddess in divine communion within me.

I felt their union become waves of energy, blending, becoming light circulating through my *chakras,* channeled through the inner meridians and passageways of my body. Then the energy was released in a joyful eruption through the crown of my head into the universe.

In that extraordinary experience my inner male and female, my need for doing and being, became integrated at a new and deeper level than ever before. When I returned home I noticed in myself a new, more meditative way of "doing," a more dynamic state of "being," and a much deeper contentment. And more and more often, being alone does not mean being lonely or incomplete. Now I can share my wholeness with my partner, rather than seek my wholeness through him.

I have since discovered working with people in my trainings that you do not have to endure three weeks of sensory deprivation or isolation to experience and unify your inner polarities. Your inner man and woman wait for you to call forth their creative and ecstatic potential.

CHAPTER FOUR

THE ENERGY-ECSTASY CONNECTION: INTEGRATING BODY, MIND, HEART, AND SPIRIT

"I am the cup . . . I am the wine . . . I am the ocean . . ."

                         ▶ Shaykh Sidi Muhammad

The marriage of our inner man and inner woman is a profound integration that allows ecstasy to permeate, transform, our daily life. This experience goes far beyond a temporary flash of insight to become part of our four centers: grounded in the body; deeply felt and accepted in the heart; witnessed and understood in the mind; and awakened in the Spirit.

When we are in tune with life, our body, heart, and mind function as a team. Energy flows through our whole being and we fall in tune with our own rhythms, beyond struggle and contradiction.

Our *body*—our physical self—is the vehicle through which our emotional, intellectual, and spiritual selves find their own expression. Through our *heart*—our emotional self—we move outside ourselves and connect and relate to the world of others. Through our *mind*—our intellectual self—we perceive, think, reflect, and interpret our own perceptions. And through our *Spirit*—our essential self—we find our Buddha nature: a positive, wise, and loving guide who reminds us of our true nature, which is ecstatic.

Our four centers are meant to interact with each other, but they are often in conflict. Our intellect wants to rule the show. Our emotional self often carries the wounds of our inner child. Our body often reflects and manifests the conflicts between these two in the form of stress and dis-ease. And our spiritual self flashes through in moments of inner peace. Each of your four centers is an abode of ecstasy. In movement and dance your body becomes fluid and alive; in love, your heart expands; in "knowing," your mind understands experience and becomes wise; in spirit you receive guidance and healing. The life force moves through each of our centers in a different way. And each center can be an abode of ecstasy or a place of suffering. Our body can move, dance, work, and make love; neglect and abuse can sap its vitality and make it a lifeless shell. Our heart can love and give warmth; withhold love and a wounding coldness develops. Our mind can perceive, understand, and create; yet projection, misinterpretation, and delusion cause untold mischief.

When your body is relaxed and grounded, when your heart is innocent and open to trust, when your mind is clear and your thoughts are nonintrusive, you can expand beyond the boundaries of self and meet others with compassion. To the degree that we are balanced and whole in these three centers, they are doorways to realization, and our Spirit shines through them into life.

BEFRIENDING YOUR BODY

Tantra teaches the first thing: Be loving toward your body, befriend your body, revere your body, respect your body, take care of your body—it is God's gift. Treat it well, and it will reveal great mysteries to you. All growth depends on how you are related to your body.

                       ✐ Osho

The body is a living miracle. It is an alchemical laboratory of seventy-five trillion cells. It is capable of astonishing feats of endurance, grace, and self-healing. It is a family of organs working together, circulating and digesting life, eliminating wastes, endlessly re-creating itself. Even our language reflects our sense of unity with our body: sorrow is a "broken heart," rage is "hot blood" or "vented spleen," and confession is "spilling our guts."

How we think about our body affects our body's health. If we are obsessively concerned with looks, always worrying about being too fat or thinking we need to buff up to be attractive, we end up at war with ourself.

In Love and Ecstasy Seminars, we discover as a group that often, when we think badly about a certain part of our body, it is not the body we are talking about but ourself. These "bad body thoughts" need to be decoded. For example, when a man says, "I hate my fat belly," he really means "There is something wrong with me. I feel like a slob." If a woman says, "My breasts are too big," she really means "If I'm too big, I'll be too much. I won't be accepted." "My chin is weak" can mean "I feel I'm not enough. I look weak, I want to be strong."

Often the frustration we feel and project on our bodies comes from not having a good sex life or not feeling loved by our parents when we were children. Our most common experience has to do with the "you should be this or that" admonitions we grew up with. To heal the body, we need to question *everything* we have ever been told about who we are supposed to be. We need to examine these shoulds with patience, courage, and tenderness.

Be gentle with yourself. Allow your spiritual self to step in. Discover the nurturing caregiver inside of you who can say, "I love you just the way you are." Yes, you were ashamed, you internalized the harsh criticisms you heard growing up. But now, see them for what they are: your own parents' programming, which they passed on to you because they didn't know better. Let it go. Start afresh. Step by step. Love yourself as you are. And day by day, listen to what the physical self has to say.

LOVE YOUR BODY AS IT IS

The first step toward integration is to make friends with your body, to love your body *just as it is*—fat, skinny, tall, short, in shape or out. When you honor your body as your friend, you begin to appreciate it in a different way: it moves, it feels, it senses, it keeps you alive. It is not a servant to do the mind's bidding, but a living entity with its own consciousness.

Whenever your body feels uncomfortable—tense, hungry, itchy, achy, sensuous—it is giving you a message. Learn from it. For example, instead of saying, "I have a headache" and taking an aspirin, ask your head, "What are you telling me? How can I help you?" Talk to your body, listen for the answer, and change the body through the impact of your dialogue with your friend.

OPENING TO PLEASURE

When you listen to your physical self, you open the door to pleasure. Observe, for example, how you make love. Sexuality is a metaphor for life, and how we approach our sexuality is a good indicator of how we approach the rest of our lives. In my experience, orgasm, the ecstasy of the body, lies at the root of our creativity. Yet many people have an ambivalent relationship with their sexuality. We want to be great lovers, we want to have great orgasms, we want to be totally alive and seductive; yet at the same time, conditioned by Judeo-Christian thought, we have renounced the very idea that we have inside us a wildness that is good and that is essentially inspirational. As a result, instead of tapping into the ecstatic potential available through lovemaking, we usually remain lukewarm and we don't feel "well-comed"—in all senses of the term! Tantra teaches, as Miranda Shaw quotes in *Passionate Enlightenment,* that

> *When one enters the palace of the sense organs,*
> *Experiencing abundant delights*
> *This very world attains*
> *The singular taste of spiritual ecstasy*

This poem teaches us how we can bring the orgasm out of the bedroom into our daily life. For we can learn how to generate "abundant delights" independently of the sexual context, simply letting the energy of sensual delights and love enliven the body, open the heart, clear the mind, and heal the spirit.

BEFRIENDING YOUR BODY

PURPOSE

 To heal, love, and honor each part of your body, each part of yourself.

PREPARATION

 Set aside at least one hour for this sensual feast, during which you will not be disturbed.

 Prepare a warm, comfortable bath and add your favorite essences: lavender for relaxation, eucalyptus for clearing your lungs, mint for sharpening the brain, gardenia and rose for opening the heart, sandalwood for the spirit, and so on.

 To welcome your body home, turn your bathroom into a gorgeous temple, with candles, incense, music, flowers. Create a sensuous and pleasing atmosphere (see Chapter 5).

PRACTICE

 Begin with a Heart Salutation (page 75).

 Rest in the bath for five minutes, breathing in the scents and letting your tensions drain away. For the next twenty minutes, gently caress yourself. Touch every part of your body. As you touch each part, inhale deeply. Feel that part, visualize it, see all that it does for you, how it helps you in your life.

 Begin with your feet. As you caress them, say, "Thank you for carrying me to my goals and supporting my journey."

 Move on to your legs. As you caress them, say, "Thank you for carrying my weight in the world and supporting my life."

 Move on to your knees. As you caress them, say, "Thank you for your unique mobility. Without you, I could not dance, ski, run, sit in meditation, ride horses, and a thousand other joys."

 Move on to your thighs. As you caress them, say, "I like your strength, your willingness to be pillars of support to connect my pelvis to my legs. I know I sit on chairs all day, so it's not always fun for you. But you are a great help to me."

 Move on to your buttocks. As you caress them, say, "I like your roundness. You protect my spine from shocks, you are sexy."

≈ Move on to your genitals. As you caress them, say, "You are my healer. The portal of pleasure, power, and fertility."

≈ Continue in this way, moving on to your belly, your diaphragm (solar plexus), breasts, chest, arms, elbows, hands and shoulders, neck and throat, face, mouth, eyes, ears, forehead, and scalp, and finally give a special blessing to your crown, at the top of your head.

≈ Then, caress your entire body and say, "Thank you for being the temple of my Spirit. Tell me what you need, and I will listen."

≈ As you emerge, dry yourself, rub your body vigorously with a special brush for the skin to enhance circulation, perfume yourself, and apply a hydrating cream. Now you and your body are allies. You have honored the ground of your being.

≈ Now the time is right to celebrate this new relationship with your body through dance. Select two favorite pieces of music that have a slow beat, so you can dance without pushing or forcing, to warm up. Then play two pieces that are wild, strong, rhythmic. For added fun, stand in front of a full length mirror and dance with your own reflection. If you feel tense spots, don't avoid them. Breathe in them, stretch them lovingly, dance with them, around them.

POINTERS

≈ If you don't have a bathtub, you can do this exercise in the shower.

≈ If you want to try this exercise with a partner, I suggest you first do it three times on your own so that you are secure in your practice.

≈ Then, taking a bath together, you caress your own body and your partner caresses your body as you pronounce the invocations out loud. In this way you receive added encouragement for your meditation. Then do the same for your partner. Finally, show your partner how you move, how you inhabit your body. Your partner will then do the same for you.

Opening the Heart

Being alive means having a heart and expressing it.
In freeing the body, we free the heart to experience
the power of love.

                                 ✿ Gabrielle Roth

The way of the heart is to be gentle and loving to yourself first. We heal the wounds of the past not by rejecting who we are and hating ourself, but by embracing even our "shadow" parts, our difficult emotions. Sometimes we don't even know that our heart is veiled. We simply feel out of touch. This was the case for Myra, a client who told me this story:

> I was driven by ambition, focused on my career, dedicated totally to my business—teaching seminars, giving speaking engagements, appearing at conferences internationally. I would come off one plane, change suitcases and leave again the next day. By the end of the year, I had earned a lot of money, but my life was in shambles. I couldn't concentrate. I was speeding all the time, trying to do twenty things at once, I didn't even know how to slow down, until I collapsed.

I asked Myra to look inside and ask herself how that activity nourished her.

"Well," she said, "I love to get up there on stage and impress everyone. I love to wear cool clothes, be brilliant."

Then I asked Myra to look inside and ask, "Are there any aspects of your occupation that do not nourish you?"

"Yes," she replied. "People's appreciation is skin deep. I am just another passing teacher, here today, gone tomorrow. Who really cares?" Myra was on the verge of tears. Her voice was trembling, deep grief wanted to surface as she was becoming more vulnerable. "And I am just a good marketing product. I sell. So I am invited. It brings bucks to everyone. But what about me?"

"Which 'me'?" I asked.

"The 'me' that's not on stage," she said quietly.

"Would you talk about that one?" I asked. "Does she have a name?" I guided Myra to close her eyes, go deep into her breathing, focus on her heart. Her hands moved to her heart. She became very sad. A small child-like voice emerged, hidden, shy, as if reluctant to reveal herself.

She said, "My name is Michou . . . I have been hiding for a long time. Myra doesn't pay attention. Her parents didn't pay attention either." And Michou went on to tell the sad story of growing up with a very strict mother who lived by the book of rules and roles and never paid attention to Myra's real desires and needs, and an emotionally abusive father who was only interested in her school marks and good behavior.

"So what would Michou need now, to heal?" I whispered.

"I would like to feel cozy, warm, loved and cared for."

"Good. How will you create this?"

"I don't know. I feel I don't deserve this, nobody can give it to me."

"What about Myra," I asked, "is there anything she could do for Michou?"

After a while Myra and Michou entered into a dialogue with each other. Myra acknowledged that she hadn't taken Michou seriously and had repeated the same behavior with Michou that her parents had with her.

As the gentle, long-repressed girl/woman in Myra emerged, she spoke more and more decisively about the changes she needed. Changes in lifestyle and attitudes but, especially, changes in values.

"Your life is not a life," she was saying to Myra. "Look at you! Are you happy? If only you could let me in, I want to love you. We need to support each other. I call for a life that is quiet, in harmony with the seasons, a life where there is time to daydream, cook, stay home, be in love, hang around. There is no need to be successful. You did it already! Stay home now! It's time to be cozy. You don't need to prove yourself, to perform, to be an expert, to talk in public, to push. To become a nobody is the most ecstatic thing you can do for yourself, for us!"

As I listened, I was amazed by what I heard. The voice of Michou now was growing stronger and wiser every minute. Myra was deeply touched, exhausted, relieved, and ready to listen. A new balance had been achieved. A sense of peace filled the room.

When you begin to touch that soft spot inside your heart, you discover how much innocence, warmth, and gentleness is there. Suddenly, the world is more spacious. You don't need to avoid your fear, but you are willing to know yourself at this deep level. With your heart open, your emotional well-being no longer depends on whether someone likes you, or loves you, or whether you are famous or unknown.

THE HEART SALUTATION

PURPOSE
As you touch your heart in the Heart Salutation and feel the warmth there, you may feel also that love has a message: "You are part of the larger creation, connected to all others, love is endless, infinitely available." To acknowledge to your partner and your friends, "I am lovable and so are you" will establish a sense of respect between you and them and open you to the dimension of the sacred. This ritual salutation is a wonderful way to begin and end each of the exercises in this book. You can do this ritual alone, with a partner, or in a group.

PREPARATION
☙ Allow five minutes of sacred, uninterrupted time.
☙ Do the salutation face to face with your partner or alone with yourself in front of a mirror.

PRACTICE
☙ Sit face to face, eyes open, with your spine straight but relaxed.
☙ Inhale, cup your hands slightly, and bring your palms together in front of your heart, with your thumbs resting gently on your chest.
☙ Bend forward slightly until your foreheads touch. Feel the heart connection between you.

꩜ Look into your own or your partner's eyes and say, "I honor you as an aspect of myself."

꩜ As your partner reciprocates, appreciate and receive the devotion and respect that is conveyed through this greeting. Both of you, in this moment, share the fullness of being; and despite the differences between you, you have called the presence of your Spirit to bless each other's hearts.

꩜ You may choose, instead of words, to sing the sound *Ooomm,* the root of all sounds. Let the sound resonate from deep within your belly. Feel the centering and cleansing effect it has on your psyche.

꩜ When you sit up again, exhale, let your hands rest in your lap. Simply gaze in each other's eyes for a moment, feeling the healing effect of this ritual. Feel how this gesture reconnects your body and Spirit.

POINTERS

꩜ The Heart Salutation is a most wonderful practice to center yourself when you are about to go into an intense or difficult situation.

꩜ This ritual teaches you detachment for the grasping of the ego: you are creating, in five minutes, a sacred space outside of all preoccupations.

꩜ To really feel the power of this practice, be totally present, inhale and exhale deeply, feel your body, your forehead, and forget the rest.

꩜ If you feel strange, at first, with this unusual way of greeting each other, use any words that seem suitable. Hindus say "Namaste." Christians say "Amen." Jews say "Shalom." Muslims say "Salaam." These are all forms of blessing.

꩜ You can do this standing, sitting in a chair or on a pillow, kneeling—anything that feels comfortable.

Spiritual guides say, "You must know yourself before you can truly love another." Christ said, "Love thy neighbor as thyself." Our relationship to ourself determines how we relate to others. When you accept yourself, you begin to recognize how lovable you actually are. You begin to hear the voice of your heart, your inner lover who will tell you that life is on your side supporting you, teaching you, helping you grow. And you may remember, in such a moment, that love, lust, and godliness need not be separated: they belong to the same team.

CLEARING THE MIND

Nan-in, a Japanese master during the Meiji era (1868–1912), received a university professor who came to inquire about Zen.

Nan-in served tea. He poured his visitor's cup full, and then kept on pouring. The professor watched the overflow until he no longer could restrain himself. "It is overfull. No more will go in!"

"Like this cup," Nan-in said, "you are full of your own opinions and speculations. How can I show you Zen unless you first empty your cup?"

          ~ Paul Reps

Our cup is overflowing with opinions and beliefs that interfere with our clear vision—"You can't do that." "It's impossible." "I'll never survive this." "I don't deserve this." Our mental traffic is often as dense as an LA freeway during rush hour. We live in a world of hyperstimuli, bombarded daily by a nonstop stream of high-tech info-missiles: buzzwords, advertising slogans, sound bites, propaganda, and political spin, all designed to snare, hold, shape, and control our attention to empty our wallets, get our votes, muffle our rebellious voices, and put us to sleep with distractions and trivial concerns.

And our mind, being obsessed with thinking, analyzing, planning, and rehearsing endless mental scenarios for incidents that will likely never happen, is in opposition to life. What to do?

WALK OUT OF YOUR MIND!

Our minds function like a bio-computer, often interrupted by useless programs. For instance, we're ready to make love, but our attention wanders and we think, "Did I turn the oven off?" Our worry and concern breaks the flow. A potentially delightful moment dissolves before it has begun. Unwittingly, we feed our computer with a negative program that says, "It won't work. You don't deserve pleasure. Business first." If we don't catch our negative programs they become self-fulfilling prophecies and our ecstatic potential is lost.

But you can change this. Become aware when negative thoughts arise. See yourself literally deleting that negative program from your bio-computer and replacing it with another program that says, "Relax. Everything is taken care of, you can enjoy this moment fully, you deserve it."

Enhance your shift in consciousness with deep, slow breaths. When you shift your thoughts to a positive and supportive internal dialogue and consciously watch your breath, you create space. Remember: You cannot think your way out of your mind any more than you can leave a forest by climbing a tree. Merely thinking new thoughts, even positive thoughts, is futile. Positive affirmations in a chaotic mind are like roses thrown into a tornado. You must leave the mind directly. But how?

Call on your heart and body centers as partners. Notice, when you are overthinking, that you have stopped feeling. You have disconnected from your body and heart. You cannot think your way out of a chaotic mind, but you can *feel* your way out, into the body and the heart. Reestablish feeling contact with these two centers. Change your state with deep, slow breaths. Relax. Feel deeply, with great attention. Be fully present in your living, breathing body. Feel into the center of your heart. Notice how this calms the mind. When you bring your mind into your body and your heart through feeling attention, your whole being naturally relaxes and opens up. There is a deep peace in heart and body when the mind relaxes. You can always find it there.

Theophan, the Recluse, wrote in *The Art of Prayer,* "You wish to grow wise in discernment of thoughts? Descend from the head into the heart. Then you will see all thoughts clearly as they move before the eye of your sharp-sighted mind."

Slow, deep breathing and simple relaxation allow you to enter the silence between thoughts. Here you can choose; direct your thoughts; stop your internal dialogue; and set new, positive programs through simple awareness and intention. This is the space of being I call Sky Mind, the clear, calm, silent awareness that underlies the chatter of our ego-mind.

YOU HAVE ALL THE ANSWERS

From your Sky Mind, while feeling your body and your heart, notice the world around you through the perceptions of your five senses. What do you hear? Voices, cars, the wind, your lover rattling dishes in the kitchen? What does your body feel like in this state of rest? What do you see, taste, and smell? Notice how the simple, direct experience of life is soothing, even healing— the sensations of your body; familiar smells, colors, and forms; the light and shade all around you.

The rich textures of our perceptions of life are like a symphony of being. When witnessed and felt with effortless attention, this symphony calms the mind, opens and aligns our four centers, and brings us into harmony with ourselves and with life. In such moments, our true nature is revealed as a vast, free, spacious state of being, of consciousness. This is our Sky Mind, which is always there behind the clutter and chaos of our subjectivity. This is the space that invites ecstasy. The Sky Mind is the mirror of the heart. It is receptive, creative, intuitive, opened to information from other centers and dimensions of being. It is the visionary mind, the fertile mind of divine inspiration.

PRACTICE INNER KNOWING

Every moment is pregnant with ecstasy, pregnant with infinite possibilities. When you relate to life through the awareness of all four centers, the right choice is revealed to you naturally. There is a simple way to receive guidance from within. When I worked with Robert Gass, a spiritual guide and organizational consultant, we practiced what he calls Inner Knowing. He explained:

> It begins with the assumption that we already know almost everything we need to know, particularly about our own journey, our own unfolding. That information is there, is available at a moment's notice. To access it,

you have to learn to tune to the right frequency, just as you adjust the dial to tune in a radio station.

❧❧❧❧❧❧❧❧❧❧❧❧❧❧❧❧❧❧❧❧❧❧❧❧❧❧❧❧❧❧❧❧❧❧❧

INNER KNOWING

You can use Inner Knowing at any time, every day, especially when a situation feels unclear to you.

PURPOSE
❧ To access your inner wisdom on any question.

PREPARATION
❧ Set aside at least fifteen minutes when you will not be disturbed. With some practice, you can access Inner Knowing in a few minutes.

PRACTICE
❧ Formulate your question. Express it clearly in your mind. Now put it aside for a moment.

❧ You will ask your question from a centered place below the level of everyday thought. To center yourself, inhale, exhale, and breathe deeply until you feel in touch with your body and your heart.

❧ Direct your question into the centered place in your heart. At the end of your exhalation, ask the question.

❧ Listen for the answer. Accept what comes. The first information is usually the clearest. You may get one word (yes or no) or a wave or burst of fifteen or thirty seconds of very focused information. It may be in the form of words, images, or feelings. The more experience you have with the process, the longer you can stay there before your mind comes in to question the validity of this information. When thoughts start intruding, end the meditation for the time being.

❧ Now you will work with what you received. What does that tell me? What questions does that raise? What does that really mean? How do I know if the answer is true? You don't. All you can do is listen as clearly as you can, try it out, and see what happens.

🙊 With practice, you will be able to center yourself and listen from within with a simple inhalation and exhalation.

🙊 Don't judge the content of the message as much as the quality: Is it light, loving, clear? Then it's probably your true voice.

🙊 Learn to taste the quality of the energy of the message. For example, you ask the question, "Should I keep teaching or should I do something else with my life?" You hear, "Time to let go of teaching and time to go inside and write." The quality of this voice is very straightforward—it's not trying to sell you anything. This is the quality of your inner guidance. On the other hand, you might hear, "You can't teach. You're no good at that." What's the quality of that second voice? It's contracted, judging, it sounds suspiciously like your mother. This is the voice of your ego-mind, your inner critic. It is a sign that you need to go deeper, to your heart.

🙊 Wait for some time and go through the process again.

Each moment of the day provides an opportunity to practice the art of Inner Knowing. You can approach any situation in your life as a teaching, an opportunity to respond with the awareness and understanding of your whole being. For instance, you're on a first date, you have had a good time, and you begin to kiss passionately. You are touching each other randomly, your hands wandering over each other's body. If your body tenses up, your heart beats wildly, and your mind races a mile a minute— Is this too much? Is this too soon? Do we even like each other?—an Inner Knowing session is in order. You can run through this dialogue in a few seconds. In fact, simply taking a moment to center yourself ("Just a minute—I have to go to the bathroom" is the easiest one in this situation!) will probably open you to your authentic feelings and choices.

∾ *Check in with your body.* "How does this touch feel to you?" Listen to your body's response. It might say, "It feels soooo good I just want to melt" or "Too rough" or "Just right" or "I don't feel anything. I'm too tense" or "I am contracting. I am afraid it won't feel right so I don't want to feel anything."

∾ *Check in with your heart.* "How do you feel when you are touched in this way?" Listen to your heart's response. It might say, "I am opening, it feels tender and safe, just let go!" or "Are you in love? Are you falling for this person?" or "I am scared, I don't feel safe" or "I don't feel a heart connection."

∾ *Check in with your mind.* What are your thoughts saying? "Just enjoy yourself and breathe, it's okay. You deserve pleasure" or "I really don't want to be doing this, but I don't want to hurt his feelings" or "Be clear. You haven't communicated clearly about boundaries."

∾ *Check in with your Spirit.* "What would be for my highest good in this situation?" Your Spirit may say, "I feel honored in my body and soul." or "I don't feel we have created a sacred space to honor this moment."

Once you collect the impressions of the four centers of your being, you can begin to integrate their messages:

∾ *Review your body's feedback about sensation.* My body feels contracted. My muscles are tense. This means I am holding back.

∾ *Review your heart's feedback about the emotions associated with the sensations.* I am afraid of something. What is it? I don't feel a heart connection between us, I can't let go.

∾ *Review your mind's feedback as it analyzes the situation.* Something's wrong here. Nothing feels right emotionally or physically. I really don't want to be doing this right now. I need to be clear and communicate what's going on and remember to be loving and enjoy myself. Make him or her feel welcome.

∾ *Review your Spirit's message.* Reflect. Observe. Witness. Expand. Assume my partner has good intentions, and as an initiation I will use this opportunity to teach him or her the skills of love! I'll speak my truth lovingly.

Now you can take responsibility to create what feels just right to you, and you can do it from a place of assurance and non-blaming. And you won't be responding from the past ("He's just like all the rest of my boyfriends, he only wants me for my body"; "She probably just wants to get married, or use me to get her pregnant") or from the future ("Well, this doesn't feel totally right but I'm *so* ready to settle down. Maybe I'll try to make it work anyway"). Work from the present. Hold the vision of the positive outcome you want to create, the situation that is comfortable for your body, your heart, your mind, your Spirit.

Use this integration during every moment. Your four centers are your support team, here to help you create a balanced life. For example, when you find yourself reacting out of habit, become aware of it—"I hate that." "Why does this always happen to me?" "If this line doesn't start moving I'm going to scream." Instead of reacting negatively, consciously wake up each center (and remember to change the program in your bio-computer!).

> ❧ *Body.* "I am grateful for the ability to feel my energy in this situation, pleasant or unpleasant." Now watch your body's responses. Is your heart beating fast? Is your throat feeling constricted? Just observe the wondrous workings taking place in your body.
> ❧ *Mind.* "I am grateful for my ability to watch how I respond in this situation." Observe your internal dialogue. ("I can't believe I have to stand in this line. My feet hurt. Why didn't I realize this was going to happen and pick another line? I always pick the wrong line.") Observes the silent gaps between the thoughts.
> ❧ *Heart.* "I am grateful for my ability to receive this situation in my heart." Observe how you are feeling right now. Sad? Contented? Consider all these emotions in your heart; your options about how you feel at any moment are wide open.
> ❧ *Spirit.* "I am grateful for my ability to be choiceless in this situation because I trust the guidance of my

Spirit." Appreciate your life this moment, exactly the way it is right now. Feel the clear breeze saying yes to your Spirit, welcome the spaciousness of your Sky Mind.

WELCOMING YOUR SPIRIT EVERY DAY

Real fulfillment comes only when we first tune into our inner direction and divine guidance. . . . That helps unite heaven and earth.

James Redfield

When body, heart, and mind function as a team, wondrous things happen: The body expresses the emotions of the heart and does the bidding of the mind. The heart is strengthened by the aliveness of the body and guided by the wisdom of clear mind. The mind expresses the acceptance of the heart and allows the tension to flow out of the body. Our true nature is revealed: ecstasy.

With each center participating equally and fully you are no longer fighting yourself, sabotaging your own ecstatic potential. You allow the energy to flow where it needs to go. And into this restfulness, Spirit comes in, with its divine energy.

But it is not the bliss that we experience in meditation that is the most important. Bliss alone does not free us from a negative pattern. In fact, an ecstatic experience can be used by the ego. We may despise our humdrum daily life, thinking it takes us away from our meditation and our blissfulness, imagining that only states of heavenly bliss are our true spiritual home. This fallacy is what the Tibetan Tantric master Chogyam Trungpa called "spiritual materialism."

The difficult work of inner transformation is not about transcendence but rather about awakening in the very midst of our difficulties and seeing through the illusions, recurring patterns, and dramas that we take to be true, recognizing that they are but a dream.

It is said, "If you meet the Buddha on the way, kill him!" This means, if you meet ecstasy on the way, let it go. Do not be attached to dramatic or exalted states. We can know a more deeply integrated, more permanently awakened state, a steady flow of energy, and joy in life, that I call EveryDay Ecstasy. Here our thoughts and emotions arise, come, and go; yet we don't believe the pictures they present us. No big deal and no big waves. And in a simple and discreet way we begin to live in a stable, ongoing state of contentment.

PART II

EveryDay Ecstasy

CHAPTER FIVE

COMING HOME: CREATING A SACRED SPACE

The world is imprisoned in its own activity, except when actions are performed as worship of God. Therefore you must perform every action sacramentally . . . and be free from all attachment to results.

                            Bhagavad Gita

We create sacred space to bring our spirit into harmony with life in our daily environment. When our mind is clear and we are fully present to life and the world around us, we are *in* sacred space. And creating sacred space, by ritually changing and rearranging our outer environment, is a means both of focusing our mind—becoming present to the sacred, which is always within us—and of anchoring and aligning the flow of Spirit in our physical environment.

I first began to understand this concept when I lived in a Tantric ashram in southern India. The temple there had statues: Lord Shiva, destroyer of illusions; goddess Shakti, mother of creation; and Ganesha, the elephant god, remover of obstacles and bestower of abundance. The live-in temple guardian was a man named Suresh Ananda, which means "guardian of bliss." He watched the temple, kept it clean, aired it out, replenished the bowls of food offerings and water, kept the candles lit, burned incense to the statues of the deities, offered flowers, and recited regular prayers. He fed the temple with his life force and his attention. He became a vehicle through which sacred space occurred in relation to the temple environment and the temple deities.

Suresh Ananda's job was to make these deities feel welcomed, nourished, and honored, so they would remain in the temple. Money seemed to flow in. The ashram built a school and a yoga room. Every day it fed the thirty members of its community, and it spearheaded many social services. Everyone knew all this came by the grace of the temple deities.

Tantric philosophy holds that our body is the temple of our Spirit; our five senses are the doors through which we perceive the world. When we travel through these doors consciously, we can rediscover our true nature, which is ecstatic. Our environment, as our "greater body," is an extension and a reflection of our Spirit. And it can, through ritual, be made to resonate with and emanate the power and presence of the sacred.

The Inner Temple: Honoring Your Body

To worship a deity, a man must become the self
of that deity through dedication, breath control,
and concentration until his body becomes the
deity's abode.

                         ∾ Gandharva Tantra

To be a true guardian of our own bodily temple, we must serve it well. We can enliven and balance body, mind, and emotions through holistic hygiene; exercise; healthy diet; conscious breathing; and alignment of our attention with spirit through some form of meditation, contemplation, or prayer. To the degree that we live these healing disciplines, treating our mind and body as living temples, we magnify our Spirit and we exist in a sacred space.

To the degree that we serve our temples poorly, by taking toxins into our bodies and minds, by not exercising or breathing properly, by not releasing the cumulative stresses of living, we fall into unconsciousness and our inner and outer environments grow cluttered and chaotic. Then we fail to notice the sacred dimension of life, the ecstasy that is always in us. We can magnify our Spirit through conscious living, or let it go out like an untended fire. Through abuse or neglect, our inner and outer temples may fall into disarray. Yet our Spirit yearns to manifest fully through us.

Perform the following ritual to make your body a welcoming home for your Spirit.

RITUAL: PURIFYING YOUR INNER TEMPLE

Feel free to adapt this ritual as feels right to you. You may speak silently or aloud. The point is to send the healing energy to your body. You may use physical touch, visualize light, or other forms of focusing attention.

PURPOSE
∾ To sanctify your body as the temple of your Spirit.

PREPARATION
∾ Set aside fifteen minutes to half an hour of undisturbed time and create a sacred space.
∾ Have on hand healing and calming essential oils, such as lavender.

PRACTICE
∾ Begin with the Heart Salutation (page 75).
∾ Breathe slowly and deeply. Relax and feel into your body and heart. Let your mind and energy grow calm and centered.
∾ When you are ready, say to your body, "I honor you as my dearest friend. You have always been patient with me and supported me. Now I want to befriend you, listen to you, and receive your guidance. Let us first heal your wounds."
∾ Scent your hand with a special healing essence such as essential oil of lavender (to promote relaxation and healing), inhale the scent of that essence and direct the breath/scent mentally to the area you wish to heal.

✺ Now go to every part of your body that has been wounded, cut open, or operated on (for example, dental work, abortions, falls, broken bones, plastic surgery, scars, cesarean cuts, pains in the joints) or has suffered any pain that reflects emotional stress (for example, headaches, intestinal upset, acid stomach, bodily tensions, muscle cramps). Touch each spot and rub it gently with your scented hand—caress it, rest your hand on it, hold it, and breathe into it.

✺ Breathing deeply and slowly, say, "Dear [name the body part: stomach, heart, tooth, jaw, wrist], I am sorry you were hurt. Here is what happened." Explain the circumstances surrounding whatever caused the pain. Then say, "I am sorry I didn't listen to your pain then. But now I send you my love. Please feel it now."

✺ Mentally, direct your energy to this body part and say, "Now, together, let us heal you."

✺ Inhaling deeply, send light and love to this area. Hold your breath gently for a few seconds and imagine this area is filled with love. Exhale, letting go of tensions in this area.

✺ When you have healed every body part, sit quietly for a moment and feel the healing energy refreshing and restoring your body.

✺ End with another Heart Salutation.

THE OUTER TEMPLE: SACRED SPACE

So how do you make your life sacred? You say
"This is sacred," and you treat it that way.

✺ Stuart Wilde

We are accustomed to thinking of sacred space only as a church, a shrine, or a temple. But our conscious intention can make any space sacred, including our home, bedroom, car, or office; a hotel room; or even an elevator (make floors one through six an "uplifting" ride for everyone). A sacred space is an empowered sanctuary where we can integrate and harmonize our body, heart, mind, and Spirit and learn to enter our Sky Mind, our natural, sacred state of being.

NATURE IS SACRED SPACE

Nature is the primal, original sacred space. We are nourished, sustained, and enlivened by Mother Earth. Learn from the "Song of the Sky Loom," from the Tewa Pueblo Indians:

> O our Mother the Earth, O our Father the Sky,
> Your children are we, and with tired backs
> We bring you the gifts that you love.
> Then weave for us a garment of brightness;
> May the warp be the white light of morning,
> May the weft be the red light of evening,
> May the fringes be the falling rain,
> May the border be the standing rainbow.
> Thus weave for us a garment of brightness
> That we may walk fittingly where grass is green,
> O our Mother the Earth, O our Father the Sky!

This is the song of a people in primal relationship to nature as Spirit: Mother Earth and Father Sky. They had no feeling of separation from the earth or the Spirit realms. When we lose contact with the natural world, we lose our fundamental roots in life in a way. Our relationship to life and nature becomes distant and abstract. Recently, I heard a Manhattan radio host say, "For many of us New Yorkers the environment just doesn't seem *real*."

Our cities bury the magnetic current emanating from the earth beneath tar and concrete, literally disconnecting us from its healing power. Nature heals us spiritually, emotionally, and physically. When we spend time in nature, we harmonize with her rhythms and cycles. Gaia, Mother Earth, is a living being of pulsing, breathing, flowing, circulating energy that is nourishing us with her current of life-giving power.

The ancient Chinese sage Zangshu said, "The *chi* of yin and yang breathes forth as wind, ascends as cloud, falls as rain. . . . This living *chi* circulates within the earth, and animates the ten thousand things." To understand what our original sacred space feels like, spend time in nature. Breathe with the earth. Feel the energy that animates the earth, the hills, the rivers, the trees, the grasses, and yourself.

꙾꙾꙾꙾꙾꙾꙾꙾꙾꙾꙾꙾꙾꙾꙾꙾꙾꙾꙾꙾꙾꙾꙾꙾

NATURAL BLISS

In The Long Road Turns to Joy, *Vietnamese Buddhist monk Thich Nhat Hanh says, "In order to have peace and joy, you must succeed in having peace in each of your steps. Your steps are the most important thing."*

PURPOSE
- To heal and renew yourself in contact with the earth, plants, green fields, wind, and trees.
- To detach from the pressure of purposeful activity.
- To enjoy simply being in movement and being aware.

PREPARATION
- Set aside an hour and go to your favorite natural spot: a beach, a park, a field, a pathway in the woods.
- Leave everything behind: no portable music, book, or notepad; just take yourself alone.
- Wear loose comfortable walking clothes and shoes.

PRACTICE
- Begin your walk slowly, breathing deeply, in step with your body's walk.
- Pay attention to the way your joints feel. Sense that your spine can be aligned with your pelvis. Allow your knees to be soft, loose, and elastic; create a step that bounces off the earth, effortlessly.
- After a while, when you have reached a natural rhythm and feel at ease, in a flow, begin to pay attention to your surroundings. Now open your senses completely, so that you perceive everything fully and sharply. Do not pay attention to thoughts, just to what you see, hear, smell, touch, and breathe within the range of your moving body.
- Now focus on what you see. Really look around with full, yet relaxed and receptive attention: notice the sky, the clouds,

the details of the landscape, the bark of a tree, the movement and color of a bird. Take it all in as you inhale deeply. Be filled with this beauty and recognize how it nourishes your soul.

❧ Now focus on what you hear. Open your ears, with full, yet receptive attention, listen to the songs of the birds (how many can you hear at once?), the whisper of the wind, the crackling of the leaves in the trees, the crickets, and all the myriad sounds near and far, and let yourself receive them until you are filled with them.

❧ Now focus on what you smell. With every inhalation, become aware of the scents or smells in the air: what is carried by the wind; the plants you pass by; the animals around; the fresh salty, wet, smell of the waves crashing on the shore. Pick a leaf from a tree. Roll it between your fingers and smell the essence, the juice.

❧ Continue in this way for fifteen minutes or more, enjoying a relaxed attention, bathing your body, heart, and Spirit in this symphony of nature.

❧ With every inhalation, feel renewed. With every exhalation, let go of thoughts and tensions and feel how you can enjoy yourself, simply, step by step.

POINTERS

❧ If thoughts invade your natural space, simply watch them as you watch the flowers and the trees. They are part of your inner landscape; let them go.

❧ After you feel renewed and relaxed, enjoy focusing loosely and softly on a creative topic or a question that needs answering. As you walk, wait for an insight, an unusual word, a new connection you might perceive.

❧ If you get tired, look for a beautiful clearing or a special vista and sit there to rest.

❧ If you have an insistent problem, sit or lie by a stream. Imagine the water is running through you and cleansing your Spirit and filling your awareness with gurgling, watery sounds, until all within becomes fluid and flows.

❧ When you get ready to return home, take this beauty with you and remember it throughout the day.

YOUR HOME IS SACRED SPACE

The concept of sacred space is ancient. In China, people have used *feng shui* (pronounced fung shway) for thousands of years to align the energies of environment, self, and universe. *Feng shui* understands that our environment affects us at an energetic level. If it is disharmonious, its effect is negative, and we can be thrown out of balance. If harmonious, it literally conducts the energy around us, bringing us into alignment with its flow. We have all had the experience of cleaning our house and feeling cleansed and energized as a result. This is an example of *feng shui*. When we organize or cleanse our outer environment, we purify and harmonize our own psyche.

You can create sacred space in your home by eliminating clutter and chaos, arranging things into harmonious patterns, and surrounding yourself with objects of power and beauty.

Recently, a Manhattan musician friend of mine complained that he was creatively blocked. "I'm not surprised," I said, looking around his loft space. "Your whole place is cluttered." Old music reviews, files, clothes, piles of letters, and cassettes lay everywhere. It was dark. The windows were at street level. No sky was visible. There was no space for his Spirit to soar.

He called in a *feng shui* expert who helped him free the flow of energy and found ways to circulate and magnify the *chi* to counter the darkness of his space (installing mirrors, hanging crystals, changing the colors of walls). With the adjustments made, my friend felt inspired and began composing new music. He even got a band together to record an album of his songs.

CREATING SACRED SPACE

I laugh when I hear that the fish in the water is thirsty. You don't grasp the fact that what is most alive of all is inside your own house.

☙ Robert Bly

To create sacred space arrange it so that your Spirit feels welcome. Clean it up. Put things in order. Use your intuition.

Arrange things, new and old, in a way that pleases and inspires you.

My friends Ramana Das and Marilena say:

Our home is our temple. "Cleaning the house" may sound dull. But "preparing our temple" is a joy. Our home is our temple because we are gods and goddesses in the flesh and our everyday life is sacred. We create power spots or altars in every room. We place each thing carefully, crystals, flowers, and candles. Before love-making, we light candles and play music. Things are always set up and ready at hand.

Rituals empower our space and deepen our connection to or-dinary life. My friend Kate has established a friendship with her home using the technique of Inner Knowing:

I work with the four directions. I stand and face each area of my home and silently ask, "What is it that you need from me?" Then I listen receptively to what comes—ideas, feelings, images. Sometimes I hear, "I need a curtain over half of the window." Or I will see an image of moving something, a plant, a lamp, a chair, to a different place. An area can literally tell you what it needs.

When your house is your temple, vacuuming, sweeping, and scrubbing becomes a meditation. Listen to Brenda Peterson, in *Nature and Other Mothers:*

There is no more comforting sound to me than the spinning of that washer or dryer. It is the whole world spinning in there, cleansing itself and me. As long as the washer and dryer spin, I tell myself, I am safe and those I love may choose to keep living alongside me. For there is laundry to be done and so many chores— chores of living. There is so much to be remembered under the dust of our old contempt for cleaning up af-ter ourselves, picking up our own socks. There is much to be swept away and shined bright and scrubbed down to its deepest, most illuminating level. Think of all the chores we have yet to do, quietly and on our knees—because home is holy.

＠＠＠＠＠＠＠＠＠＠＠＠＠＠＠＠＠＠＠＠＠＠＠＠＠＠＠

CLEARING YOUR SPACE

PURPOSE
Clearing out is a fundamental part of creating sacred space. Make it a conscious ceremony, you are not just cleaning a room, a house, or an office. You are in a participatory relationship with your environment, raising its energy level, its vibration, and that of your body and mind at the same time.

PREPARATION
✿ Before you begin, take a moment to center yourself with a deep breath.

PRACTICE
✿ Begin by clearing the physical space. Remove all clutter. Give or throw away anything that robs your space of light and energy. If you can't bear to part with it, store it neatly in a drawer or closet.

✿ Sweep, vacuum, dust, mop, or do whatever else you need to do to clean the room. Open doors and windows. Let in fresh air.

✿ When you are finished cleaning, purify yourself by washing your face and hands or by taking a bath or shower. Now you are ready to clear the energy of the space.

✿ Standing in the center of the room, close your eyes, breathe deeply and evenly, and go inside yourself. Say out loud, "I purify this space, my home (or office, or . . .), my temple and invite my Spirit to dwell here."

✿ Envision the room filled with a protective white light. See that light fill every crack and corner, permeating the walls. See the same light surrounding the house, protecting it from the outside.

✿ Clear out the old, static energy with sound (not from a

stereo but from real instruments). Ring bells, clap hands, sing, chant, make sounds of joy all around the room.

❧ To purify and neutralize the space, burn incense, light candles, spray a gentle mist of water. Put fresh flowers in the room as an offering.

❧ Now put on some favorite music and dance around, completely uninhibited and abandoned. Fill the room with your life, your voice, your breath, and sweeping movements that fill the space as if you were the wind blowing through and churning the energies.

ENHANCING THE PLEASURES OF THE FOUR CENTERS

Your body, mind, heart, and Spirit should all feel comfortable in your sacred space. Take the following elements into consideration when you create your space.

SPACIOUSNESS ❧ For the body, one of the most important elements is a sense of freedom. If your space is harmonious and you have room to move, your body feels free and its energy can flow. If you are worried about knocking things over or getting things dirty, you will feel inhibited and so will your guests. Consciously walk around your space. See if you can trace the flow of energy around the room. Remember, your room doesn't have to be large to be spacious.

FRESH AIR ❧ Fresh air brings in fresh energy. Open the windows whenever possible. If you live in a polluted area and can't open the windows, use an air purifier or negative ionizer. Make sure you pick a machine that is quiet!

TEMPERATURE ❧ A comfortable room is not too cold, not too hot, not stifling or drafty. Avoid air-conditioning and artificial heat or cold if possible, especially motor or furnace sounds.

COLOR ❧ Make your room beautiful, a delight to the eyes. Choose colors that inspire you. In my bedroom, for example, I use bright hand-painted drapes and sheets from Bali. Every morning I wake to vivid jungle scenes, bright landscapes with birds and rivers. My first impressions are of the exotic beauty of nature. Choose scenes, images, and colors you resonate with. Notice your responses to different shades. Subdued whites and beiges are nonintrusive. Soft colors let your Spirit soar. Bright colors evoke passions and emotions: reds are for life and eros; greens for heartfulness and hope; blues for expanded consciousness and peace.

PLANTS ✍ Fresh flowers bring color, life, and joy to a room. Living plants not only are beautiful but also emanate life energy, exude the oxygen we breathe, and provide a soothing quality.

LIGHTING ✍ Let the lighting be soft and indirect rather than harsh and bright. This creates an atmosphere of gentleness and mystery, a play of shadow and light. When possible, rely on natural sunlight. Instead of overhead lights, try wall sconces or lamps with dimmer switches. At night, have candles ready to create a sacred mood. Replace fluorescent lights with incandescent light. (If you cannot do this, try wearing glasses with colored lenses.)

SOUND ✍ Sacred space should not be noisy. Keep motor noise to a minimum whenever possible. If you work in a noisy office or live in a noisy apartment, consider buying a machine that emits white noise—sounds of nature, water, and wind that neutralize disturbing noise.

FRAGRANCE ✍ Our sense of smell is related to inspiration. So use fragrances and aromas that lift the spirit. Incense and essential oils evoke various pleasant moods. Different types of diffusers help spread the aromas of essential oils through a room. For example, if you want to stay awake and energetic for long periods, use mint or eucalyptus; to open the heart, use rose or gardenia; to expand the Spirit, use sandalwood; to enhance relaxation and awareness, use lavender; to create a sensual mood, try ylang ylang or amber.

SACRED MEMENTOS

Traditional cultures customarily integrate sacred experience into physical reality. The Huichol Indians made yarn paintings of visions received in sacred ceremonies and hung them in their homes. Many ancient cultures weave rugs in intricate patterns of exquisite beauty and wholeness. Many stained-glass church windows seem to emanate a heavenly radiance. Tibetans hang in front of their homes and temples multicolored prayer flags covered with verses of sacred mantras or invocations to deities.

My friend Ryan, who has a masters degree in environmental design, belongs to a community of Sky Dancers whose members are dedicated to bringing ecstasy into everyday life. He says

> The three-dimensional space actually seems to soak up the vibrations of our rituals and celebrations—our homes, our kitchens, our living rooms—so we are living and breathing these ecstatic states. I notice that our homes have grown more beautiful since we practice sacred rituals together. This work allows us to find in ourselves what is truly and authentically *us* and bring it into the space. For example, my house in the mountains is filled with Native American icons—a medicine wheel on the wall, an eagle painted on the barn door. The medicine wheel reminds me of the path I am walking, the man I am becoming. The eagle reminds me of a higher perspective—I see the river to the left, the mountain range to the right, I see where I fit into the landscape.

Sacred mementos need not be esoteric or overly serious. We can be playful and sacred at the same time. Internationally known artist, sculptor, and painter Niki de Saint Phalle has an exquisite house near Paris. She made her dining room chairs in the form of a woman's body. Her plates are welcoming hands. The American artist Judy Chicago has designed a dining room set with plates that depict different *yonis* that look like graceful flowers. Artist Daniel Spoeri, after sharing a meal with his friends, glues leftover objects to the table: cigarettes, napkins, cups, glasses; he even paints leftovers on the plates. Then he cuts the legs off the table and hangs them on his walls.

Mementos that remind you of moments of joy, pleasure, and holiness can be objects you have bought, found, or created. Arrange them in your home. Acknowledge them as sacred, even ceremonially, by waving incense before them, praising their beauty aloud, speaking to them as if they understood you. (Perhaps they do. Swiss psychologist Carl Jung, an avid chef, talked to his kitchen utensils and claimed they served him better and lasted longer!) Here are other ideas my friends have done to create sacred space:

> ❧ "I took a bowl and put sand inside, and feathers, and a little lake for water. Also incense, and a little candle for the East. I keep it in my living room.
>
> ❧ "I put fragrant potpourri in the ashtray of my car, and I keep it open while I drive."
>
> ❧ "I put charms on my necklace that remind me of messages I have received in important dreams."
>
> ❧ "I collect at least one special rock or shell from every place I visit. Then I display them on shelves and in baskets and even in my yard to remind me of times and places that have brought me joy."
>
> ❧ "I put up photos of all the people I love and who love me on my refrigerator. I include pictures of inspiring people I don't know personally, but whom I'd like to know.
>
> ❧ "I play sacred music in my car, during my commute time: great mantras—sacred verses sung and repeated—and I sing along. My car becomes my cathedral, my place to pray and sing. By the time I get home, I am high, clear, and rested."
>
> ❧ "I have a picture of the Dalai Lama on top of my computer. When I'm trying to connect to my e-mail, I look at his picture and remember that there's an even greater web beyond the World Wide Web!"
>
> ❧ "I designed a rainbow-colored canopy and had it made to hang above our bed, to symbolize protection."
>
> ❧ "I hang a colorful cloth over the door to our bed-

room to remind us that we are entering this space with intention and purpose and that our lovemaking is sacred."

WHAT INSPIRES YOU?

When you create sacred space, allow your personal environment to reflect the energies of the archetypes, gods and goddesses, heroes, people, ideas, and symbols that are most meaningful in *your* life. Experiment as follows.

    ∺ List things that make your life worth living: beauty, love, health, nature, family, money, art, etc. Now examine your life closely and see to what degree you have integrated these energies in your life. Are you fed or undernourished in these areas? How can you bring them more into your daily experience?

    ∺ Find pictures that powerfully symbolize these things for you. For me, *The Kiss* by Gustav Klimt represents love; Botticelli's *Venus,* standing shy and naked in a shell, represents beauty. A picture of an athlete in motion can represent aliveness and health, a picture of a waterfall can represent energy, a beautiful sunrise can represent hope, a forest can represent nature, and so on.

    ∺ Collect photos of people you love and admire and put them on a wall.

    ∺ Look for words, music, and poetry that move or inspire you. Recite, memorize, or write them on paper in your most beautiful handwriting.

    ∺ On a large piece of poster board, create an energy map of your visions and desires. You can do it as a collage. Find images that inspire you, that symbolize your hopes and dreams. Be colorful and creative. Add to it whenever you like. Make it, like your life itself, an ongoing process or a series. Put it where you always see it.

Guardians of the Sacred Space

The natural progression of purifying the energy in
your home is to make all your life sacred so that
everything has a meaning and a purpose. You start
with your home and then you'll want to go further.

                     ✎ Karen Kingston

Your sacred space should be a sanctuary: clean, beautiful, and charged with your sacred intent. Invoke Guardians of the Space whose energy and presence will protect and envelop you. Declare yourself the living Guardian of Your Space and Life. Here are some of the roles and tasks that I have established in my life and in the Love and Ecstasy Trainings.

THE GUARDIAN OF THE TEMPLE

As Guardian of the Temple you have primary responsibility for creating, serving, and maintaining a sacred space. You oversee cleaning, monitor the temperature, keep the air fresh, the environment beautiful, the aroma sensual and spiritual, the atmosphere charged with your life force. From time to time you may purify the space by burning incense, singing and chanting, sprinkling or spraying water, and so on. In the Love and Ecstasy Trainings, three new people daily join in this function, to bring their love, creativity, and energy into the group's space.

The Guardian of the Temple and assistants decorate the center of the room, especially important in a ritual space. The center should be a focus of attention and a power spot. Candles, colored scarves, crystals, flowers, special stones, etc. can be used. It is a pleasure for a group to enter a room creatively blessed by the Guardians of the Temple.

If you live alone, you are Guardian of your Temple. If you live with a partner, roommates, or your family, invite them to share this role with you.

THE GUARDIAN OF THE RITUAL OBJECTS

The Guardian of the Ritual Objects is responsible for the altar, musical instruments, crystals, and any other sacred objects and mementos provided by the group. This guardian creates and decorates the altar, keeps the flowers fresh, and changes and lights the candles.

THE GUARDIAN OF THE TIME

The Guardian of the Time is like a metronome—in charge of the beat, the rhythms in which a ritual unfolds. A sacred ritual— whether it's meditation, artistic creation, sexual Tantric practice, or music playing—usually has a beginning, a middle, and an end. The Guardian of the Time finds subtle, creative ways of reminding the leader of the ritual that "it is now time to. . . ." This way, the leader can let go into timeless space and fully surrender to the spirit of the ritual.

THE GUARDIAN OF SOUND

The Guardian of Sound is in charge of providing music that enhances the sacred space during a ritual. It can be through musical instruments or a selection of tapes. If a sound system is used, this guardian must know how to operate it. If subdued lighting is required for a ritual, have a small flashlight nearby. This guardian chooses and organizes music to support the mood of the moment—from dance to sensual massage to meditation.

CUSTOMIZING THE GUARDIANS

The guardian concept lends itself to all sorts of occasions. Here are some ideas.

IN LARGE GROUPS ∾ A team of guardians, each with a specific assignment, works wonderfully.

IN YOUR HOME ∾ If you live alone, you are all guardians as needed. If you have a partner or a family, each of you can be a guardian for various functions. Rotate guardianship every week or two. This keeps your relationship to your function fresh and pleasurable. The Guardian of the Time, for example, can go through the house ringing a bell to call family or housemates to meals, meditation, or gatherings.

TRAVELING 🐌 When traveling with your partner, one of you be the Guardian of the Temple, in charge of preparing your hotel bedroom as a sacred space. The other can be the assistant. Perhaps set out candles, massage oil, and lubricants for lovemaking; drape scarves around the lampshades for soft lighting; wave incense; set out water to drink and a bowl of fruit to eat; provide extra pillows and towels. Bring favorite pictures or power objects to set up in the room.

As religious historian Mircea Eliade says in *The Sacred and the Profane,* the experience of the sacred reorganizes our lives in unique and fundamental ways. It is important to recognize these moments and consciously work to integrate them in our daily living.

To do this, recognize and maintain your body and home. When you wake, feel that the sacred dimension is within you and all around you. Keep a melodious bell by your bed and ring it first thing each morning. Trust that life brings into being just what is needed for your growth. Through the power of ritual, conscious and creative awareness create magic daily and manifest your dreams and intentions.

CHAPTER SIX

CALLING ECSTASY:
RITUAL MOMENTS TO CELEBRATE DAILY LIFE

*Ritual provides the bridge between inner and outer
worlds, and creates a context for connecting to the
seat of our souls. The end result of all ritual is
increased balance, strength, energy, and comfort.*

              ∽ Angeles Arrien

Our lives involve myriad rituals whose deeper meanings we
have long forgotten. We wave, hug, shake hands, clink glasses
before drinking, offer gifts. We carry lucky objects or repeat
special words to ensure success at critical moments. We spontaneously perform ancient rituals or make up new ones at important moments. We celebrate birthdays, anniversaries, retirements,
and life transitions with gifts, songs, toasts, and speeches. We
burn an ex-lover's letters in the fireplace to ritualize a moment
of moving on.

    We have a number of official rituals in our society, yet few
are imbued with their original mystery and sacred dimension.
Yet through conscious use of rituals, we can recapture and rein-
voke the power of the sacred in our everyday lives.

    In all these special moments we have a choice. We can miss
the mark because we are in a hurry and we don't pay attention
or don't take others into consideration. Or we can live the mo-

ment with heart and with inspiring words that convey a sense of reverence for the sacred meaning of this moment and the learning potential of this transition.

This chapter contains a map with clear guidelines for creating your own rituals. Numerous elements and aspects of ritual are presented here in a way that allows room for improvisation. Once you learn the basics you can adapt them to your needs in a creative manner, as the Spirit guides you.

WHAT IS RITUAL?

Whenever human beings are faced with challenges alone, in groups, or in societies, they develop rituals. Rituals give significance to life's passages. They provide form and guidance to our lives in times of grief, peril, uncertainty, and celebration.

Jeanne Achterberg, Barbara Dossey,
Leslie Kolkmeier

In its simplest meaning, a *ritual* is a series of actions performed in a prescribed manner. But when we act with deep awareness and dedication to a higher purpose, it is much more than a simple convention. Whether we create an elaborate mythic drama or make a simple, heartfelt gesture, ritual can open the door to the sacred.

One meaning of the word *Tantra* is "weaving." And rituals in every tradition and culture weave the varied yet simple strands of life into a tapestry of beauty, harmony, wholeness. Dance, song, music, prayer, purification, meditation, invocation, and sacred offerings, by these means we gather and focus our Spirit to impart a sacred dimension to our deepest intentions. In *Performing Inside Out,* author and director William Pennel Rock says that in ritual, we "channel the unnamable gods." When the power of our intention unites with the power of our Spirit, miracles occur.

Through ritual we can honor and release the past and create new futures by becoming present to the invisible Spirit, the web of life, the locus of infinite possibility in which past and future are parts of a single strand. There we can feel the divine within us, invent new selves, access other dimensions, visualize and manifest our dreams.

Full participation in ritual *expands* us, calls forth and gives expression to dormant parts of our nature: artist, teacher, lover, healer, visionary, shaman, wild-man or -woman, god or goddess. A ritual performed in the sanctuary of our sacred space is an initiation. It empowers us to express our wild, ecstatic, visionary selves.

Ritual activates, magnifies, and integrates the energy of our four centers: our body (through movement, gesture, and dance), our heart (through feeling, music, invocations), our mind (through holding a vision, invoking sacred speech), and our Spirit, which manifests through all of the above. Ritual binds love with spirit. It is the language of ecstasy.

We perform rituals for many reasons:

- To open ourselves to Spirit.
- To leave the mundane world and enter the realm of the ecstatic.
- To mark a significant event, a passage, a transition, an ending, or a beginning.
- To express through choreographed gestures our love for life, the divine, and one another.
- To exorcise past traumas and generate renewal, creating healing transitions.
- To mourn, celebrate, pay tribute, or express gratitude or deep regard for another.
- To unite with the past, our tradition, and our ancestors.
- To regenerate ourselves and our world.

RITUAL IS HEALING

A ritual is a powerful forum for healing: for uniting the divided parts of ourselves. A ritual need not be complicated to effect true healing. My friend Tia remembers:

When I was in college, my parents had a great ritual to welcome me home on vacations. Summers had always been a huge transition for me, and I usually came home in a panic. But my parents really smoothed that out for me. They would hang my college flag on our house so that when I returned the message was "The Queen is coming home, raise the flag!" Then I would come back to the familiar comfort of my house and family. The dinner table was set with candles, and we would have a moment of silence, and then share what was happening in our lives.

RITUAL CAN BE SPONTANEOUS

The way you decorate your home, serve a meal, greet or say good-bye to a friend, or read a story to your child can express the sense of heart-full welcome of returning home, which Tia described. Children do this spontaneously. My friend Isobel told me this story:

> To celebrate my mother's birthday, she and I hiked down a path to the sea. We walked along talking. Suddenly a snake appeared on the path. My mother immediately said, "Let's go back."
>
> But I was riveted to the spot. The moment seemed inherently symbolic. I asked my mother, "If you dreamed that you were walking on a path, a snake appeared in front of you, and you turned around and went back, how would you feel when you woke up?"
>
> "Disappointed," she said.
>
> Then I told her, "Snakes symbolize energy from the unconscious, a symbol of change and transformation. Snakes are sacred to the Goddess—*she* wouldn't turn back because of a snake! Are you not a goddess? This is a gift!"
>
> She thought a moment and said, "Yes!"
>
> We both started laughing. "Happy Birthday, Mom!" Then we saluted the snake and continued our walk. Coming back, our path was clear.

RITUAL CAN MARK TRANSITIONS

Moments of transition can be disorienting: The past is over, the future is unknown. Who are you without these stable anchors? Now is the time to welcome new opportunities, to discover new meanings, to respond in a fresh way to others and to the world. For instance, when you end a relationship, you might move to a new house, plant a new garden, or travel abroad.

When she was a child, Leila's family moved often. Here is how they handled their many transitions:

> Moving often was very disorienting for us kids, but my family had a great ritual for dealing with this. Just before we moved away, our whole family would go around the old house with candles and incense. We'd sit together in each room, sharing our memories of that room, and what felt special about it for each of us. Then when we arrived at the new house we'd do the same thing, only now we'd talk about what each room was going to be for us, what our expectations and desires and hopes were for that room—creating our personal meaning and connection with that room. Also, we'd bring a crystal and some earth, rocks, and plants from each place we had left to each new place we moved to. And we'd put the "old" earth in the ground, arrange the crystal and the rocks, and settle the plants from the old house into the new soil. As we bridged the past and the future, we established a sense of grounding and stability that was healing for all of us.

Marking significant moments of transition enables us to live with one foot firmly planted in two worlds, visible and invisible. And simple moments taken to express sincere gratitude to life, for all it has given and will continue to give us, restores us to a sacred relationship with all that is.

RITUAL IS COMPASSIONATE

To be truly effective, a ritual must be compassionate at heart. Rituals designed to cause harm or acquire power over others are called black magic. I have seen such rituals harm those who performed them, alienating them from life, people, and their own spiritual nature. They invite grief and destruction. We are all interconnected, and we cannot harm another without harming ourselves. A true ritual promotes healing and transformation for everyone concerned. Susan's story is an example of a spontaneous and compassionate ritual performed between her and her husband, Jim, in a moment of painful transition.

Jim and I had a bitter breakup after ten years of marriage. When I arrived at his new apartment to sign the divorce papers, I felt very vulnerable. I felt in that moment that we *had* been a part of each other's life for a decade, and yet we had done nothing to acknowledge that.

I longed to reach back to our original friendship and make this divorce a healing transition rather than a wound to carry into the next relationship. I took a deep breath and said, "Jim, we have shared so much over the last ten years, and we both know that not all of it was bad. I want us to keep something of each other that reminds us we have loved each other, and that we value what we have learned from each other." I thought he'd say something derisive.

But he sighed and said, "You are right."

I asked him to sit face to face with me. Then I looked in his eyes and said, "Jim, I want to thank you for being my friend during all these years; for taking care of me when I was sick, even though we weren't getting along; for teaching me how to organize my business; for being available and open even in the worst of times. Thank you for encouraging me to climb mountains and go rafting even though I was afraid. You helped me to develop my confidence. I'm grateful for all the gifts and delights I received from you. And I release you into your new life with my blessings."

Jim was visibly touched. He answered, "I never thought we'd be having this moment. Thank you for accepting me as I am, even though you feel hurt, and for being willing to let me go. I appreciate the emotional support you gave me when I lost my job, even though I know you were angry and scared. You taught me to pay attention to my feelings and to listen more deeply. You helped me organize my art studio and inspired me to be creative. I'm grateful to you for everything I learned from you, and I know I'm richer inside for having been with you."

Then we hugged each other. It was simple but deeply healing for both of us.

KEYS TO CREATING A GREAT RITUAL

*The process of ritual follows the same basic stages
we experience in life. These stages of unfolding are
paralleled by the seasons and their changes. . . .
Each of the seasons . . . is unique. But when we
look at the whole cycle of the year . . . we see the
larger beauty of balance and rhythm in creation and
in life.*

                          ～ Renee Beck and
                     Sydney Barbara Metrick

In the last twenty years of teaching SkyDancing Tantra, I have lived all over the world and participated in and developed hundreds of rituals. The fundamental question in all of them is how do we, as adults, reconnect with the enchantment of the soul, the magic of innocence, and the fun of childhood? The delight of creating feasts that express these qualities is unsurpassable. For me, creating them with the members of my SkyDancing Tribe, my team of teachers and co-workers, is among the greatest joys of life. We proclaim our intention and blessing through poems and invocations, using music and performance. We call forth the archetypes through dance, using Tibetan singing bowls and other ritual objects. We weave beauty, fun, depth of meaning, and spontaneous improvisation all in one. And no ritual is ever the same twice, even when we have performed it dozens of times.

Remember these guidelines when you create a ritual:

   ~ *Keep it simple.* Omit everything that is not to the point. Let your heart be your guide, not your mind.

   ~ *Make it fun.* It's easy to get bogged down in solemnity during a ritual. But the God and Goddess love humor!

 ◈ *Stay centered and remember your intention.* Breathe easily, move fluidly, know where you came from and where you are going.

 ◈ *Remember that you are bridging the visible and invisible worlds.* Think of your ritual as a mythic, heroic journey and yourself as the bridge between heaven and earth. You will not be the same person at the end of the ritual as you were in the beginning.

 ◈ *Honor the four centers.* When your body flows, your heart stays open, your mind is clear, and your Spirit soars, each moment is a gift.

Rituals are a dynamic and creative process. They offer a way to weave spiritual transformation with everyday living. The rest of this chapter will give you new perspectives on creating moments for the Soul.

LISTEN TO YOUR INTUITION

Before you begin, bring yourself to a place of stillness. Meditate; practice Inner Knowing (page 80); or simply watch your breath, feel your heart and body, and let your mind come to rest. Then examine the issue your ritual is going to address. In a relaxed manner, ask within:

 ◈ What situation am I addressing? Name the issue— a new job, a new house, a separation, accomplishing a vision, and so on.

 ◈ What is the essence—the most important need or goal—of the situation? For example, celebration, renewal, trust, healing, or releasing attachment.

 ◈ Do I or the other people involved in the ritual have any dilemma around this issue? If so, name it: shyness, fear of being hurt, fear of the unknown, fear of failure, fear of loss, or fear of death.

 ◈ What can I include in the ceremony to heal these feelings? For example, a hug, a blessing, an invocation to a bright future, or a formal acknowledgment of gratitude for what was good and precious from the past and seeing how this still helps me today.

   ❧ What clear result do I want from this ritual? For example, healing a wound of rejection, loss, or betrayal; integrating or resolving a difficult lesson; gaining the courage to jump into a new circumstance; or finding a new vision of my future.

WHO IS THE RITUAL FOR?

To set the right mood for the ritual, consider who the participants will be. If it is for your lover or mate, the ritual can be erotically intimate. If it is for your parents, the mood should be convivial, honoring and acknowledging the past and expressing gratitude. A ritual for your friends can be a celebration full of wild humor and fun. In a ritual for your children, you can reassure them, empower them, care for them, and teach them how they are a part of the fabric of the family and community. If the ritual is with business associates, it will be more formal and low-key, mentioning helpful strategies that might connect the players in a creative way. If it is a support group or a seminar, you can involve all the players with music; dance; and creative participation in invocations, blessings, appreciations, and visioning.

WHAT ARE THE PREPARATIONS FOR A RITUAL?

Virtually all of the rituals in this book call for two or three basic preparations.

   ❧ *Set aside a period of time when you will not be disturbed.* The time that belongs to your ritual should be contained by the ritual. Minimize as much as possible interference from phone calls, doorbells ringing, children running in, and so on.

   ❧ *Create a sacred space.* Depending on the nature of the ritual, your space can be as elaborate as a ballroom or as simple as a candle. The important thing is to set the space aside from its daily use for the use of the ritual (see Chapter 5).

   ❧ *Gather your tools.* Be sure to have on hand everything you will need to perform your ritual.

The other two preparations you will need to consider are timing and overall structure.

TIMING. ❧ A ritual must have a clearly established structure (but one that integrates the possibility of spontaneous change along the way), especially if it involves other people. The idea is this: Have a clear intention, yet do not be attached to the outcome. To offer a clear container that supports people's joy and gives new meaning to *this* moment, now, is more important than being attached to a fixed goal. Make a simple script. Generally, spend the first quarter of the time warming up, building the energy; two quarters of the time in the crescendo; and the last quarter of the time in the serene or winding-down phase, basking in the ritual's afterglow.

If you are creating a complex ritual involving a group of people, you may need assistants or guardians. It is useful to have someone you trust help you with logistics, create and review lists, call people, coordinate the timing, help with music, and so on (see Chapter 5).

GENERAL STRUCTURE. ❧ Think of a ritual as a symphony, with a beginning, a middle that builds to a crescendo, and an end that diminishes to a serene conclusion. (It is similar to a session of lovemaking.) Like a symphony, a ritual also involves theme and repetition. It is a journey into poetry, movement, music, and sounds that expresses and invokes the ineffable.

The content of your ritual may vary, but the basic structure should stay the same. In a wedding, for example, people come together to witness the event in the beginning; the sacred joining takes place in the middle, with the kiss of bride and groom being the crescendo; then feasting and dancing to celebrate makes up the end. Strive to create a clear beginning, and a crescendo building to a strong yet relaxed ending. This process of creating conscious, potent, well-formed rituals will help you create special moments in your life that you experience as works of art.

PRACTICE
Creating a ritual is like choreographing a ballet. As you read the following steps, imagine you are creating your own ritual. How

would you incorporate the guidelines to best express your spirit and suit your needs? What would you add or eliminate? See the Afterword (page 276).

HEART SALUTATION ⬥ I like to begin my rituals with a Heart Salutation (page 75), to open the heart to expanded possibilities.

INVOCATION ⬥ An invocation is a form of prayer in which you call forth the qualities and energies you want to bring into the room and into your life. You can invoke a mood of reverence, expanded receptivity, gratitude, celebration, surrender, urgency, or forceful power; you can acknowledge or release the past or set boundaries.

When you make your invocation, express yourself clearly. Be bold and adventurous. Improvisation can add a delightful energy to a ritual. Choose a few sounds or words that express the essence of the situation or of the energy qualities you want to call forth. It is okay to make "mistakes." You are not performing at the Metropolitan Opera, you are invoking the Spirit in a cathedral of your own making. Here are some themes you may want to address.

Call the Four Directions ⬥ To evoke a sense of our connection to the cosmos. Dedicate the north to mind; the south to heart; the west to body; the east to Spirit; the center to the merging of inner man and inner woman; the above to your inner teachers and guides; and the below to unconscious and primal forces, dreams, and ancestors.

Invoke a Spiritual Guide ⬥ If you wish to establish a sense of protection, invoke the invisible presence of a great Spirit, a beloved teacher, a deity. For instance, "O Vajrasattva Buddha, clear light of the Diamond Mind, may you bless us with healing, may we share your light with all sentient beings." Or "We invite the presence of the goddess Aphrodite that she may shower us with love and beauty."

Invoke Protective Energies ⬥ Call forth any archetype with which you resonate: the Healer, the Lover, the Wise

Woman, or the Wise Man. Call forth the help of your ancestors who paved your way: your mother who gave you birth, your father who helped conceive you. You may also call on animal spirits who embody the power you wish to incarnate, for example, the eagle, a symbol of clear vision.

Invoke Healing ❧ Call forth the difficult moments, the wounds that you wish to heal. The lessons they have taught you, the wisdom they now bring you: "May your anger now be transformed into an ally, and open the door to your sense of power and clarity. May it teach you forgiveness. This is your chance to discover how to let go, and to trust your wisdom and be guided."

Invoke the Spiritual Function of the Ritual ❧ Examples of invoking spiritual function are, "I dedicate this erotic joy to the renewal and inspiration of our relationship" and "I dedicate this ritual to the enlightenment of all sentient beings."

BEGINNING ❧ Begin slowly and gently. See and feel your vision and open to spirit. Take time for silence and stillness. Let people reconnect with their soul and become conscious of their personal place in the ritual. State the purpose of the ritual in a single sentence (We are here to celebrate my daughter's entry into womanhood" or "We are here to honor the God and Goddess within each of us"). Welcome them with simple words or gestures; touching their heart is appropriate here. You may clear the energy with a hand clap, a chant, or by ringing a bell. A good way to enter into sacred time is to light a candle, guide the players to their positions, put on soft music, and begin with a Heart Salutation.

MIDDLE ❧ The middle is when the vision and purpose should be clearly manifest in ritual context, whether it is the coming together of male and female, the transition from childhood to adulthood, or the celebration of our divine nature. You create order, align your inner centers, give deeply felt acknowledgments.

CRESCENDO ❧ This is when every part of the ritual—the participants; their feelings, energies, and actions; the visible and invisible worlds—is woven together to produce a great fusion, a grand communion of energy and intention, a celebratory climax that releases the participants into a healing sense of harmony, union, ease, and a certainty of accomplishment and of connection with one's "tribe."

END ❧ It is time to bring things to a conclusion, to wind down from fire to water or earth, to ground in your body the energies released in the ritual. Visualize taking into yourself and incorporating into your everyday life these expanded, sacred energies. The end of the ritual should be a firm closure, so that the energy created by the ritual is fully absorbed by the participants and not dissipated through casual, unconscious speech and behavior. You might have a celebratory dance; a silent meditation; a group acknowledgment of transformation that has occurred; or a concluding ceremony thanking the Spirits and directions for their power, presence, and support. Ring a bell, chant, or extinguish the candle to welcome people back into temporal space.

End with a song or a Heart Salutation (page 75). Be silent and still for a moment.

POINTERS

At the end of the ritual, note for yourself the things you will need to watch for next time, what might have been handled more skillfully, the effect of the ritual, its consequences, what to expect, and so on.

GATHERING YOUR TOOLS

When body, heart, mind, and Spirit are in harmony, we experience ecstasy. As we have seen, ritual is a powerful way to establish that harmony. Much of the power of ritual is in the symbols, which I call the tools of ritual. Some of these you can hold in your hand—bells, candles, wands—others are more abstract—fresh air, the four directions, your own clarity and intention.

ECSTATIC SPACE ❧ A sacred space is an environment for bliss. Bliss flowers when the base or the container of the experience is solid. It is helpful to mark the space by naming the seven areas.

North ⤚ The north is the place of the mind. At its highest point it is guarded by the eagle, which soars above the landscape and sees the big picture. When you create a ritual, invoke this awareness and open to the mind at large and infinite possibility. Air is the element of the north.

South ⤚ The south is the place of the heart, emotions, playfulness, vulnerability, and innocence. The guardian of this space is the dolphin. In your ritual, when you want to honor the space of the heart, you say, "I invoke the guardians of the south, the dolphins who remind us of our playfulness and of the innocence of the heart." Water is the element of the south.

West ⤚ The west is the place of the body, nature, the seasons and their cycles, health, fertility, strength, and balance. The guardian of this space is the deer or buffalo. Earth is the element of the west.

East ⤚ The east is the place of the Spirit and enlightenment of consciousness. It symbolizes courage, passion, moving through obstacles, seeing the truth, the hidden meaning behind the obvious, and acknowledgment of the spiritual dimension. The guardian of this space is the lion. In your ritual, invoke this dimension by using sacred objects that awaken your Spirit (photos of masters or guides, crystals that purify, incense, candles). Fire is the element of the east.

Center ⤚ The center is the place of integration. Here your inner man and inner woman merge to create a balance between energy and awareness, love and power. Feel your receptive and active qualities blending as you stand in the center of the space. (The center should be a strong visual focus, so decorate it with candles, colored scarves, crystals, flowers, or other similar objects.)

Below ⤚ Creatures of the earth, the demons (our obsessions, our egos, our doubts, our lies), and the serpents (the unconscious, the obscure, our blind spots, our dreams, our delusions) live below. In your ritual, you may need to address these issues. For example, make friends with anger or penetrate self-deception. Acknowledging what is below expresses your willingness to transform and heal.

Above ～ Your teachers, the people who inspire you and guide you on your path, your spiritual guides, the deities you feel connected to, and your archetypal sources live above. In your ritual, address them and invoke their presence, support, and blessing. Try to incorporate their teachings. As you prepare the ritual, ask yourself, "Would this action honor their teachings? In doing this, am I aligned with my path?"

RITUAL SOUNDS ～ We are like wondrous musical instruments that vibrate and respond to musical frequencies. Our bodies, hearts, and Spirits can be tuned and harmonized by specific musical compositions. Choose the music for your ritual accordingly to evoke wonder, delight, lightness, depth of heart, peace. Sometimes a piece of music that is played during an ecstatic moment anchors this state in your psyche. By playing the same music again later you create an automatic recall and effortlessly rekindle the same state.

Music ～ Choose your music according to the moods you want to elicit in the ritual. Choose a variety of music that supports the phases of the ritual: dance music, sacred mantras, simple songs of the heart that everyone can sing, gentle background music when people need to recite poetry or read text, light and spacious and gentle for the end. Provide drums, bells, wooden flutes, and rain sticks, and encourage people to participate.

Recorded Music ～ Be sure to have a selection that expresses a wide range of feelings and moods: longing, sadness, sexiness, joy, awe, awakening, lightness, laughter, power. Choosing the appropriate music is a skill you can develop by listening to many kinds of music as often as possible and noting your body/mind's responses. Usually, strong drumbeats help your pelvis and your legs to feel the earth and give you strength. Flowing and romantic musical compositions with string instruments and voice open the heart. Calm, ordered music, such as that of Bach or Mozart, clears the mind. Light, high-pitched flute sounds and bells inspire spiritual moods.

Percussion ❧ Percussion instruments are perfect for purification: clearing the mind of intrusive thoughts and the space of stagnant energy. Percussion instruments ground the energy and remove people's fears. Use these sounds at the beginning of a ritual, using clap sticks or hands, rattles, shakers, drums, or feet. Claps and rattles create a call to attention: "Be here *now!*" Claps are a good way to clear the air in a room after an argument.

Singing ❧ Singing opens the throat and allows your true voice to emerge. You do not need to have any training to sing during a ritual. Start to enjoy singing when you are taking a shower, in the kitchen washing dishes or preparing breakfast, driving in your car. Sing notes. Try different pitches. Slowly sing one note at a time and quickly sing many notes. Do this until you find a tone, a note, and a speed that inspire you. Classical Indian singers I have studied with tell me that singing for ten minutes everyday when you get up cleans your blood.

RITUAL ENERGIES AND OBJECTS ❧ Ritual invests ordinary objects with symbolic meaning or power, making the invisible dimension visible. Use whatever you have on hand—stones, photos, crystals, candles, flowers—anything that has personal meaning to *you*. My partner used to say, "If you are naked and empty-handed in a parking lot, you still have earth (body), water (heart), air (mind), and sun or moon (Spirit)!"

Consecration and Purification ❧ A ritual will be more effective if you empower your objects through ritual means:

❧ Hold the object in your hands and consecrate it through a prayer.

❧ Hold the object to your solar plexus (or your heart or third eye) and imagine you send your power into it, charging it with every exhalation.

❧ Leave the object in the sun, under the light of the full moon, or in a running stream to purify it.

❧ Give the object a simple blessing ("I bless this [water, bell, etc.] with the power of Spirit") to consecrate it.

THE FOUR ELEMENTS ✑ Each element represents a certain energy that can be evoked in different ways, depending on the intention and goal of the ritual.

Fire ✑ Fire symbolizes the Spirit: joy, the distillation of experience into timeless wisdom, the bright illumination of the mind, ecstatic awakening, and the refinement and transformation of raw energies into the more subtle light of awareness. Fire also represents passion, eroticism, the infusion of Spirit in the body that transforms orgasm into ecstasy. It is also enthusiasm, courage, willpower, motivation, and purification. It gives us the power to lead, the quest to awaken, and a passionate appetite; fire ignites the ecstatic self. Use fire (flames, candles, a bonfire, a fire in the fireplace) to burn away the old and welcome the new. Throw into the fire representations of those things you no longer want in your life.

Water ✑ Water symbolizes emotions, flow, surrender, the playfulness of a child, and adaptability. Water suggests the flow of life and emotions, the journey to ecstasy, and the cleansing of impurities. It offers refreshment, rejuvenation, baptism, the birth of Spirit, pacification of the mind, reflection, assimilation, and gestation. Water nurtures us, heals and balances our emotions, prepares us for pleasure, and gives us dreams and intuitive guidance. Use water as a symbol of purification, clarification, and blessing. Mist the room (use a plant sprayer) or sprinkle it from a ceremonial bowl (use your fingers or a flower). Add a drop of essential oil to the water to elicit a particular mood (lavender for relaxation, mint for mental clarity).

Air ✑ Air symbolizes breath, inspiration, intelligence, thoughts, freedom, dissolution, new beginnings, humor, wisdom, clarity, subtlety, flight, the expansion of consciousness, and detachment. Use air (the fresh air around you, or air scented with incense or essential oils) to elicit a sense of spaciousness in your ceremony.

Earth ✑ Earth symbolizes solidity, health, manifestation, feeling at home, and a strong foundation. Earth also symbolizes the body, your own physical body and the greater body of Mother Earth. Earth suggests building, construction, and concretizing an idea. The qualities of earth are caring, healing, nurturing, grounding, stability, security, belonging, sensuality, pleasure, and touch. The Earth gives birth to abundance, harvest, and sustenance. Use earth (place it in a bowl, sprinkle it on the floor) to ground the past and anchor your understanding of a situation.

HOW TO CREATE AN ECSTATIC RITUAL

You can use this model as a basic structure when you create your ritual, but you don't need to go through all these steps each time. Just read through this exercise to remind yourself of the points you might need to address for your particular ritual. Remember, you can keep it simple.

PREPARATION

ᕙ What is your intention for this ritual? State it clearly.

ᕙ Write your script (optional). If your ritual is complex or you think you may forget something important, write down the sequence of events. Keep the paper handy so you can refer to it as needed.

ᕙ Create the ritual space: dedicate a sacred space for the ceremony (see Chapter 5).

ᕙ Determine which tools you will use for your ceremony, gather them, purify them, and consecrate them.

ᕙ Be specific about the timing and the steps you will follow and remember to notify the participants at the beginning.

PRACTICE

ᕙ Welcome the participants.

ᕙ Perform the Heart Salutation (page 75).

ᕙ Mark the transition into sacred time. Light a candle, ring a bell, or use one of the suggestions in this chapter.

ᕙ State your intention. Hold this intention throughout the ritual, letting it empower the ceremony.

ᕙ Call forth protection and guidance from your spiritual

teacher, a deity, the four directions, your inner guide, your higher self, your ecstatic or wild self, any archetype with which you resonate (the Healer, the Lover, the Wise Woman or Wise Man, and so on).

᷒ Invoke the Guardians of the Place, the gods, guides, wisdom, spirits, feelings, ideas, or archetypes you wish to represent.

᷒ Perform the ritual. Begin with something to ground the energy: shaking, dancing, stamping feet, drumming.

᷒ Bring the ritual to its crescendo and allow it to subside in serenity.

᷒ End the ritual gently, slowing down the tempo, the sounds, and the words. Let everyone sit in silence, feel their heart, and integrate the experience.

᷒ To bring everyone back to normal consciousness, ring a bell and simply say with a smile, "Welcome back!" as you stand up and blow out the candles.

᷒ Encourage people to exchange a hug and talk to each other about their experience and what they learned.

᷒ Take a moment to express how you feel and what you learned.

POINTERS

᷒ Remember your intention throughout the ritual.

᷒ Dedicate your ritual to the healing of those you love and to the good of all sentient beings.

᷒ Remember that the well-being of the participants comes before the design or performance of your ritual structure.

᷒ Remain open to your intuitive guidance during the ritual and be willing to adjust and improvise within your structure.

᷒ Rituals are like medicine: they work best if you believe they have healing power. Your faith in the outcome is important.

᷒ If someone has strong emotions during the ritual, be gentle and supportive and encourage the person to release them.

PART III

THE ANATOMY OF ECSTASY

The chakra system is a symbolic map of our energy system, a blueprint of of our pathway to ecstasy.

The information in this section offers new guidelines that can lead to experiencing life more fully. As you work through each chakra, take your whole self into account in any situation; relationships, your work, and your spiritual growth.

The next chapter is an introduction to and an overview of the chakra system; it will show you how energy is transformed, refined, and expanded. Each chakra is a door to a new quality of awareness preparing you for the following chapters that offer concrete rituals, meditations, and exercises for working with each chakra. May you understand and master the power and potential in each of your chakras and create abundance and joy in your daily life.

CHAPTER SEVEN

THE SEVEN TANTRIC KEYS TO ECSTASY:
OPENING THE CHAKRAS

Again and again the sacred texts tell us that our
life's purpose is to understand and develop the
power of our spirit, a power that is vital to our
mental and physical well-being. . . . We are
biological creations of divine design.

Caroline Myss

Imagine: You are going to visit your best friend who has built a
new house. You enter "*Chakra* House" through a long hallway.
On earthen walls hang pictures of your friend as a boy, of his
close family members, and of his ancestors. You gaze at the pictures and feel connected to his origins and roots.

The hallway leads into the bedroom, a sensual space deco-
rated in erotic red silks. Your friend shows you the bed and says,
"We call this place the Root of Creation, because every time we
make love we feel renewed and creative." This is the temple of
the first *chakra,* the sexual center, where sex connects you to the
earth, the roots of life, and your origins.

Voices call you into the garden. There the rest of the family
plays around a big swimming pool. You see a picnic table laden
with fruits, breads, vegetables. The aquamarine water invites you

in. In the warm, buoyant water you easily connect with the others on a feeling level. The kids fight and play and laugh. Your friend is in continual motion, kissing his wife, clowning, diving into the pool, throwing a beach ball to the children. His wife takes it all in, quietly making sure everyone is at ease. This is the terrain of the second *chakra,* the belly center; here life is experienced as energy in motion, emotions, digestion, assimilation, and balance.

Now your friend leads you to his office. Clearly, it is his place of power, with a large, solid desk and bold geometric patterns on the walls. Sun pours in through an open window, revealing an imposing view of the hills. Here he works, thinks, creates, plans, makes money, and directs his ideas into the world. You are in the temple of the third *chakra,* the solar center, the place of self-empowerment, will, leadership, and achievement where we incarnate in the world through action.

"Come," your friend says. "I'll show you the heart of our home." He leads you to the mezzanine and opens the door to a spacious family room. Here large sofas are strewn with soft pillows and the walls are warmed by soft light streaming through stained-glass windows. This is where he sheds the cares of work and worldly obligations and meets his wife and children to share loving moments. This is the room of the fourth *chakra,* the pulse of life, where love nourishes and transforms the energies of the first three *chakras.*

And now your friend takes you to a room filled with musical instruments. He picks up a guitar, and you choose a drum. Together, you play, sing, and laugh, improvising beautiful harmonies, thrilled by the music that pours out of you like liquid honey. This is the temple of the fifth *chakra,* the song of the soul, where you create, improvise, dance, and express your truth.

Now you climb a spiral staircase and enter a simple room, where you kneel before a low table covered with flowers and candles. You breathe deeply, serenely seated, bathed in the clear light of this space. In this moment of stillness, deep insights come to you regarding a long-standing problem. In the face of its simplicity your whole perspective shifts. Now you know what to do. This is the realm of the sixth *chakra,* the third eye center, where you perceive all things through the intuitive powers of inspiration and imagination.

Finally, your friend takes you up to the penthouse, an open patio; the only roof is the sky. You look around at a spectacular 360-degree view of the entire countryside. You see how the roads, houses, streams, mountains, blend into the horizon and the sky. They all seem connected, part of a whole. You feel your place as a link in a great chain. With gratitude, you relax into the bliss of being simply who you are, at peace with the world. This is the vision from the seventh *chakra,* the crown center, where you surrender and melt into your Source and feel one with the universe.

You marvel at this house, how smoothly one room leads into another, how clear of obstruction and clutter it is. You feel stronger, more alert, and energized as you flow from room to room, each one perfectly expressing its essence and function, making the next more powerful by its presence. Your journey through *Chakra* House resonates inside you long after you leave. How could you refine your own dwelling place along such simple yet magical lines?

The Path of Vibrant Energy

Look at these worlds spinning out of nothingness.
That is your power.

☙ Rumi

As the power of the life force moves through the *chakras,* the energy generated awakens a new awareness of who we are and how we deal with our world. Day after day, just as our heart beats and our lungs breathe, our *chakras* spin, drawing in the life force, the *prana,* from the invisible energy fields all around us and "out of nothingness" replenishing, harmonizing, and attuning.

HOW THE CHAKRAS WORK
You can't see your *chakras* as you can see your body. But as you learn more about them, you will gradually recognize their presence and power in your life. The *chakras* propel *kundalini,* (*prana, qi,* or the force of life) toward its destination of consciousness.

Yoga master B. K. S. Iyengar describes the *chakras* in this way: "As antennae pick up radio waves and transform them into sound through receiving sets, *chakras* pick up cosmic vibrations and distribute them throughout the body."

The moment we understand our world as a dynamic interplay between energy and consciousness, we begin to see life as a dance of energy in constant flux and ever-changing forms, pulsing, expanding, and contracting. Each *chakra* is a rung on our personal evolutionary ladder, resonating with a frequency of life energy that we learn to master and integrate on our way to wholeness. In each *chakra* we learn to master a unique aspect of life and human experience, to live and function freely at that level so that our energy can rise to the next rung. Each *chakra* brings unique gifts and abilities and also challenges, dilemmas, and demands for our functional and relational participation in life.

ORGASM IN THE SEVEN CHAKRAS

For me, making love is a metaphor for everything we do in life. And when we make love, we re-create physically what happens energetically in each of the seven *chakras*.

This idea of building up a charge—of containing and allowing energy to flow through the body, and eventually releasing it, as we do in orgasm—applies exactly to our *chakras*. In each *chakra,* a marriage between energy and consciousness, power and awareness, Shakti and Shiva takes place. The ancient Tantric scriptures tell us that Shiva and Shakti, in their wild lovemaking, caused the *chakras* to spin and churn, "agitating all." This reminds us that orgasm is not just sexual: it is the building, churning, and rising of the life force that is occurring at all times in every living being.

Just as each of us has an inner male (emissive, active) aspect and an inner female (receptive, attractive) aspect, so do our *chakras*. The female aspect of each *chakra* attracts energy and draws it into its center; the male aspect propels or directs the energy outward and circulates it through the rest of the *chakra* system. These two motions create the spiraling, spinning, orgasmic movement of the *chakras*. And just as in sex—the more energy we have available, the more intense the excitement and the greater the orgasmic response. The expansion and contraction generated by this merging of the male and female is the very movement of life. And the more the life energy flows through each *chakra,* the greater that *chakra's* power to generate and transform energy and consciousness at each level.

As we master the energies and issues of each *chakra* and balance the dynamic tension between its active and receptive components, there is an intensification much like the buildup of sexual energy between a man and woman that leads to orgasm. An open *chakra,* one that freely conducts the life force, irrigates and enlivens our whole being with its power. And the energy flows and rises to the next *chakra.*

At times, a deep, spontaneous opening of our *chakras* may occur, perhaps through a sudden release from fear, pain, sorrow or when our energy is intensified through dance, exercise, work, strong breathing, intense orgasm, powerful emotions, deep meditation, or even our total presence and receptivity to the moment. Then our life force flows unobstructed through our *chakras.* Our body feels vibrant. Our heart is open. Our mind is clear and free of negative thoughts. And our Spirit feels embodied in life.

Such moments are privileged glimpses of what is possible, yet the *chakras* rarely open all at once in a perfect, unobstructed flow. In any given moment, one *chakra* may be relaxed and open while others are not. Their energy fields are in constant flux.

The experience of energy transformation that takes place through the *chakras* is not limited to lovemaking. Every experience in life contains energy that our *chakras* are designed to process.

UNDERSTANDING YOUR TANTRIC CORPORATE PARTNERSHIP

As with our endocrine gland, which functions as an interactive network to form the endocrine system, each *chakra* interacts and influences the others. When one *chakra* opens, all the others are beneficially affected, along with our bodies, minds, and emotions. To understand this better, imagine how they might function as a team on the "Tantric Board of Directors" of your "Corporate Body."

🍂 The crown center is the guardian angel, watching over the others, dispensing light and love.

🍂 The third eye center is the visionary, making sure that everyone gets the big picture, understands the goal, stays on track, and is motivated to reach the highest potential.

🍂 The song of the soul is the speaker, giving a creative voice to all the others and allowing them to speak their truths.

🍂 The heart is the mediator, looking for common ground, embracing and accepting all as they are, trusting and keeping the peace.

🍂 The solar center is the administrator, empowering and supporting all to do their best and generating the necessary energy for accomplishment.

🍂 The belly center is the guardian of right action, looking after everyone's health, rhythms, timing, and cycles and advocating change or creating completion.

🍂 The sexual center is the founding parent, keeping track of origins, ancestors, laws, and rules of behavior. This director is a rock or an anchor for the system and the passionate one who keeps the team juiced up.

This board of directors meets regularly, and each director has one vote. Ideally, for your corporate body to function properly, the power must be shared equally and all the directors should agree on every issue. Often, however, this is not the case. Sometimes one director gets too controlling and makes a power grab (a corporate takeover! That greedy *chakra* must be stopped!), leaving the others weak and ineffectual. If one or more *chakras* are ill, in pain, in need of attention, and unable to exercise their authority, their responsibility falls back on the others, adding an extra burden to the system. Sometimes the various functions of the *chakras* become blurred or displaced altogether. For instance, when the fourth and sixth *chakras* are confused, feelings become intellectualized as the heart is controlled by the mind—as in the case of a friend of mine who said of a woman he was dating. "I *think* I love her."

Although each *chakra* is a separate entity, they function holographically: each contains an aspect or reflection of the others. This means that to be fully open and vibrant, a *chakra* must be tuned to the other *chakras* and be supported by them. For instance, to love fully and be alive in the fourth *chakra,* the heart, you need the generative passion of the sex or root *chakra,* the balance and flow of the belly *chakra,* the empowerment of the solar plexus *chakra,* the voice of the throat *chakra,* the vision of the third eye *chakra,* and the receptivity and surrender of the crown *chakra.*

TED'S STORY: AN OPENING
OF THE FIRST CHAKRA

When a *chakra* opens, it can be a transformative experience. My friend Ted had a spontaneous opening of his first *chakra* (the center through which we feel grounded and connected to our roots). Ted had been doing *chakra* work with me for a while, when he noticed feelings of longing and of being out of synch in his belly and a ball of tension in his solar plexus. He told me:

> I started doing the *Chakra* Tuning Meditation every day [page 142]. At first it was difficult to breathe and move in the area of the belly and solar plexus. It was as if I had to protect something that didn't want to come out. Then, one day at the end of the meditation I had a vision. I saw what was connected to these blocks. I relived the entire episode.
>
> I was born seven weeks premature. I saw my mother only two times on the day I was born and I never saw her again for seven weeks—until the day I was scheduled to be born. During that time I never had the chance to bond with my mother. I was just passed around from nurse to nurse, and I always had the feeling I had been abandoned.
>
> For forty-seven years I stumbled through life, rootless. I never really felt at home anywhere.
>
> During the *Chakra* Tuning Meditation, I felt the despair and longing I experienced as an infant. It was cold, dark, nobody was there. It was very lonely. After crying for a long time I suddenly realized that I hadn't really been abandoned—there were people all around me, wanting to help me . . . *people who had saved my*

life! But as a newborn baby, I just wasn't able to perceive them. Now at last I knew I'd been loved and cared for and saved.

Knowing this was tremendously healing. Every morning for forty-seven years I woke up with that sense of loss. Every day I was trying to compensate for that abandonment. This meditation gave me the missing link. It generated enough energy to allow me to rip through the pain. It forced this experience back on me so I could heal it.

I feel relieved of an enormous burden. The pain of not knowing what happened and feeling blocked in my action and my career is gone. I feel confident now that I can create a new life for myself. I finally opened enough to receive the message that I had not been abandoned, but saved.

Ted deeply and fully experienced his pain, grief, and sadness. It was digested and its energy was processed and integrated through his *chakras,* which are no longer blocked by old unexpressed pain.

THE CHAKRA TALK: RECEIVING THE MESSAGE OF YOUR CHAKRAS

Did you know that your *chakras* can speak to you? The most direct way to understand your *chakras* is to listen to their messages. You can tune your intuitive, receptive intelligence to each of these centers. Your *chakras* are messengers of your body and mind's deeper truths. They are poets. They can participate actively in your healing.

In the Love and Ecstasy Training, I practice the *Chakra* Talk Meditation with a group of fifty participants over a period of one week. We work in groups of three people, each of whom takes a turn as the "speaker," the "witness," and the "silent listener." The speaker has seven minutes to let the *chakra* talk; the witness writes down the words in a notebook or tape-records the talk; and the silent listener is a supportive presence. The group explores one *chakra* a day, giving a voice to the *chakra,* which speaks directly. Here are some excerpts that will give you a flavor of the variety and depth of the *Chakra* Talk.

Some Voices of the Fifth *Chakra*, the Song of the Soul

JOAN ❧ I am your throat. I need more space from you to speak freely. I want to be free, you're holding me back. Let me say what I feel, let me feel what I say. . . . I invoke the Spirit into the body. I am the sounding board of the soul. I am the regulator of vibration.

JACK ❧ I am the throat. I have to hold everything together. I have to make sure everything is coordinated, everything is happening right. I am tight. I want to be free. The artist sits here. I have the choice. I can express, call out, *be, be me!* [Long silence.] Now I am still. I feel energy throbbing in my throat: there are streams of electric currents going through the spine, bright colors flowing, merging. . . . The energy is so subtle, so bright. . . . There is such a fine resonance in there. . . . Now I have space . . . I feel free.

The Voice of the Second *Chakra*, the Belly Center

PETER ❧ I am the belly: I feel pregnant with vastness. I thank my roots for nourishment. I am the provider. I store experiences in my belly. I save visions in my belly.

SARAH ❧ I am big, round, full, I am the womb. All things come through me. I have power. I hide much. I am a well of hope and despair. There is no bottom to this well. I am the mother. The mother knows compassion because she has lived through the tears in her belly.

Similar themes come up spontaneously for each *chakra:* in the belly, the theme of vastness; in the throat, the theme of freedom to be creative. Poetic monologues emerge. A new voice. A dynamic and wise call to action. You can use the *Chakra* Talk to connect with each of your energy centers to receive inner guidance and to live every moment of your life more consciously.

THE CHAKRA TALK

This is a simple exercise, only slightly more advanced than the Inner Knowing Meditation. (page 80) The most important thing to keep in mind is that you are not making anything up—you are lending your voice to feeling sensations that arise in our power centers. Accessing the deeper layers of your subconscious depends on your ability to relax deeply and let the inner voice come up on its own.

PURPOSE
∾ To receive clear messages from your *chakras*.
∾ To heal energy blocks and enhance your creativity in daily life.

PREPARATION
∾ Plan about twenty minutes for this meditation. You will connect with one *chakra* at a time—one per sitting.
∾ Make sure you are in an undisturbed, silent atmosphere and will not be interrupted.
∾ Unplug the telephone and other electronic devices.
∾ If you are using a tape recorder, have it ready and turn it on before you begin.
∾ If you do this with a partner, alternate: one is the speaker, the other is the witness.

PRACTICE
∾ Begin with the Heart Salutation (page 75) and direct it to the *chakra* with which you will be connecting.
∾ Sit or lie down comfortably. Relax any tensions in your neck, head, shoulders, and spine.
∾ Now take five minutes to relax. Simply close your eyes, relax your face, and watch and follow your breath (breathing gently through the nose is fine). Let the breath be deep and gentle, no pushing. With every inhalation, feel you take in life energy (*prana*) and revitalize your body. With every exhalation, let go of any tensions. If thoughts come, let them come and go as you would watch clouds passing by in the sky. Come back to your breath. Relax.

ɞ Now, focus on the area of the *chakra* you want to connect with. Gently rest your hands over the area (for example, for the fourth *chakra* rest your hands over your heart). Breathe into that area of your body, focusing your attention. Visualize the organs that are there, or simply say their names. Imagine you are speaking to a child, the spirit of your body—gently, lightly, like a lullaby, whispering. Continue for a few minutes until you feel received. Internally, say, "Heart [name of the *chakra*], I connect with you now. I give you my voice. I welcome you. Let me receive you. Speak through me."

ɞ Now lend your voice to that energy center and listen to what it has to say. To ensure that you are directly accessing the *chakra,* make sure that you speak in the first person. For example, "I am your heart. . . . Right now I feel constricted" and so on. If you say, "*My* heart feels . . ." chances are your mind might run the show and you might not really hear the true deeper voice expressing your *chakra.*

ɞ Continue to tune in for about five to seven minutes. There may be long pauses. You are speaking from a deep place inside yourself. Let the pauses be there. Relax with what is. You will know when the exercise is over. Then take a deep inhalation and exhalation and thank your *chakra* for the messages you received.

ɞ End with a Heart Salutation.

POINTERS

ɞ You can do this out loud and record the talk with a tape recorder; you can have a friend with you to take notes (this exercise is great done in a small group of three or more friends), or you can do it silently in the way of Inner Knowing.

ɞ If you feel stressed or tense, begin by taking a walk or stretching and breathing.

ɞ You may choose to begin with the chakra most in need of healing or plan to do all seven *chakras.* I recommend starting at the sexual center, your foundation, and moving upward, one *chakra* per day.

ɞ Resist the temptation to analyze what is happening. To allow the voice of your intuition to speak, go deeper, take a few deep breaths, wait, travel mentally to the area of your body ruled by the particular *chakra,* and repeat the steps above.

ɞ When you are finished, stand up, walk around, and take a

break before you (or you and your partner) review the notes of your talk. In your review, find the essence, the central message of your *chakra*. Create an affirmation with it and remind yourself about it daily.

⨀⨀⨀⨀⨀⨀⨀⨀⨀⨀⨀⨀⨀⨀⨀⨀⨀⨀⨀⨀⨀⨀⨀⨀⨀⨀

ENERGY AND ECSTASY

If you have ever said, "Why does this *always* happen to me?" then you know the feeling of a *chakra* that is blocked, contracted, and in need of healing. Repeated thought and emotional patterns and chronic dilemmas are signs of the obstruction of the flow of life energy through our *chakras*. For instance, if our will, or third *chakra* is weak, we may experience a chronic sense of failure, an inability to complete what we have begun, a sense of being interfered with by life or others. If our heart *chakra* is blocked, we may be unable to give or receive love, be prone to resentment, or attract people who abandon or abuse us. This is partly a process of selective awareness; what we focus on, we draw to ourselves. As an old saying goes, If a pickpocket is in a crowd of saints, all he sees are pockets.

By working directly with our *chakras,* we can transform negative moods and behavioral patterns; strengthen weak areas; and improve our health, sex life, career, and relationships. Here are some examples of how blocks in each *chakra* can affect our body, mind, emotions, energy, and behavior.

BLOCKS ⨀ If our first *chakra,* the sexual center, is contracted, our connection to pleasure is tenuous, even disturbed. If our relationship to our sexuality is difficult, our life energy can be reduced to a low flame. We may find it hard to fully conduct our life force. We become vulnerable to problems and diseases of the reproductive organs. Our relationship to work tends to become a survival matter, also devoid of pleasure. We may never feel we have enough and so push ourselves, becoming workaholics. Or we may collapse and lose all motivation.

If our second *chakra,* the belly center, is contracted, our personal boundaries may be hazy to ourselves and to others. Or we may fail to establish them altogether. Unable to clearly distinguish between "ours" and "others'" we find it hard to say no. Poor self-nurturers, our health can become problematic. Through lack of flow, we may become constipated both physically and emotionally. We may find ourselves trapped in situations we feel helpless to change or be paralyzed by feelings of general hopelessness.

If our third *chakra,* the solar center, is contracted, our self-esteem suffers. We may allow others to take advantage of us, even becoming the victim who is angry at situations, yet does not want to take responsibility for changing them.

If our fourth *chakra,* the heart center, is contracted, our pain from old wounds may stop us from trusting. Our head may take the place of our heart. We doubt everyone and everything. And though the pain of loneliness may fill us with a longing for love, our fear of being hurt keeps our heart closed to love and relationships.

If our fifth *chakra,* the throat center, is contracted, we lose touch with our core of originality and find it difficult to freely and authentically express ourselves. We may be stuck in subordinate roles, biting our tongues and never communicating our truth.

If our sixth *chakra,* the third eye center, is contracted, we may feel confused or lost. Lacking a clear vision of our direction and purpose, we may become followers who look for others to guide us and give us answers. And, unconsciously resentful of our dependence, we may also tend to judge and be critical of others.

If our seventh *chakra,* the crown center, is contracted, we do not trust our higher guidance or believe that the solution to our problems are within us. Our relationship to Spirit, to the divine, is unclear. Our spirituality may be a kind of double-bind or doubtful hope. And by trying to live on a foundation of faith that we do not truly possess, we are often apprehensive and disappointed by life.

SUDDEN OPENINGS ～ Wholeness means that each *chakra* can open and operate at its highest frequency. With our *chakras* open, energy flows freely through them like water in a stream. Yet our blocks, conflicts, confusions, delusions, and physical problems can make the initial opening painful.

As the inner fire in the form of a strong energy charge (sexual or nonsexual) or excitement seeks to flow through areas of constricted physical and psychological armoring, long-repressed emotions may suddenly burst forth. Triggers include deep breathing when we have been chronically tense, reaching out for help when we have been isolated and lonely, being held and kissed deeply or pleasured intensely for a long time, being encouraged to make sounds when you have been silent and inhibited, and being massaged in tense places where you have stored strong emotions. Any of these circumstances may release sadness, deep sobbing, long-forgotten feelings and images, or ancient rage.

People sometimes feel frightened or overwhelmed by the intensity of their response to a *chakra* opening. But this emotional outpouring is a response releasing an old pattern of protection that has kept the *chakra* closed and armored. Generally, when people suppress their feelings, they are unable to access their own power.

In the *Chakra* Talk Meditation, certain pains or fears may arise. They may be the voice of the energy you held back. But if you allow it to be expressed, you may feel a sense of relief, a new aliveness, a new space within. These shadows are not your enemies. Our inner demons reveal themselves as powerful emotions: sadness, rage, or old memories or wounds coming forth to be confronted, healed, and transformed. Welcome them when they come. For every demon is an angel in exile. And when you call them back and embrace them, they may become your most powerful allies. They can, if you accept them as a part of yourself and befriend them, open the door to wisdom. For they may contain the message of your own hidden or suppressed power, which may now become available.

CHAKRA TUNING

Now we will explore playful ways to allow your conscious breath and movement to churn, vibrate, and stream through each chakra. This vibrant movement is the expansion and contraction rhythm of life that is inherent in the energy play between female (contraction/inhalation) and male (expansion/exhalation) in each chakra. The goal of this exercise is to have fun! Do whatever you really like to do: use dance, movement, creative expression, or visualization. I have also included affirmations that correspond to each of the seven chakras. These "power chants" were created by Tai-chi and Chikung master Anne Chandler.

PURPOSE

~ To open and relax your *chakras,* allowing energy to flow through them freely.

~ To empower your *chakras* with new energy and aliveness in every moment of your life.

PREPARATION

~ Find a place at home or in nature where you feel comfortable and can be alone (with yourself or with your partner) for half an hour. If you are in nature, find a beautiful, secluded spot where you can move and dance and shout freely.

~ Set up your the sound system and prepare to play your favorite dynamic dance music—African rhythms, salsa, or world beat, the music should make you want to shake, rattle, and roll! Then prepare yourself for a no-holding-back celebration dance. You are going to open your circuits and plug into the power of aliveness that opens your *chakras.*

~ If you are in nature, bring musical instruments or simply clap your hands and use your voice.

~ Even though this may seem to you an unusual practice, you can consider this the Tantric equivalent of a workout at the gym that involves aerobic movements, strong breathing, and exercising the muscles and organs associated with each *chakra.*

PRACTICE

~ Start the music.

~ Begin with a Heart Salutation (page 75).

~ Breathe deeply through your open mouth. Take the breath all the way to your belly, even to your sex. Breathing through your mouth will enhance your feelings and expand your sensations in each *chakra.*

~ Begin to dance, move, and undulate like a snake—your legs, knees, pelvis, spine, neck, all the way to the crown of the head.

Feel that everything moves. Let the deep breath carry you into the movement. Breathe as you move. Continue for about ten minutes. Let your voice make spontaneous sounds that vibrate and open up your throat *chakra*.

∾ When you're warmed up, direct breath and movements to each of the *chakras* in turn. Spend about three to five minutes on each one, starting with the first and going all the way to the seventh.

The Ecstasy of Orgasm—Going Back to Your Roots

∾ As you focus on your sexual center, begin to move your feet, your legs, and your thighs. Undulate your pelvis like a snake. As you dance to the beat, tighten and relax your sexual muscles. Let your breath, voice, and movement enliven your pelvis. Feel your sexuality as a living current, healthy, juicy, and vital. If you feel resistance—such as feeling that this is silly or feeling stiff—acknowledge it and give yourself permission to go on anyway. See if you can dance the resistance away and dissolve it through fun. As you dance, affirm that you are a powerful sexual being—or whatever words are vibrant and true for you— sing it, reciting it as a poem, or saying it silently to yourself.

∾ *Healing Affirmation:* I am safe, secure, my needs are met. I am an orgasmic being!

The Ecstasy of Flow—Being in Tune

∾ Now move your focus to the belly. At the second *chakra,* keep dancing, twisting, snaking, and breathing deep into your belly through your mouth. Now focus on balance and strength. Take on a flowing movement. Send love and appreciation to your physical body. Visualize that it is healthy, alive, well coordinated, and wonderful. If you are dealing with a particular physical restriction or challenge, envision all the other tissues, muscles, and energetic systems in your body coming to support the healing of that trauma or disorder. See it, touch it, love it, dance it, breathe it.

∾ *Healing Affirmation:* Life is play. My energy is flowing and my confidence is growing.

The Ecstasy of Power—The Radiant Sun

∾ Now focus on your solar plexus, just under the rib cage,

where the diaphragm is. Breathe deeply into that area, still undulating. Feel tingling, juicy energy pouring into your solar
plexus. Feel your emotions, your personal power, your self-esteem, your self-confidence gather there in a great ball of powerful, joyous light energy. Express this power with strong sounds
and words. Declare your power out loud. Claim your rightful
place in the world.

&. *Healing Affirmation:* I am worth it. It's my power and I use it
wisely.

The Ecstasy of Love—The Longing to Merge

&. Now focus on your heart *chakra* in the middle of your chest.
Let your breath expand your rib cage. Envision your heart *chakra*
opening and filling with bright energy and golden rays sent to
you from those who love you. Dancing the heart, extend your
arms as if you were flying. Then embrace yourself: You are the
lover and the beloved meeting within your heart. Send forth all-
encompassing love, caring, support, nurturing to those you love
and to the world around you. Allow whatever feeling you have
to be expressed—laughter, shouting, tears. Let it melt your
heart.

&. *Healing Affirmation:* I am loved. I give love, I receive love.

The Ecstasy of Creation—The Song of the Soul

&. Now focus on your throat and explore your voice. Move
your neck and head. Yell, chant, improvise, go wild, enjoy the
ride! Experiment with ways of singing the song of your pelvis,
your belly, your heart, and so on. Really connect with your energy. Express it outwardly in all the ways that it wants to. Give it
complete freedom and enjoy the ride.

&. *Healing Affirmation:* I listen to my heart and express what I
feel. I make the choice to love my voice.

The Ecstasy of Insight—Seeing Beyond

&. Now focus behind your forehead on your third eye. Inhale
deeply; as you inhale imagine your life energy expanding outward through each of your eyes, your ears, your crown. Let your
dance become a slow, fluid glide. See yourself as an eagle flying
through space. Look around inside and outside, see the big picture as you move. What is happening in your life? Can you re-

ceive intuitive guidance right now? Tune into whatever images, visions, insights emerge as you dance. Can you feel a greater purpose at work in your life?

❧ *Healing Affirmation:* I look, I see, I listen, I hear. I have a vision of my life's purpose.

The Ecstasy of Transcendence—The Open Sky

❧ Now direct your awareness to the crown of your head. As you continue to dance, breathe, enjoy moving, imagine that the crown of your head opens up like a flower to receive the light of the sun. Feel the light penetrate and fill your body with radiance. Feel in this light the power and guidance of your own Spirit. Open yourself to gratitude and joy as you allow Spirit to dance through you.

❧ *Healing Affirmation:* I am becoming who I am. I am a God/Goddess in the making.

POINTERS

❧ Your success depends on your intention. It helps before you start to visualize briefly all your *chakras* opening through dance.

❧ In the beginning you may encounter resistance or blocks in one or more *chakras.* Go slowly, be gentle and patient. Talk to them: "Yes, I know this feels difficult, but that's all right. You can do it. I'm here with you. Let's do it together, breathe with me. That's it, come on, let's have fun."

❧ The effect of this dance will be to enliven your daily life and make the maps and rituals in the next seven chapters more accessible. You may enjoy them more because you will have *felt* the energy in each *chakra.*

❧ When you've done it a few times, invite the whole family to join in—children especially love this exercise.

In this chapter you learned about the seven *chakras,* the energy grid in our body that transforms your life energy into power, consciousness, and ecstasy.

The next seven chapters are each devoted to one *chakra.* Each chapter presents the "*Chakra* Map" which outlines the energies of the *chakra,* its images and archetypes, its positive and negative behaviors, and its qualities. Next we'll explore the essence and the issues connected with that *chakra.* This is followed by examples from *Chakra* Talks that show the range of voices that might be expressed. Finally, we will learn a ritual designed to help us empower that *chakra.*

CHAPTER EIGHT

THE FIRST CHAKRA:
THE ROOT OF CREATION

THE FIRST TANTRIC KEY:
YOU ARE AN ORGASMIC BEING

*I am the source of life. The passion of life. The voice
of life. I connect you to the ground of being.*

            ❧ The voice of the first *chakra,*
from a *Chakra* Talk

THE CHAKRA MAP

ECSTASY ❧ The ecstasy of orgasm.

IMAGES ❧ The coiled snake; the roots of the tree of life.

PHYSICAL LOCATION ❧ The base of the spine, the
pelvic floor, the legs and feet.

BODY PARTS ❧ The genitals (penis, vagina, clitoris) and
uterus.

ENDOCRINE GLANDS ❧ The prostate, testes, and ovaries,
which make up the Taoist House of Essence.

MAIN FUNCTIONS ஃ Sensation, reproduction, survival, transformation.

POWER ஃ Orgasm (an intense churning movement that generates heat, fire, explosion, release, fulfillment, renewal). Also, the power of attraction/desire, gravitation/grounding, birth/belonging.

ESSENCE ஃ Renewal.

FEARS ஃ Survival fears: of death, of change, of not having enough, of penetration, of sexual pleasure, of being or accepting "too much"; incapacity to contain energy.

MASCULINE POWER ஃ Erection, emission, impregnation, individuation.

FEMININE POWER ஃ Attraction, birthing, manifestation, oneness.

OPEN AND RELAXED ஃ "I am the source," "I am fulfilled," "I am orgasmic," "I have enough," "I create."

BLOCKED OR CONTRACTED ஃ "I feel empty," "I feel left out," "I don't have enough," "I don't belong," "I am not loved," "I am not fulfilled."

Positive qualities ஃ Feeling connected to your origins: honoring your ancestors and valuing where you come from; able to connect to a family, a tribe, a group, and feel a sense of place and belonging. Strong sexual connection: at ease with your own sexuality and that of others; understand orgasm as a sacred and valuable energy; creative; able to connect with the new possibilities of the moment, situation, or person. Feeling grounded: knowing how to evaluate the "bottom line"; understanding the essential point in any situation. Feeling grateful: positive sense of knowing where you come from and where you are going. Feeling "at home" in life.

Negative patterns ஃ Feeling not enough: anxious to please, compliant, do-gooder; self-loathing. Feeling unable to hold onto life or to pleasure, unable to contain energy: premature ejaculation or weak or nonexistent orgasms. Feeling pleasure and lust are "bad": force feelings through violence, abusive sexual behavior (sexual molestation, rape, uncontrollable lust). Feeling no sense of foundation: unreliable, avoid commitments, neglectful, never on time, forget appointments, indecisive. Afraid of not having enough: spendthrift, chronically in debt; preoccupied with greed, envy, possessiveness; wanting more and never having enough; compulsive/addictive behavior (addiction to sex, gambling, drugs, shopping, food bingeing).

THE CHALLENGE ✎ Feel yourself as the source of your own orgasm.

HEALING AFFIRMATIONS ✎ "I am the source," "I have enough," I have what I need now," "I am fulfilled," "I'm safe, secure, my needs are met."

QUESTIONS FOR GUIDANCE ✎ "Do I belong here?" "Does this turn me on?" "Am I getting what I need?" "Do I feel connected to this [person, project, place, and so on]?"

ARCHETYPES ✎ The erotic lovers; Shakti and Shiva; Eros and Aphrodite; Attraction and Beauty; Ganesha (the elephant god of India), the remover of obstacles.

The Essence of the First Chakra

You don't have to spiritualize sex to make it valuable, because by its very nature sex is a deep act of the interior life and always brings with it a wealth of emotional and spiritual meaning.

✎ Thomas Moore

Our *chakras* contain all qualities and states of being, from darkness to light, madness to enlightenment, pain to ecstasy, hatred to love. Our task in the first *chakra* is to become rooted in our natural depth, grounded in our sexual nature, renewed and enlivened by the pleasures of the body that partake of the joys of the Spirit. Here we discover our sexuality and the capacity for orgasm, and experience the raw, elemental life force as pleasure and conception, generated in the act of lovemaking.

Our genital sexual development begins in early childhood. Curious and absorbed by genital sensations and the awakening currents of sexuality, we naturally direct this new energy toward the parent of the opposite sex. If our parents are maturely grounded in their own sexuality, then our primal sexual overtures are met by them with maturity and understanding and we are nurtured and empowered in our awakening as little sexual beings; our natural impulses are neither exploited nor suppressed. With such healthy mirroring, our relationship to our sexuality is less likely to become a source of conflict and alienation from self and others. Free of shame, or obsession, our sexuality becomes a source of joy and play in relationship, a positive aspect of our wholeness and our self-identity in the world.

But parents and cultures unfailingly project their sexual dysfunctions onto their children. As children, we are shaped more by who and how our parents are than by what they say or intend. We are imprinted by their desires, inhibitions, and conflicts. We absorb and take on their unhealed wounds. All the issues and aspects of love and sex become apparent facets of a single and absorbing dilemma. And they all have their source in the division between sex and love, between the genitals and the heart. Sex is often in dilemma below the heart. And it must be healed in every *chakra* to rise into the heart.

Each *chakra* has a function, an energy that can manifest in positive or negative form. In its dark side, first *chakra* energy can be an infantile, devouring hunger, devoid of tenderness or love. The positive root energy of the first *chakra* is orgasmic pleasure, the creative and life-affirming power of sex. When your first *chakra* is strong, you are rooted in Gaia. You are at peace with natural pleasures. The surge of the life force pours through your genitals as you make love. The power of primal creation flows through you and your being is continually renewed. Your limbs are mobile and alive. Your survival is not in doubt, for you know with inner certainty that all your needs will be met in the natural course of your living.

If we suppress our first *chakra* power, we may wilt like unwatered flowers. And if we chronically overindulge in pleasure, we may be emptied like leaking buckets. The energy of the first *chakra* was meant to be enjoyed through sex *and* harnessed as a creative power to flow through us in both forms. When we find this balance, we can fill rooms with our dynamic energy and natural authority. People will be magnetically drawn to our charismatic aliveness.

THE ROOT OF THE LIFE FORCE

The first *chakra* is our Source, the door to our conception, our umbilical cord to Mother Earth. It is the root of our life force, whose symbols in ancient Taoist and Tantric teachings are the dragon and the coiled snake. The snake is the power of undulation, transformation, and renewal and the movement of energy through the body. The dragon is the fulfillment of power in its most dynamic form, breathing the fire of life as it soars between heaven and earth. The snake and dragon are both masculine and feminine.

In the ancient Goddess religions, the oracles of Delphi and Eleusis associated the serpent's bite (a metaphor for sexual penetration) with the awakening of clairvoyance and mystical insight. Hence lovemaking was honored as a sacred path to wisdom and revelation, a form of communion with the Goddess, the Mother of Creation.

HONORING ANCESTORS

When we make peace with life and all it has given us, acknowledging with gratitude our past, our parents, our grandparents, and our ancient lineage that has carried life current into this body, at this time, for a purpose we alone can fulfill, then we can open ourselves to the present and flow into the future, dynamically alive. Here is how my friend Vinit accomplished this.

> Driving home after a wonderful weeklong hike in the Oregon mountains with my parents and my sister, suddenly, I felt my deep love for my parents, and gratitude for their many gifts to me. I thought, *What if this is the last time I see them?* And I realized I came through them, they raised me, and it was very important to acknowledge this. I turned around and drove back.
>
> I told my parents what I was feeling and how grateful I was. They were deeply touched. They had tears in their eyes. We all hugged, and I said spontaneously, "I'd like to do a ritual to honor our ancestors." So we all sat at a round table in the garden.

In the middle of the table I lit a candle to symbolize the invisible Spirit. Beside it I put a large quartz crystal, representing the transformation of the earth energy into clarity; a goblet of water, symbolizing flowing emotions; and a stick of incense, symbolizing the penetrating fragrance of the life energy all around us.

We invoked Spirit and I said, "We are here to acknowledge the lineage of our ancestors, from whom we have all received so much. They gave us all they had. Now we have a new consciousness to pass on. We are part of this unbroken chain of beings. Let us take a few minutes to hold them in our hearts with reverence— our parents, grandparents, great-grandparents, great-great-grandparents, uncles, aunts and cousins, our entire lineage—with gratitude and love."

Then I spoke about nature and the cycle of becoming and renewal—how rain forms in the clouds, falls to the earth, into the rivers, nourishing all life on the planet, then evaporates back up into the clouds to fall again; an endless cycle. I closed the ritual, invoking Spirit in a prayer for healing. I expressed our gratitude that our ancestors were integrated in our beings, our hearts, minds, and Spirits.

Afterward, we were silent. Nothing more needed to be said.

TOWARD AN ECSTATIC WAY OF LIFE

When our first *chakra* fully opens and we bring its force into balance, our life is infused with its passionate, creative, regenerative power. Both creativity and orgasm are rooted in sexuality. Orgasm is the epitome of pleasure and satisfaction, the very fountain of life, the pulse of generative passion in the human body.

The universe itself is in a state of constant orgasm at the level of pure energy, and full sexual orgasm brings us into greater harmony with the vibrant energy of universal life. In the fullness of orgasm, every cell in our body dances, electrified, and we resonate with all life at the level of vibration. We make love with trees and stars and with existence itself. Such true pleasure can heal old wounds and fill us with a "peace that passeth understanding."

For each *chakra,* there is usually an issue to resolve, a wound to heal, a skill to master, and an orgasmic potential to be realized. And how we relate to our sexuality directly affects our totality: our creativity, our health, our self-esteem, our relationships, even our relationship to life.

The religious and cultural repression of our sexuality makes our first *chakra* a Gordian knot that must be somehow undone. How can we be happy and fulfilled if we are at war with the body in which we live, full of guilt over the natural pleasures for which it was divinely designed?

Every day we can choose to be intimate, to act bodily, to participate in life passionately, to appreciate desire, to seek deep pleasures rather than superficial entertainments, to live as lovers rather than mere doers, observers, and judges. We can choose to be a part *of* life, rather than apart *from* life.

SEXUALITY AND HAVING ENOUGH

If we are not fully nurtured and loved as children, we learn to guard and grow miserly with our life force, fearing its depletion. If we were neglected as infants, we grow up with a raging hunger to be touched, loved, and filled. Our parent's neglect imprints the fear of scarcity into every fiber of our beings, a deeply ingrained belief that there is not enough. From this spring many compulsive hungers, drives, and behaviors; disturbing preoccupations, with often unreasonable ideas and beliefs; and desperate urges and feelings for which we seek some outlet or release. This is the source of a multitude of compulsions, obsessions, and addictions.

In our efforts to guard our precious store of vitality, we may turn inward and away from life, the very source of vitality itself. Or in our efforts to acquire the life we feel we were denied, our search for pleasure may become an obsession as we squander our life force through orgiastic self-indulgence. Either path is an expression of our already wounded and alienated relationship to life. And our sexuality suffers in one way or another. Perhaps we cannot reach high levels of arousal. Or perhaps we give too much importance to the sexual performance, the mechanisms of orgasm, yet remain separated from the possibilities of intimacy and love.

We can heal our primal wounds through therapy, Tantric

sexual practices, yoga, deep tissue body work, emotional work, etc. We can open our first *chakra* and be restored to a positive relationship to desire, pleasure, and the body. Desire, pleasure, and the body are not our enemies. Life-negating asceticism is the half-truth of half-men who may have been holy but were certainly not whole. Nor are desire, pleasure, and the body the ultimate answer. Let them become our friends, and it will be enough.

Our mistrust of life and the body creates pain and fear, and goads our futile efforts to control or exploit our experience. Then we cannot tolerate the energy charge of arousal or the demands of intimacy. We cannot surrender to love. Why not give yourself permission to lose control? Let yourself be consumed in the joyous fires of love and bodily pleasure. Be swept away by life!

Johanna and Paul came to the Love and Ecstasy Training. They had been married for twenty-six years. Ten years into her marriage, while she was traveling abroad on her own, Johanna experienced traumatic sexual abuse. When she came to the training, she complained that she could not access her full ecstatic potential in lovemaking. "It's just a trickle," she said, "and I want fireworks!" Through patient and delicate work over time, using the Tantric sexual practices and exercises of the training, she discovered and fell in love with a new Johanna: erotic, alive, joyful, and free. A while ago she sent me the following letter:

ECSTASY ON THE FOURTH OF JULY

On my most recent self-pleasuring experience, I encountered the snake, who said: "I am your energy; pleasure me, pleasure yourself."

Self-pleasuring. Alone, loving myself, in Paul's and my Sacred Sexuality room. On the futon with the floor-to-ceiling mirror in front of me, I lie naked, legs spread wide, awkward, vulnerable. My first time really looking at my *yoni,* that part of myself which has felt so much pain, whose pleasure has so often left me feeling shame. But I'm looking! It only took me forty-eight years. I caress myself, my arms and legs, lavishly stroking a rose-scented massage oil onto myself. I feel the juice of my own arousal as I pinch my nipple and finger the tip of my emerging clitoris.

"Yes," I whisper aloud to myself, "I'm here. I'm in a body! I'm alive! I am woman! Yes! I embrace all of me—ordinary human, everyday woman, Goddess, slut, bitch, lover, and beloved. I let go; I surrender—to myself, to life in all its complexity and mystery." Breathing through my mouth, breathing from my belly, I open myself. I caress my body.

Self-pleasuring. Alone, loving myself. I smile; married twenty-eighty years, Paul and I are happy beyond our most hopeful dreams. Vibrations spread throughout my body. Tingling in my chest and all the way down into my feet. Tingling in my scalp. I feel a fullness in my head. Pow! My whole body spasms, orgasms. Again and again. Exquisite pleasure right at the edge of pain. Wonderful nectar oozes out of me like an underground spring rising through marshy ground—my own nectar soaking the sheet. Sounds come out of my mouth, loud and free. It feels so good, wild, joyful. A spring tightly wound since the beginning of time at last unsprung! I did it! I pleasured myself to full body orgasms.

Waves of bliss roll through me. Energy moves through my body like ocean swells—cleansing, clearing, healing. All my cells feel vibrant. Expanding, I feel part of the space beyond my body, merging with all that is. What a Fourth of July! What an Independence Day!

I feel myself and I feel my female lineage, my bond with all women. I feel myself and I feel my connection with all men. And I cry with joy and gratitude. I am free at last.

Johanna expresses the essential discovery of her deep powers as a woman. Through the opening of her first *chakra,* she found new levels of trust in herself and her creativity in the world. As a result she was able to take over her aging father's foundering business and bring it to a new level of dynamic success. Then she handed the business over to her younger brother so she could pursue her soul's call to become a writer and a teacher.

The Chakra Talk

When you do the *Chakra* Talk (page 138) with your first *chakra,* you will hear the voice of your roots, your beginnings, your sexuality. The following examples from my students will give you an idea of the range of voices and images you may experience.

BARBARA ❧ I am the voice of Mother Earth. I am the pulse beat of the earth. I am the womb of the earth. I am the womb of my mother and my grandmother and all my ancestors. The womb of life. The source of life. I am wild energy. I connect you to the body of life, to orgasm undulating through your body. I am the entrance to new life. Going deeper and deeper inside me, you will find your origins. The roots of life. The connection to your ancestors. In me, you will find your source.

DON ❧ I want to be an authentic, wild, unfettered being, but I am feeling restricted in expressing joy without shame or embarrassment. I hold resentment against parents and authorities. I'm dangerous, outlawed, not good for you. I carry shame and guilt from eons back. I struggle to connect to a forgotten past of celebration.

LYNN ❧ Let me dance life to the beat of the drum. By the fire. Wild nights of drink and ritual and naked love beyond the mind. I am the door to Dionysus. Stay in me and I will bring you endless pleasure, nurture you, fulfill you, give you everything you need. I am hungry to be filled. Stay with me, fill me up.

FIONA ❧ I am a tiger. Wild. I am the fire of sex. I am the dance of *Yoni* with *Vajra.*

KEN ❧ I am the primal lover. My testicles are plants that grow from deep in the earth. My *vajra* is the sun. *Yoni* is a universe. Together we are one.

THE ART OF ECSTATIC LOVEMAKING

When we bring lovemaking into the sacred dimension, all the chakras work in unison, allowing sexual pleasure to flow through each chakra and be transformed into the delight of the heart and the ecstasy of the Spirit. Creating a ritual for lovemaking is a statement that we are ready to heal our anti-ecstatic patterns regarding sex and love and an opportunity to create the optimal conditions for lovemaking. Play with this ritual. Make it longer, shorter, simpler, or more sophisticated. Discuss with your partner how you can adapt it to your needs. More suggestions can be found in my books The Art of Sexual Magic *and* The Art of Sexual Ecstasy. *If you don't have a partner, use it as a ritual for self-pleasuring. Allow your sexuality to flower.*

PURPOSE

&. To create the best possible environment for sexual loving so that your sex, your body, your heart, your mind, and your Spirit can be in harmony.

PREPARATION

&. *Timing.* Allow yourself enough time to relax and play. I suggest two to three hours of uninterrupted time. Make a date with each other in advance. Prepare ahead: make child care arrangements; allow time to freshen up, make food, gather tools, and create the sacred space (see Chapters 6 and 7).

&. *Tools.* Gather all the tools you may need for creative lovemaking. Use your imagination!

&. *Foods.* Choose the luscious ripe fruits, plates of delicacies (such as lychees, crystallized ginger, chocolates, or whatever you like), wine, special aphrodisiac teas, water, glasses.

&. *Scents.* Wear the most erotic perfumes—try different ones for different parts of the body (both musk and ylang-ylang are reputed to enhance sexual arousal; definitely use musk for the genital area). Scent the air with essential oils or incense.

&. *Environment.* In your sacred lovemaking space you may want flowers, candles (don't forget matches!), pictures of spiritual guides and loved ones, poetry, one magic blanket to put on the bed or the floor and to sit/lie on, stones and shells from the beach, sensual silk sheets, plenty of pillows, Tarot cards, feathers and pieces of fur for stroking each other's skin (see Chapters 6 and 7).

∽ *Music.* Have instruments to play and music to listen to: flutes, bells, drums, or your favorite instruments; CDs or tapes.

∽ *Costumes:* Determine in advance what you are going to wear. It is great to dress for sex. Once you are dressed, you may undress and dance and strip tease in front of each other. You may also want silk scarves, special jewelry, or velvet wraps.

PRACTICE:

∽ Begin with the Heart Salutation (page 75).

∽ Now, using your intuition, go inside and ask yourself: Where are we going? What is our intention for this lovemaking session? My students in the Love and Ecstasy Training have expressed these intentions: to bring healing and abundance to our love life, to develop my capacity to surrender to the flow of excitement without inhibition, to learn how to guide my partner to what turns me on, to feel comfortable giving pleasure totally and receiving pleasure totally, to bring variety to our love life, to open our minds to create new possibilities to merge and melt, to lovingly move through fears and allow more pleasure, to honor my partner as a God/Goddess, to dissolve boundaries between me and my partner, to go-glow-grow with the flow, and to experience spiritual communion through sexual union.

∽ With your partner sitting or lying opposite from you, in silence or with soft music, let yourself sink to a deeper place within yourself, beyond the usual traffic of thoughts. Breathe together, harmonizing your breathing. Do this until you feel yourselves breathing in harmony.

∽ With your partner, agree on your intention and state it together in this form: "This ritual is intended to . . ."

∽ Now say the invocation, expressing your intention to honor the highest potential in each other. For instance: the man says to the woman, "I honor in you the Wild Woman, that she may feel loved when she is ready to let go. I honor in you the Mother, that she may feel supported when she nurtures our children. I honor in you the Goddess, the Shakti, that she may surrender to her pure energy, and know she is the Source of creation." Or the woman says to the man, "I salute in you the poet, that you may sing the beauty and grace of our love. I salute in you the lover, that you may be blessed by my delight and receive it a thousandfold. I salute in you the God, Shiva, may your divine Spirit be a source of creativity and inspiration for us both."

Grounding: Honoring the Chakra of Orgasm and New Beginnings

᪣ Caress your partner's body, touching every part and speaking sweet words of appreciation about your partner's body. For example, the man might say, "Beautiful Shakti, I love your soft skin, your brown, erect nipples, your breath rippling through your belly, your strong legs. I love to touch and feel your strong muscles, your limber body. To tickle and scratch your chest. What a beautiful body you have." Then the partners should reverse roles.

᪣ When every part of your body is touched, it feels accepted, enlivened. And now it is easier to trust the body and to feel that the body can be the vehicle of your love because you have acknowledged it and made a loving connection with it. Touching each other's body everywhere opens the door for renewal. Your body is refreshed, renewed with the potential of love, care, and acceptance. This fosters trust and welcomes healing, and the ecstasy of flow.

The Chakra Empowerment: Honoring the Chakra of Flow

You will now bless your partner's chakras, and your partner will then do the same for you. As you give a blessing to each of the chakras, you empower these energy centers. Symbolically, you are opening these doors through these invocations, which connect the Spirit to the body. Simply receive the empowerment with joy. Feel free to express your blessings in your own words. Sitting opposite each other, begin.

᪣ *Touch your partner's sex:* look at it and say, "I honor the door to our delights. May your sweet flower of love, or your powerful scepter of love, feel empowered with pleasure, moist with lust, charged with passion. May we get out of the way, so they are free to do their dance with each other."

᪣ *Touch your partner's belly:* look at it and say, "May your strength come forth and sustain our love, may you feel welcomed, comfortable. May the love that we share heal past frustrations or resentments so that we may feel connected and in the flow with each other."

✎ *Touch your partner's solar plexus:* Look at it and say, "May you feel centered and secure in yourself. I empower you to fully enjoy all that you are: wild, radiant, lustful. I love to see you this way."

✎ *Touch your partner's heart:* Look at it and say, "I welcome your love, I love you. I welcome your feelings and I accept all that you are."

✎ *Touch your partner's throat:* Look at it and say, "Let us open the door to sound and song. May our love sing, and shout . . . may we feel free to ask for what we need: your desire is my pleasure, your pleasure is my desire."

✎ *Touch your partner's third eye:* Look at it and say, "May we be wise in our lust, generous in our love, expanded in our visions: filled with light and love."

✎ *Touch your partner's crown:* Look at it and say, "May the power of your lust flow through your body, bring health and vitality to all your *chakras.* May we merge as One in ecstasy."

✎ *When you have both received the empowerment:* Say in unison, "We dedicate our pleasure and orgasms to the well-being of all sentient beings on earth. May they be happy!"

Arousal: Honoring the Chakra of Empowerment

Sex is first and foremost a matter of energy, and energy grows as arousal grows, and arousal grows when we move away from thinking to breathing. We do this by watching and deepening our breath, breathing through the mouth to be closer to our feelings. We spread the energy of excitement through the whole body by moving the body and by making sounds of delight that give a flavor and color to our energy and a message of approval to our partner.

✎ Lying in each other's arms, playfully begin to turn each other on. Kiss, slide over each other, let the flame of excitement grow.

✎ Let every pleasurable sensation be enhanced and expanded as you focus your breath where it feels good. As if you were going to pick up that stimulus and carry it to the rest of your body. Breathe deeply.

As your breath and your pleasure deepen, let your body respond through movement. The orgasmic reflex happens through a series of pleasurable, highly exciting movements of rocking the pelvis backwards and forwards . . . try it consciously.

Enhance your sexual sensations by tightening and relaxing your sexual muscles while you breathe deeply and rock your pelvis. Be natural and loose and playful about it. This is not a technique you are performing, you are just finding ways of expanding your pleasure to the whole body and moving beyond the mind.

Let your wild self come out: growl like an animal, talk dirty, describe what you feel, shout what you want, show your body and your sex, be proud and strong about who you are and what you feel.

Merging: Honoring the Chakra of Love and Passion

Take a moment to hold each other, doing nothing. Visualize your sexual excitement rising like a fountain to your chest and filling your heart with delight. Imagine that you become a flowing stream. Relax and allow yourself to fully receive your partner's loving caresses. Allow your heart to trust in your love, right now. Give yourself first the love you want to receive. You are the beloved. As you appreciate yourself, you know you deserve love, as much as you share it. Rest in the knowledge that this moment is your creation, your gift to each other. Feel the completeness, the perfection. Let go of all goals, directions, expectations. Just accept now. Him. Her. Here. How glorious!

Truth: Honoring the Chakra of Creativity

Now is your chance to become fully aware, to take responsibility for what you want. Ask yourself, "Is my partner touching me the way I like? Does this feel wonderful? Or do I want it deeper, stronger, slower, somewhere else?" Then ask your partner for what you want. Ask lovingly. If you don't want to speak, take your partner's hand and put it where you want it. Express appreciation when it feels good: "Aah, yes, that's it, keep going." If either of you has fears, anxieties, or unspoken feelings about lovemaking, this is the time to speak them, honor them, and let go. Avoid identifying with your partner's difficulties or feeling guilty about them ("It's my fault," "Why is my partner never satis-

fied"). Listen in silence. Lovingly, supportively, echo back your partner's feelings, and say, "I understand how you feel, it's okay, I'm here for you, we will move through this together."

Imagine: Honoring the Chakra of Vision

Become aware of your internal dialogue, your thoughts, your pictures and fantasies. Let them all be a positive support to the experience. Be clear that you will sabotage your experience if you indulge in negative judgments. Simply watch them come, say, "Next!" and send them off. Pay attention to ideas, visions, insights, or inspirations that may come up during lovemaking. You may actually see your energy in forms of colors, or symbols, or even fantasies. Remember to focus on your chakras and send light and love to each center with your breath.

Expanding Beyond the Body: Honoring the Chakra of Enlightenment

Now explore transforming and refining your connection. Lying face to face, exchange breaths. One of you exhales, the other inhales. Do it through the mouth, softly, deeply, slowly. You are harmonizing your breaths, finding a common rhythm. After a while, when you are comfortable with this exchange, you may feel that you melt and disappear as a solid body, and only the breath of Spirit remains. Feeling as you inhale, that you draw in your sexual energy, your pleasure, your excitement, to the belly, heart, throat, and when you exhale, visualize it going out, like a fountain, through the crown of your head. This is a fun, wonderful way of cleansing your chakras and connecting sex and spirit. End the session lying quietly in each other's arms, relaxing, melting, letting go, doing nothing, Feel gratefulness and appreciation for this moment.

CLOSURE

☙ *Men:* Before you disengage sexually, ask your partner: "Can I leave your wonderful garden now?" She may say, "Not yet, let's stay inside each other longer, let's just melt and relax for five more minutes." *Women:* You too can find poetic words to express the desire to end the session.

☙ *Men:* When you leave the garden, "close the door": Gently lay your hand on your partner's sexual flower for a few minutes to allow her to integrate, close her psychic and sexual gates, and feel complete. *Women:* Touch his penis gently, as a subtle message of acknowledgment.

🐚 Look into each other's eyes and say, "Thank you. It was wonderful!"

🐚 Relax in each other's arms, doing nothing for some minutes.

🐚 End with a Heart Salutation, thanking each other for the pleasure you have given and received.

🐚 You may or may not want to end the exchange with feedback: What did you discover? What did you feel? What was the most difficult moment? What was the best moment? Feedback is a great way to integrate an experience and learn about each other's sexual responses and functioning.

POINTERS

🐚 *Remember that a lovemaking ritual is a delicate challenge.* It is important not to "judge" the experience against some ideal criteria of the "perfect ritual" and "the perfect performance." What happens, happens. That's all. And that's a great teaching!

🐚 *Express your feelings positively.* Avoid negative words, criticisms, or talk about another lover while you are with each other and especially when you are inside each other. Feelings of anxiety, fear, or hurt in you or your partner will then be anchored in your sexual center and may contribute to unconscious, fearful, distrusting reactions during subsequent lovemaking.

🐚 *Learn from your difficulties.* No ritual is ever perfect. Some parts are divine, some parts may be difficult. When you can feel that this is okay you are ready to open up to your maximum ecstatic potential.

🐚 *Allow surprise.* Include something unexpected in your lovemaking. For example, set up a picnic blanket on the floor and eat naked; cover your partner with chocolate sauce and lick it off; light a fire in the fireplace and caress your partner's body with ostrich and peacock feathers.

🐚 *Become erotic in your daily life.* Let the eroticism of sex become your very essence. Let it infuse how you eat, talk to each other, touch each other, talk on the phone, and so on.

🐚 *Cultivate reciprocity.* Sexual ecstasy is a co-creation between partners equally deserving of the highest, most ecstatic sexual experience they can have. Give your partner as much pleasure as your partner gives you.

 Say yes to pleasure. Give yourself permission to receive pleasure for as long as you need.*

 The key to pleasure is to tease and take your time. Forget about sexual orgasm as a goal; just be concerned with the moment to moment turn-on of erotic caresses and arousal. Give up going anywhere, achieving a great performance. Agree that you will focus on spreading your arousal through the body. Caress your partner's (or your own) erogenous zones intensely, then tease. Go away. Brush the whole body as if you were diffusing the excitement over the whole skin. Go on teasing each other erotically until you are mad with sexual longing. Relax until you can contain more intense arousal for longer periods of time.

 Self-pleasuring. With or without a partner, you are the source of your own orgasm. As Johanna discovered, understanding your own erotic needs, and loving and pleasuring yourself can be an empowering, transcendent experience. Learn what you like through self-pleasuring. Then you can guide your partner to what you like, breathe deeply into the pleasure, move your body, enjoy yourself. You can also pleasure yourself in front of your partner as part of your lovemaking.

---

* Stella Resnick, in The Pleasure Zone, writes: "It takes time to kindle the spark into a heat that sizzles through your entire body." Show your body how much you love it.

CHAPTER NINE

THE SECOND CHAKRA: THE FLOWING STREAM

THE SECOND TANTRIC KEY: YOU ARE LIFE IN FLOW

*I am the Belly, I am the mothership, I am the door
to your mother's womb. I am the body erotic,
electric. I create, procreate, recreate. I am excessive.
Wild celebration. In me hides unbounded aliveness,
appetite for the unknown, mysterious calls of
longing and fulfillment.*

           ❧ The Voice of the Second *Chakra,*
              from a *Chakra* Talk

THE CHAKRA MAP

ECSTASY ❧ The ecstasy of flow.
IMAGES ❧ A surfer riding a wave; the yin-yang symbol.
PHYSICAL LOCATION ❧ The navel, the belly.

BODY PARTS ❧ The womb, spleen, liver, hips, lower back.

ENDOCRINE GLANDS ❧ The adrenals, which are the Taoist House of Water.

MAIN FUNCTIONS ❧ Healing, being in tune with the rhythms and cycles of the body and of nature, making choices, understanding change and transformation.

POWER ❧ Physical health and strength.

ESSENCE ❧ Balance, harmony, equanimity.

FEARS ❧ Of expressing hurt, of releasing emotions, of letting go, of risk.

MASCULINE POWER ❧ To act, to take initiative, to exercise authority and control, to create boundaries; the ability to say no; healing as science; developing the ego; being the provider.

FEMININE POWER ❧ To respond, to take responsibility, gestation, protection, nurturing; healing as caring; the ability to say yes.

OPEN AND RELAXED ❧ "I am in tune," "I know what to do," "I know the way," "I am in the flow."

BLOCKED OR CONTRACTED ❧ "I can't do anything right," "I am lost," "I am out of balance," "I feel out of step."

Negative patterns ❧ Remembering past wounds: playing the victim, feeling regret, being a martyr. Holding on: possessiveness, jealousy, stubbornness, getting attached to old structures or to dead relationships because you don't want to rock the boat, workaholic. Control issues: strict disciplinarian, wanting to be obeyed at all costs, demanding, manipulating, dogmatic, know-it-all.

Positive qualities ❧ Self-awareness: independence, sense of adventure, can take risks and try new things, ability to make choices that are right, knowing what to do and how to do it. Balance and flow: effortless creation, grace, playfulness in most situations, ability to change positions easily during lovemaking and in life. Receptive: ability to give birth easily, good mothering and nurturing qualities, honoring boundaries.

THE ESSENCE OF THE SECOND CHAKRA

The stillness in stillness is not the real stillness.
Only when there is stillness in movement can
the spiritual rhythm appear which pervades
heaven and earth.

           Ts 'ai-ken T'an

Through our second *chakra,* we relate to our bodies; and through our bodies, we relate to the world. Our lower belly is our life-energy womb, creator of egg and sperm, generator of life's essence, fertilizer of new wholeness. Our belly nurtures new beings and creative ideas. It is our body's reservoir of energy and endurance and physical health. It anchors our body to the earth. The second *chakra's* ability to reconcile opposites and conduct the flow of our life force is the source of our body's healing powers.

The essence of this *chakra* is root and flow: balance and anchor between energy and body, between our inner self and the outer world. When our second *chakra* is strong, and our boundaries are clear, we understand who we are in relation to others, and we intuitively feel and know our place in the world. We feel centered, vital, healthy, comfortable in our body and sensitive to our environment. We flow, we embrace life, we dance with obstacles, we live life naturally and effortlessly. When we move from our *hara,* as the belly *chakra* is known in the Asian martial arts, we move with sureness and grace, like a cat. We are spontaneous, transcending rigid method and form. We know and feel with our guts. We radiate calmness and poise. But when our second *chakra* is weak, we move awkwardly through life, leaking energy, feeling powerless, unstable and off balance, as if we were not in our bodies.

The gut instinct of the second *chakra* can sense tension or danger, respond correctly, and distinguish between what is mine and what is yours. The mind, guided by the belly, becomes a mirror, a witness to the instinctual flow of effortless action. Its nature is implied in the yin-yang symbol, for it contains and harmonizes the apparent opposites of energy and gravity, root and flow, and the receptive/feminine and active/masculine polarities.

PUBERTY: DIFFERENTIATING SELF FROM OTHER

I call the belly the guardian of our life cycles. Through the belly, we feel how the body changes, how our energy responds to the seasons within and without. In the belly we feel most powerfully life's great transitions: pregnancy; birth; the onset of death; and of course, puberty. The "fire in the belly" heralds the beginning of manhood, as the lunar tides of blood, emotion, and intuition herald the beginning of womanhood.

In puberty, the belly stirs, and a new cycle of awakening begins. In this crucial initiation, a trial by hormonal fire, the vital, generative impulses of the second *chakra* come roaring to life. We are challenged to balance and ground ourselves amid a flow of newly awakened energies and integrate into our systems forces that at times threaten to overwhelm us.

Puberty rites in traditional cultures are designed to honor, ground, and contextualize this disorienting life passage. But in the West this crucial transition is typically ignored or suppressed. Girls in their teens often feel clumsy and ashamed of their bodies. They slump so they're not noticed, cover their breasts with their arms, worry that their stomachs are sticking out.

Boys during puberty are suddenly told to become men. This often translates into rigidity—standing up straight, stiff, shoulders back, belly tight—or wild recklessness as a sign of manly courage.

For both boys and girls, the awakening of the second *chakra* during puberty is associated with anxiety and shame. Too often bereft of mature guidance, cultural or individual, they are left to control their raging hormones on their own. This energy, bound up with social conflicts and taboos, can become obsessive, paralyzing, even self-destructive.

The ritual acknowledgment of puberty marks the passage from boyhood or girlhood to adulthood, provides a meaningful context for a confusing transition, and welcomes children into the circle of adults as valuable members of the tribe. The ritual acknowledgment and honoring of transitional life cycles is immensely healing. It is the stuff of which community is made. And its lack in our culture is the literal lack of community itself, of tribal intimacy.

A GIRL'S FIRST PERIOD ∽ A girl's first period signals her body's awakening to womanhood, her ability to conceive new life. It is an extraordinary event! Yet most girls feel it is something to be hidden in shame. I put the following question to a group of young women: In the best of all possible worlds, when you began bleeding for the first time, how would you like to have been received and what kind of ritual could you imagine would have supported you at that time? Here is how they responded:

> ∽ It would have been nice to have had a ritual blessing for my body through the transitions of puberty and losing my virginity. Your body starts changing so quickly during this time—your hips are larger, your breasts get bigger, and you grow a couple of inches. Everything is changing. You have to relearn how to take care of yourself every day. I wish I could have had a support system and a special ritual to say, "You are beautiful and we love you exactly the way you are and whatever you choose to do."
>
> ∽ It was summer when my first period came. I would love to have gone into the ocean and bled freely there.

≈ I wish my first period had not been gross and disgusting and messy and hateful and uncomfortable—which is what it was because my mother complained about it. I would love to have discussed it intimately with her, talked about what to do and how it felt to have blood coming out of me.

≈ I wish I had been introduced to the moon cycles and how it related to my menstrual cycles and to me as a woman. I didn't know about that until college!

≈ I would have loved some quiet time on my first day, just allowing it to be secret, and feeling protected and cherished.

ON THE VERGE OF MANHOOD ≈ For boys, the awakening of sexual energy and the penis—with its suddenly random, self-determined erections, and especially its emission of sperm—can be an unnerving and uncanny encounter with the primal force of life. What is this organ doing with a mind of its own, bothering and demanding attention, tingling and hardening whenever it likes? What is the strange new juice coming out? Now he can make babies. He is no longer a child, but a man. What does it all mean and what, if anything, is he now supposed to do?

Without a wise parent/mentor or ritual to help a boy make this sudden transition from childhood to manhood, it is left to be ridiculed or celebrated at a school yard scatological level. It becomes a profane joke rather than the sacred mystery he intuitively knows it to be, and which inspires in him both dread and wonder.

Men who had a difficult transition through puberty often carry tension in the belly area. Men are taught to suck their bellies in by gym teachers in school and then in the military. As a result, the belly is a place where men store and hold deep emotions, and letting go in the belly is deep work. Men (or women who have problems with digestion) can find great release in the following simple exercise: Sit comfortably with your hands on your belly. Breathe love into your belly from your heart. Feel the warmth from your hands penetrating deep inside, relaxing tension, healing intestines. Breathe deeply and slowly into your belly. Gently massage your belly. Under your hands, feel it expand with the inhalation and soften with the exhalation. Enjoy the natural softness of your belly—let it hang out and be okay.

ENCOURAGING BODY INTIMACY

Physical intimacy is often minimized around puberty. Young children thrive on touch, hugs, affectionate bodily contact. But as sexuality dawns, parents and children both tend to draw back. Yet children *need* affectionate, nonsexual physical contact as much as ever.

Many people in the Love and Ecstasy Training find the Melting Hug, a basic practice, very difficult. It consists of nothing more than two people embracing, allowing their bodies to soften and melt in close, relaxed contact with each other. Yet the first response is usually to hug from the shoulders up and stick the buttocks out and away from the other. We call this the "Donald Duck" hug! Discomfort with human contact is often learned during puberty, when intimacy signals the "danger" of sexual possibility. It is important when puberty comes that parents do not draw back from their child, but continue their natural expressions of physical affection.

MOVEMENT AND BODY ESTEEM Do you remember how much joy you experienced as a child through simple movement? During puberty, our impulse toward unrestrained physical self-expression finds a second wind. Teenagers naturally want to move, to put on some music and move their bodies freely. "I was taught from a young age about movement," says Moira, fifteen. "It made me comfortable with my body. Parents should dance with their kids and teach them how to move in their bodies. It's a wonderful gift. Movement is an amazing way of processing things without thinking."

Movement is key in developing a healthy relationship to our bodies. And so is comfort with our own nakedness. Rituals involving nudity, such as family or communal saunas and hot tubs, common in Japan and some European countries, can teach children more powerfully than words the simple and ordinary beauty of the human body. Being naked with others in fun and natural ways reduces the negative charge our culture imposes on nudity.

BOUNDARIES Through our second *chakra,* we intuitively differentiate between self and others. We explore and set boundaries, which contain our energy and allow us to exist and act within an accepted parameter of safety. We live within numerous boundaries: the walls of our house, the fence around our property, the amount of time we are willing to work or give to others, the personal and societal rules and laws that govern our social interactions, even the amount of pleasure and excitement we allow ourselves to experience.

Boundaries begin with our sense of who we are and with our ability to say no. When our belly center is weak, our boundaries are unclear—we may have trouble knowing where we end and others begin. We may be insecure, allowing others to invade our personal space. We may be overly concerned with others, attending to their needs and neglecting our own. Or we may be too rigid, too demanding or intrusive or not allowing others in.

Boundary setting involves making choices. As an exercise, for one day examine everything you do in terms of what you choose to accept or reject moment to moment—both emotionally and physically. "Do I *choose* to impose my needs on my partner, or will I take my partner's needs into consideration?" "Do I choose to let others impose their agendas onto me, or will I draw the line and say no?" "Do I choose to make this agreement now or am I saying yes to please someone else?"

As you ask and answer these questions, the nature of your own boundaries will become more clear.

A STATE OF FLOW

Athletes speak reverently of being "in the zone," those moments of flow that come like magic, when the body moves beyond the mind and seems to function at an almost supernatural level. Richard Moss, author of *The Second Miracle,* referring to the pleasure of flowing down a ski slope, calls this state "being the skiing." In such moments there is no doer, only the witness of the body as energy in motion, our form moving like a shadow in a shifting light, in a perfect dance with what is. You may have experienced it playing golf, tennis, or skiing down a challenging slope. "Out" of your mind, guided by your *hara,* you fall into your center of gravity as breath, muscles, movement, and awareness become one in action. As Richard Moss expresses it, "Thinking collapses into feeling. Doing collapses into being. There is alertness, aliveness, flow."

Flow is a state of dynamic absorption, of *being as action,* unmediated by mental processes. Time may seem to stand still or to move very fast. Flow is lucid action, a state akin to ecstasy, an effortless condition in a body that seems to have melted into its origins. Pure instinct. When we move spontaneously, our mind stops and we truly become our body. For our bodies, composed of 70 percent water and reared in the amniotic fluids of the womb, flow in motion is a natural state.

Sometimes we experience flow spontaneously, but usually it is the result of years of disciplined practice—in dance, gymnastics, or martial arts; in pottery making or painting; in public speaking or acting; and even in everyday activities from driving a car to cleaning the house. You can practice flow with great benefit while making love. Instead of thinking ahead, racing toward orgasm, relax into feeling in the present moment. Don't worry about the next moment, whether you are doing it right, whether he will come too soon or she will come at all. Release all thought and judgment by feeling, surrendering to the energy of each moment. When you enjoy the simple pleasures of touch, feeling, breathing, and expressing love in the act of love—instead of effort and concern for results—flow happens.

SNAKE TIME IS FLOW TIME &. Many people today find their lives are tightly scheduled, we feel boxed in by the squares on our calendar planners. When we live in "calendar time," it's difficult to be in the flow. Do this simple Snake Time exercise to experience a new kind of flow chart. All you need is a large calendar page of the current month, a jar of brightly colored water-based paint, and some colored pens.

&. Dip your index finger in the paint and let your finger flow like a snake through the days of the month. Admire your work.

&. Now dip your finger in the paint again, and beginning in the box that marks the first day of the month just zigzag down through the day-boxes like a snake. Don't look at the numbers. Just make sure to touch every square that has a number on it. Imagine that your life is like this snaky line, going where the energy takes it.

&. Now write in your appointments for the month.

With the colored pens, give each one a symbol that represents the energy or the potential of that moment. You
don't have to stay inside the boxes! Draw a sun with
bright yellow rays expanding to the other boxes, or a
climbing vine, or a glass of wine spilling a few drops, or
a question mark. Let the flow of the month, symbolized
by the snake, connect them all and flow through them.
➣ When you are all done, look at the calendar to get a
sense of how the month will flow, what your expectations are, what surprises may be in store for you. Then
put it up where you can see it every day. If you really
want to have fun, you could even dance on the calendar!

Flow occurs when we are consciously present in our body
with feeling and attention, balanced and centered in our belly.
A boat floating on the water naturally rests on its center of
gravity, adapting to the waves and currents with perfect ease. It
doesn't try to balance, to float. Being centered in our second
chakra, our *hara,* is like this.

Here is an example of how movement, flow, and balance can
harmonize our Spirit and open our heart. My friends Ann and
David Chandler are both teachers of Tai Chi, and run the Eagle's Quest Tai Chi Center. They have been together for twelve
years. The story of their courtship is a study in patience.

When we first met, I knew instantly I wanted to marry
David. We became really good friends and David became my Tai Chi teacher. We had a very Tai Chi friendship—it was very slow, sort of "on" for a few months
and "off" for a few months. But I was learning the Tai
Chi form. After being apart for a year, we met again; still
in the flow, we went to a field to do Tai Chi together.
We continued the form, David was reciting poetry
while gliding with me into the round, fluid movements.
We each felt as if our Spirit/energy circle opened up
like a golden ring to encompass and join with the
other's circle. All in movement and in flow, the two
rings interlocked and came together as one. And spontaneously, without a word. We knew, at this moment,
that our Spirits had merged in holy matrimony and

union. We had this intimate ecstatic experience, yet no one said anything.

Six years went by . . . and we finally decided to get married. The day of our wedding, he wore a tuxedo and I wore a white dress; and at the end of the ceremony, in front of everyone, we repeated the Tai Chi form again, in the same way we had, six years ago, reciting the same wedding poems which once again filled my heart with love. It was beautiful. I learned a lot from this about patience. Patience is a part of balance. So many people today are impatient. They can't trust. If we are true lovers, if we are meant to be together, it will happen. We need to be a little more patient.

Flow is not always a matter of patience or peak performance. It is sometimes a matter of survival necessity, of doing the right thing at the right time in exactly the right way. For example, in the nick of time, you perform a sudden complex maneuver in your car and avoid a serious accident. An example of this flow of necessity was told to me by Doug, a martial artist friend who worked as a landscape gardener:

I was digging on a hillside when it suddenly collapsed. The earth started sliding down the hill onto the driveway, and me with it. Rather than fall, I stepped onto a post and leaped out, thinking to land on the driveway on my feet. But there was an iron bar sticking out of the top of the post, and as I pushed off, the bar caught my foot and tripped me off balance. My leap carried me off the hillside as I'd intended, but I found myself in midair in a horizontal position, eight feet above a concrete driveway and falling facedown. I was in the classic "Superman" position, only I couldn't fly. And there was no way to right myself. I saw everything in an instant. My mind was crystal clear, and I was falling in slow motion. I knew if I fell in that position, I would be badly hurt. So as I fell, I turned in the air onto my side, almost leisurely it seemed, and went into a martial arts "fall" position. I hit the concrete driveway in perfect form, on my right side, in the way I had practiced ten thousand times, slapping my crossed arms, one thigh and the sole of one foot on the ground to absorb and spread the impact throughout my body. From the adrenaline, I felt no pain, not even the shock of impact. An eight-foot horizontal fall onto concrete, and I was all right. I stood up and walked away.

Here are the keys to experiencing flow:

- In your mind's eye, have a clear vision of your goal (I am going to ski down this slope; I am going to clean the house in one hour; I am going to speak in front of this group). But do not be attached to the outcome. Accept that it might turn out differently.
- Consciously relax, breathe, and release any resistance or complaints you may have.
- Watch your breath rather than your mind.
- Choose, moment to moment, to focus your attention *only* on what you are doing. Forget yourself. Don't *try*. Surrender your mind and your body into the experience.
- Trust in yourself. Relax everything.
- Don't worry about success or failure.
- Surrender to your body in motion.
- Feel moment to moment what is happening.
- Do not compare with what was yesterday or project what will be tomorrow.
- Do this as meditation.

GUT INSTINCT ∾ In a difficult situation, listen to the guidance of your gut. It speaks with the voice of instinctual connection, with the wisdom of true feeling. Our minds tend to lead us away from our instinct. But in any present moment, when the mind has had its say, we can focus on our belly, listen to our gut and follow its instinctive flow.

To feel the guidance of your gut, try this simple exercise: Imagine that your gut has an antenna, an invisible umbilical radar growing out of your navel. As you go through your day, feel and move from that place, letting that cord from your *hara* draw you and guide you. When you want to make meaningful contact with someone, send that cord from your belly to his or her belly. Pay attention to the quality of the connection, to his or her response, and the feeling in your gut.

HEALING

Our second *chakra,* unifier of opposites, is a natural locus of healing, of bringing together, of making whole. Merely being *present* in our body when we are sick can change our condition and speed up the healing process. And by actively talking and listening to our body, nourishing it with our feeling attention, we can heal it.

An important element of healing is taking down time—consciously relaxing, going deep to a place of rejuvenation when you are tired, overwhelmed, or sick. Winston Churchill claimed his daily naps gave him the resilience to bring England through World War II. Napoleon was also famous for his ability to take refreshing naps between battles. Modern sleep research shows that the body takes three to five hours to release the stress of the day and achieve the relaxed state in which rejuvenating sleep begins. But it takes only five to ten minutes of conscious relaxation to release the same amount of stress. Thus five to ten minutes of conscious relaxation before going to sleep allows us to go straight into a rejuvenating sleep cycle. Practicing down time when we need to recharge our mental, physical, or emotional batteries is an invaluable asset to health and well-being.

Here are some other secrets of healing I would like to pass along to you:

    Never label a person as sick. What you see, think, and project with your mind affects physical reality. Instead, visualize and feel the person in radiant health.

    Your centered, loving, supportive presence will sometimes do more for a sick person than any medicine. Shower him with energy. Talk to him, hold him, love him, make him laugh.

    Have faith in her self-healing capacities and impart your faith to her. But don't pressure her to recover. Accept her as she is. Some people have something to learn from their illness and don't need to be pushed back into health.

🕭 Make sure she is in a joyful, sensual environment with fresh air, flowers, music, natural light, and good food.

🕭 Let her rest or move as much as she needs to.

🕭 Create a healing ritual together, or with his permission, perform one of your own. The guidelines in Chapter 7 and the ritual at the end of this chapter are useful. You can clear his energies and his room with Tibetan singing bowls, incense, chanting, fresh air, and invocations.

🕭 Regard illness as a purification. Participate with it in this Spirit by purifying and clearing your thoughts, your words, your feelings, your personal space.

THE CHAKRA TALK

When you do the *Chakra* Talk (page 138) with your second *chakra,* invoke the voice of your belly, your *hara,* your center of flow and healing. The following examples from my students will give you an idea of the range of voices and images you may experience.

NICOLE 🕭 I am the belly, the source and the womb. All things are born in me. I am an ocean of the forces and powers of life. There is no beginning and no end to my vastness. My feelings are true. I am the mother of compassion.

JENNY 🕭 I hold a power energy. My urge is to create. I am the provider that sustains life. I am pregnant with myself.

RON 🕭 I am the belly. My fierce center is a cauldron of fire, boiling with vitality and strength. I create form from formlessness. I protect, I trust, I act, I exist, I teach everyone through flow.

JUDITH 🕭 I feel food inside me. It doesn't nourish me. It's rotting. Becoming poisonous. It forms a tight ball of pain. I am afraid. I am clenched. I am insecure. I don't know how to be alive, how to be centered. I have no boundaries. I'm absorbed and violated by everything around me. I'm afraid to be born.

TRACY ∞ I draw the power of the root and I channel it through the rest of my being. I am a spinning top, very stable in my spinning. My spinning is vast. I am the gut, the place that decides. No one else decides. That is my true power.

PETER ∞ Everything is cooking inside me. Movement and energy stream through me into life. I contain thunder and lightning, turmoil and storm. I turn chaos into form. I cleanse and heal.

KATHERINE ∞ Out of me, the belly, cords extend everywhere, in all directions. I want to merge with the whole world. I'm here, alive, present. Sometimes I am warm and sleepy, full of food. Sometimes I am empty and full of energy. So much life and power reside within me.

VINCENT ∞ I feel pregnant with vastness. I thank my roots for nourishment. I am a storehouse of experiences and visions. I receive cosmic nourishment from the universe. I am connected to reality.

CHAD ∞ I am the center, the still point, eye of the storm. I am the sun in this body. Everything radiates from me. I draw power from the roots and channel it through the whole being. I am the place that decides.

A RITUAL OF HEALING AND BALANCE

This ceremony is a powerful tool for healing any painful situation, illness, relationship, or situation where it is necessary to bring difficult emo-

tions to your awareness and embrace them so they can be transformed. Such a process lies at the root of all healing. Before you begin the ritual choose a specific area of your life, a difficult issue that you want to heal: your relationship, your body, your sexuality, etc.

PURPOSE

༅ To heal a painful situation or relationship.

༅ To transform difficult emotions.

༅ To find balance and integration at any moment in your life.

PREPARATION

༅ Reserve one hour when you can be alone and uninterrupted.

༅ Prepare your sacred space—light a candle, burn incense, or scent the room with a soothing essential oil (see Chapter 6).

༅ You can do this ritual alone or with a partner, with or without music.

PRACTICE

༅ Sit comfortably on the floor or in a chair with your legs parallel—do not cross them. Make sure you have good back support.

༅ Begin with the Heart Salutation (page 75).

༅ Rest your hands loosely on your lap with the right hand on the right thigh, the left hand on the left thigh.

༅ Relax your body, close your eyes, and begin breathing deeply for a few minutes. When you are in a state of calm relaxation, turn your right palm up toward the ceiling.

༅ Focus on all the difficult moments you have had in your relationship, or times when you have been ill, or whatever situation you are healing. For the next few minutes, let memories, feelings, visions, and thoughts come forth. They may be of times you were frustrated, not seen, or misunderstood; or they may be moments of separation, longing, dissatisfaction. See the specific situations. Continue to breathe deeply. If difficult emotions come up, allow yourself to accept them for now. Be with them without chasing them away or fighting them. You are going to create healing, and it is good if what needs to be healed comes forth.

☙ Imagine that you bring all these difficult situations to rest in your right hand, one by one. Let them gather there.

☙ Now ask yourself, "What did I learn from these experiences? How did they transform me?" Remember that the most difficult times are often our best teachers. Can you find some positive effects, such as teaching you patience, compassion, discrimination?

☙ Now take your attention away from the right hand and focus it on the left hand. Let the left hand rest on your left knee, palm up.

☙ Call forth in your awareness all the positive experiences in this part of your life: times when you felt loved and protected, when you felt comfortable, healthy, happy, and healed. See those moments clearly now. If no vision comes forth, think in your mind or feel in your body how it was, and live it again now.

☙ Now bring all those moments into your left hand and let them gather there.

☙ Ask yourself, "What did I learn from these experiences? How did they transform me?" Listen for clear answers. You might feel that you received courage, self-trust, the power to take initiative, open your heart, surrender to love. Whatever comes forth, feel it, listen to it, and learn from it.

☙ Now take your attention away from the left hand and take a deep breath. Very slowly, breathing deeply, begin to move your hands toward each other. Cup your hands together when they touch. At this moment of touching, a symbol will appear to you: it may be an image, a form, an energy sensation, an unexpected thought, a color. Whatever it is, hold it in your hands. This symbol represents the healing of this aspect of your life.

☙ Hold the symbol for a few minutes and feel the energy that it carries for you. Breathe deeply. Stay with it.

☙ Now take that symbol to your belly, slowly, resting your hands on your belly. Let the healing go to your belly as you store the symbol there. It is now a healing resource that you can call on any time you need it.

☙ End with a Heart Salutation.

POINTERS

☙ Make sure you don't rush through this process, take your time, let your breathing be slow and deep, without forcing.

꙾ In most cases, the symbol will appear either right away or after you have practiced this ceremony two or three times. If you don't see anything with your inner eye, you may instead receive feeling impressions or thoughts. Thinking it or feeling it are fine.

꙾ You may want to play very soft, unintrusive music in the background during this ceremony. It might help you to focus without being distracted by thoughts that are not relevant to the process.

꙾ If you like, share your experience with your partner: what happened, what you learned from the difficult and the beautiful experiences. Speak of your impressions of the symbol.

꙾ If you like, you can write your impressions of the ritual and the symbol you received in your journal.

꙾ Remember the symbol throughout the day. Draw it on a piece of paper that you keep by your desk or on your altar.

꙾ Repeating this ritual daily for a week will enhance its healing powers.

CHAPTER TEN

The Third Chakra: The Radiant Sun

The Third Tantric Key: You Are the Source of Power

I am the bright and shining sun. I am creation;
I am your life force made manifest in the world. I
give you direction and power. I give light to all
chakras below and above. I am will, determination,
and I serve myself up on the altar of the heart. I
am the feet walking steadily on the path.

               ❧ The Voice of the Third *Chakra,*
                         from a *Chakra* Talk

THE CHAKRA MAP

ECSTASY ❧ The ecstasy of power.
IMAGE ❧ The sun radiating warmth, giving life; the radiance of light.

PHYSICAL LOCATION ⁓ The solar plexus.

BODY PARTS ⁓ Digestive system, liver, and lower and middle spine.

ENDOCRINE GLANDS ⁓ Pancreas, which is the Taoist House of Transcendence.

MAIN FUNCTIONS ⁓ Transformation and self-empowerment, independence, determination, and will.

POWER ⁓ Courage and enthusiasm.

ESSENCE ⁓ Empowerment.

FEARS ⁓ Confidence based: fear of rejection, of control, of being taken for granted, of being criticized, of not being respected, of not looking good, of being unable to honor commitments.

MASCULINE POWER ⁓ Self-inquiry, will, manifestation, charisma, courage, discrimination.

FEMININE POWER ⁓ Assimilation, self-respect, surrender, cooperation, solidarity.

OPEN AND RELAXED ⁓ "I am okay as I am," "I have the power," "I am free," "I honor myself," "I love to show myself."

BLOCKED OR CONTRACTED ⁓ "I am not sure," "I can't decide," "Tell me how to be," "I need your permission to . . . ," "I don't dare."

Positive qualities ⁓ Leadership: clear and inspiring leadership skills; holding a clear vision and moving toward your goal; intention wedded to action; discrimination; decisiveness; ability to organize groups, places, jobs, and people. Self-respect: independent spirit, feeling free, able to surrender and let go. Generosity: able to share power and co-create, able to honor others, enthusiasm in action, great charisma. Good money management skills.

Negative patterns ⁓ Powerlessness: feeling unworthy and undeserving, acting helpless, being a loser, being neglectful, being dependent or submissive, feeling sorry for yourself. Control issues: manipulating others; being a control freak, bossy, or authoritarian; showing off.

THE CHALLENGE ⁓ Expand your power but don't impose it.

HEALING AFFIRMATIONS ✿ "I honor myself," "I am worth it," "I look good," "I believe in myself," "It is possible," "I radiate energy and light," "It's my power and I use it wisely."

QUESTIONS FOR GUIDANCE ✿ "Who is in charge here?" "Is this truly what I want?" "Do I feel my power and express it in this situation?" "Am I trying to please him or her or do I really mean it?" "Who is it that desires, that wants, that decides here?" "Is this [person, job, money, belief] worth my while?"

ARCHETYPES ✿ Creation and destruction: Brahma, lord of creation; Saraswati, embodiment of nature, patroness of the arts and sciences; Shiva, lord of transformation through destruction; Shakti Lakini, who establishes the connection between the physical and the celestial plane of existence and inspires manifestation. Action: Mars, lord of action; the Sun, symbol of fire.

THE ESSENCE OF THE THIRD CHAKRA

By God, when you see your beauty
You'll be the idol of yourself.

✿ Rumi

Our third chakra, our solar plexus, is a reservoir of power. By directing the full force of our intention toward our chosen goals and moving creatively into life, we leave the womb of childhood and are transformed.

We transcend our childish dependence on others and discover a more reliable source of joy in life: our own power. And we learn our own true value by living with integrity, by working to bring our dreams to fruition. Just as a child learns to walk or to ride a bicycle, we persist; and each fall teaches us who we are, what we want, where we are going.

In our solar center we confront life directly and meet ourselves. We wrestle with fears of failure, rejection, loss of face, and death; with feelings of hopelessness, inadequacy, and despair. When we avoid healthy challenges, abandon creative projects, give up on our visions, or remain silent when we should speak, we lose our power, our capacity for strength, happiness, and pleasure; our joy and power leak away through our belly.

As we grow stronger in our third *chakra,* our wrestling with life takes on a quality of intimacy. Instead of an enemy, life becomes a worthy opponent, then a mentor. And at some point, we realize that all our struggles have really been with ourselves. Like Jacob with the angel, we wrestle with life until it gives up its blessings, one by one.

This is how we grow. And it is how we earn self-respect. For self-worth is *not* a free gift. It does not come from feel-good resolutions, positive visualizations, and affirmations. We generate our self-worth through concrete acts, over time. We *earn* it for ourselves. If our will is weak, we *will* have low self-worth. Even if others praise us, our belly will not contain it. We make the sun rise in our own belly by proving ourselves in life in a fundamental sense, by developing the qualities of courage, strength, integrity, and will in our third *chakra.*

YOU ARE THE SOURCE

True power is the willingness to tell the truth; to feel what we feel; to drop our self-destructive programs; and to admit our ignorance, pain, and fear. It can be very challenging to say "I don't know," or "I'm scared," or "I hurt" and then to find a way through the dilemmas. The courage and strength to do this is born in the solar center.

Sometimes, lacking a strong fire in the third *chakra,* we feel powerless to create or to effect change. We may look to others to carry our weight, to save us, to be powerful in our stead. We may hide from responsibility and risk, fearing to make mistakes, to be criticized or rejected. We may long to submit eternally to powerful gurus, guides, and lovers, imagining their radiance will give us the warmth and power we have failed to generate for ourselves. But no outside power can put fire in our empty belly any more than we can be nourished by watching another eat a seven-course meal. There are practical ways to empower ourself in daily life and strengthen our solar center.

ACT IN ACCORDANCE WITH YOUR OWN VALUES ❧ You give away your power when you allow yourself to be influenced by outside opinion to the degree that you compromise your own values.

It is useful to make an inventory of your deeply held beliefs and values, and then ask yourself how close you are to living them. In what areas do you make decisions based on what others say, think, or want rather than on your deepest feelings and beliefs? Remember, integrity means wholeness. Strengthening your integrity is an essential practice in developing your third *chakra* and healing your wounds.

LEADERS AND FOLLOWERS ❧ Ron Heifetz, director of the Leadership Education Project at Harvard's Kennedy School of Government and author of *Leadership Without Easy Answers,* shared the following principles, which he feels are key in developing personal empowerment and leadership:

❧ *Don't expect others to provide all the answers.* Heifetz says, "Students in a classroom expect the professor to provide all the answers. They don't expect the professor to give *them* responsibility for their own learning." Empowerment comes from taking responsibility for your learning challenges.

❧ *Develop the capacity to face failure.* Training in leadership requires that people learn to analyze their own failures, which are inevitable, and learn to move on after learning the lessons failures have to teach us.

❧ *Develop the self-trust to be able to improvise.* Life is improvisation. "We constantly make midcourse corrections based on the unpredictability of today's actions," says Heifetz. We can learn to be flexible and spontaneous, light on our feet, in dealing with what comes our way.

❧ *Develop the habit of empowering others.* Instead of being the authority figure with all the answers, give people the resources they need to get the job done. Offer guidance and lend a helping hand. But let others use their own creativity to solve problems. Express your appreciation often. By empowering others, we empower ourselves. Merely controlling or criticizing others often leaves us feeling frustrated.

☙ *Be willing to engage in discussion, debate, and even conflict.* Says Heifetz, "Powerful people frequently don't like conflict. They don't like to be challenged. And they often surround themselves with people who support their need for validation." True power means the willingness to participate in conflict creatively, productively, and with respect.

☙ *Develop a deep sense of self-worth.* Many of us have not yet experienced our own deep essential worth and so cannot act from that knowledge when we make mistakes. "I think one ought to approach the nurturing and the acquaintance and the intimacy and the knowledge of that essential worth as part of the practice of living," says Heifetz.

WILL AND PLEASURE ☙ Feed your pleasure center as you fire your will. You need not sacrifice one to the other. The Tantric approach is holistic: balancing will and pleasure, masculine and feminine, and fully acknowledging the value of both. The liabilities of an unbalanced masculine approach to will, often mistaken for strength or spirituality, are revealed in the experience of my friend Bruce:

> By the time I was thirty, I had been celibate for ten years, a strict vegetarian practicing daily yoga, meditation, and general self-denial. I thought being spiritual required abstinence from every kind of pleasure. At that point in my life, I was utterly dry—juiceless, emotionally starved, and unhappy. After a period of despair, I saw clearly that my asceticism, though condoned by classical spirituality, was in fact an expression of deep fear and mistrust of life itself. I had been living as if life were the enemy. When I saw this, I stopped all my "not-doing" cold turkey for two years: no meditation, no vegetarianism, no abstinence, no righteous self-denial. I started going to parties, socializing, dating women, drinking beer, and dancing. I started enjoying life as a gift I had unwisely rejected. As balance came back into

my life, it released tremendous energy. I met an amazing woman, fell in love, got married. And for the last ten years, I have been happy, productive, creatively fulfilled beyond my wildest dreams.

DARE TO RISK ❧ Many people, through fear or lack of self-trust, crave father figures: leaders who promise simple answers and solutions to life's complex dilemmas. They seek in outer authorities a substitute for their own undeveloped will. If we have learned useful lessons by following the guidance of others, well-intentioned or otherwise, we can learn at least as much from charting our own course in life and accepting the responsibility for our own successes and failures. When we do this, we leave the well-defined world of convention and enter the world as it is, unpredictable, exciting, and filled with the potential for ecstasy.

TAKING RESPONSIBILITY ❧ Even when we have developed our will or authority, we may unconsciously use those who depend on us as scapegoats for our own failures. Natalie, a successful motivational speaker and seminar leader, fell into this trap. At her conferences and workshops, something always went wrong: unmet schedules and deadlines, missing microphones and materials. She perceived herself as the victim of her "inept office staff."

I guided her through a meditation in which she focused on her solar plexus. She saw and felt a dark "ball of contraction" in that center. Upon closer examination, she expressed that this "dark and heavy place" represented her hatred for business administration and leadership. She saw how she had been avoiding responsibility for running her business. Natalie saw that all of her business—the people she chose, the way it was managed, the level of financial success or failure—was her creation, a reflection of her own psyche. I invited her to relax and breathe into the dark place, in her solar plexus. Gradually, she saw light coming through, growing, dissolving the dark place until it felt open and the tension was gone.

Eventually, she saw a sun in her solar plexus radiating light with every exhalation, surrounding and energizing her team, her director, and her office. I asked her to do this for three days.

And I suggested she take concrete actions to remedy the things that were going wrong: communicating to her staff, giving clear guidelines, and making specific agreements and hard decisions when necessary. Natalie set herself to this task with a determined will and an open heart. Within three months, her organization shifted to a new level of success.

PRACTICAL EMPOWERMENT

DRESS FOR SUCCESS: PLAYING ROLES One of the most important keys to self-empowerment is *Do not define your self-worth through the eyes of others.* What is it that most readily identifies us with our role in the eyes of others? The answer, of course, is: the clothes, the costume we choose to wear.

We can learn to play the role and wear the costume without taking it seriously. "Be in the world, but not of the world." Combine this with the saying "In Rome, do as the Romans do" and it is possible to avoid identifying with your costume and even to feel playful and relaxed in almost any role or costume. You can also choose to wear clothes that make you feel strong, sexy, or powerful. Throw away old clothes that don't reflect who you are inside. Use what you wear creatively, playfully, as a costume of empowerment in the theater of life!

PERSONAL FENG SHUI Simple as it may seem, your physical appearance and your health directly affect your self-esteem. You feel better when you look and feel your best, and others respond accordingly. The Chinese call this your "spirit appearance," a kind of personal feng shui. The next time you are feeling low, emotionally or physically, take greater care than usual with your appearance. Go for a brisk walk or a run, do aerobics, stretch or do yoga, work out at the gym. Notice the difference in your energy level and how you feel about yourself. You can change your state in such simple ways.

LIFE AS PRACTICE Programs for strengthening the third *chakra* must involve concrete action. Just as sitting on the couch and thinking about skiing is not enough to get our bodies into shape; visualizing, affirming, or positive thinking and speaking are not enough to strengthen the solar center. Practicing a new skill is a powerful ritual for strengthening this *chakra*. In an October 1997 interview in *New Age Journal* on Contact Yoga, teacher Nateshvar Ken Scott noted:

> There is light at the core of every cell, there is light between every joint, and that light gets released as we are opened. So each time you practice, you have a chance to find the doorway to your ecstatic state—to release that light. Your yoga might be swimming, it might be putting on rock and roll music and dancing—whatever it is that opens up your channels. If you approach your practice daily in a sacred, curious, unlimited way, you begin to make space in your life for transformation.

So choose an issue, a project, a skill that you wish to learn, something in which you are strongly interested or that holds deep personal meaning for you. Dedicate this as your "Will and Self-Empowerment Project." It could be a book you want to write; an art, sport, or other skill you wish to learn; or a specific problem area you wish to work on.

Now, *make a concrete plan*. Enroll in a class. Or create a weekly schedule incorporating regular practice. Commit yourself to a minimum of one hour, three times a week. Notice when resistance comes up. Notice what fears, obligations, or beliefs interfere with your commitment. See everything that arises as a challenge. Here are two examples of practical empowerment.

My friend Doug, with whom I worked on a writing project, told me how he became a professional published writer:

> I'd been writing countless small pieces for years, short stories, essays, and performance pieces. But I'd never completed a big project. I'd been working as a laborer for ten years, but my dream was to make a living as a writer. It became a real crisis for me. I knew I had to complete a big writing project, which I'd never done. And to do this, I had to develop a greater will and strength than I had at that point. I also knew that if I started a big project and didn't give up, I'd be a different person by the time I was finished.
>
> At the same time, I started running in the hills near

my house. I used these hills as a metaphor for hills I needed to climb in my life. I dedicated every run to developing my will, succeeding in my project and changing my life. I knew that if I pushed beyond my physical comfort zone every day, I'd form a habit of transcending my limitations in general.

Now I get some of my best ideas as I run those hills. I've written several books, I'm a professional editor, and I now support myself through my writing.

Empowerment is a very practical matter, as the next story demonstrates: Jamie felt that she had problems setting limits and keeping her boundaries. "I let my kids walk all over me, I let my husband plan all the vacations and how we were going to spend our money. Finally, one day, when I couldn't even get my dog to come on command, I burst into tears.

It became clear to me that I needed practice in asserting myself. I hired a dog trainer who showed me how to speak calmly and firmly, and stand my ground until I got results. I practiced with my dog every day, and soon I realized it was spilling over to my relationships with my children and my husband. I guess you can say, "Everything I learned about life I learned in dog training!"

EMPOWERMENT EXERCISES ⁓ You can enhance your sense of personal power through breathing and visualization. Try this simple exercise to develop charisma and presence. Close your eyes, breathe deeply, and relax. In your solar plexus, imagine a sun radiating light and energy. Feel warmth and light there. As you inhale, see the sun brighten and expand inside your solar plexus. As you exhale, feel this sun radiate energy through your whole body. Inhaling, charge up. Exhaling, expand. Now radiate this energy as rays of light. Put this into practice. For example, before you enter a room full of people, speak in public, go to a meeting, or ask someone out for a date, visualize this energy radiating from your solar plexus, filling the room and all the people in it. Feel your connection to them as they receive your light. Now establish contact while you feel radiant, powerful, self-confident.

Here is another meditation to help you find your power center and charge it up. Sit in a comfortable position (in a chair or on the floor) and rest your hands over your solar plexus, under your rib cage. Direct your attention there. Feel and breathe into it. Now inhale energy into your solar plexus. See and feel it light up, as a coal lights up in the fire when you blow on it. Relax and hold your breath quietly for a moment, feeling your solar plexus full of power and light. Now press against your solar plexus, forcefully exhaling all the air at once, and shout the sound *"Ha!"* with the full force of your power center. Feel the sense of your power and the pleasure of fully expressing it. Do this for fifteen minutes. Enjoy the warmth and centered feeling that results. Do this fifteen-minute exercise every day for one month to develop inner strength.

CREATIVE WORK, MONEY, AND ABUNDANCE

I love this quote from Kahlil Gibran's *The Prophet* and I have found it to be true in my own life:

> *You have been told also that life is darkness,*
> *And in your weariness you echo what was said by the*
> *   weary.*
> *And I say that life is indeed darkness save when there is*
> *   urge,*
> *And all urge is blind save when there is knowledge.*
> *All knowledge is vain save when there is work.*
> *And all work is empty save when there is love.*
> *And when you work with love you bind yourself to yourself,*
> *And to one another, and to God.*

One of the most creative opportunities for empowerment is our work. We usually associate work with obligation. But ecstatic people, like *you,* discover that it is possible to love the work you do by making it a creative expression of who you *are.* Then your work serves you, others and even the world.

Osho has commented on this passage: "Life belongs to those who are creative because life is nothing but a long, eternal process of creating more beauty, more truth . . . of creating higher states of consciousness, and finally of creating a god in your own being. There are people who think that without being creative, they can be happy. It is impossible, because creativity is the only way to relate with the ecstasy of existence."

Work as a source of ecstasy is a foreign concept to many of us. Yet when we discover our creativity, in a work that is of service, we find our power and our place in the world.

I discovered this new dimension of work as play when I lived in an ashram in India. There we were asked to do a different job every day, usually not one we had been trained for. One day I was asked to work in the kitchen, the next to translate poetry, the next to weld pipes. These new and ever-changing jobs were completely unrelated to what I normally do in life or to my professional occupation. It was a major challenge to my ego attachments about work as a career and a way to prove your worth to the world. The old questions of professionalism, success, reputation, seemed irrelevant in such a context. You worked for free, for play, as a meditation in awareness, and to serve the community. You gave of yourself for the enlightenment of all beings. Gradually, work became a meditation done out of love. I was being creative not to get results and success, but because I loved what I was doing moment to moment. I was able to immerse myself in the work, pay attention to what I was doing, be present, do the best that I could. And to make it even better, this was an ecstatic community—we danced two or three times a day, between work sessions. As Osho says, "Life is light, life is joy. Life is celebration. If you work without love, you are working like a slave. When you work with love, you work like an emperor. Your work is your joy, your work is your dance. Your work is your poetry."

YOUR TRUE WORK ✍ You may be a divorced working mother with two children to raise. You may be a husband and father with mortgage payments and plenty of responsibilities. You may be a career man or woman climbing the corporate ladder. You may be living near the poverty level. But if you find the will, there is no circumstance so dire that it cannot become the very means of your transformation.

Gurdjieff's admonition to his followers was: "Remember why you are here!" There are essential questions that we all must ask ourselves if we are to find meaning in our lives: What is my unique talent? What am I here to do? What is my true purpose?

Once we find our meaning, our purpose, and harness our will to it, miracles happen.

Kahlil Gibran wrote, "When you work you are a flute through whose heart the whispering of the hours turns to music." "It is not a question of any particular work," says Osho. "Perhaps it is just making shoes; but making them with such intensity and totality that you are completely lost in the act. The moment you are lost in work, you become almost like a flute on the lips of existence itself. Your every gesture turns into grace, and your every moment brings celestial music to the earth. You become a vehicle."

Creative work energizes and renews us, fills us with enthusiasm for life. It makes us "a flute on the lips of existence itself." This is the final stage of will, where our struggle with life gives way to our being lived by life. An occupation that inspires these qualities in us usually has the following components:

    ➳ It challenges us to bring forth something that is uniquely ours: a new idea, perspective, or special skill.
    ➳ It challenges us to find a place where we can stand outside the competition.
    ➳ It is of service to others.
    ➳ It involves all four centers: body, heart, mind, and Spirit.
    ➳ It is inherently rewarding. The money isn't the point. We feel compensated for our work by the very pleasure we have in doing it.
    ➳ It connects us with life and with our concern for the human community and the planet.
    ➳ It gives us a sense that we have contributed to life in some small way.

Finding your true work may mean leaving your current job. But it can also mean finding an identity *outside* of your present work. Your career may not meet all your "meaning" needs. Ask yourself what you can do outside of your work that fills this need, that gives you a higher purpose, a deeper meaning that is inspiring.

TAKE RESPONSIBILITY AND INITIATIVE ➳ Empowerment means increasing your capacity to take responsibility. Find your growing edge. Take small risks to make a difference. Then take bigger risks and work to keep stretching that edge. Dare to commit, to take action, to accept responsibility, to be your courageous self. For example, Carrie had long dreamed of a career as a journalist, but was never able to go to journalism school. To make ends meet, she worked as a secretary at a movie studio. She liked the studio, but not her job. She wanted to write stories and looked around to see where else she could fit in. She was particularly drawn to public relations. So she made a friend on the public relations team and asked to tag along when they went on the set to watch a film shoot and interview a star. She noticed that the PR people seemed bored: they churned out the usual stories and missed most of the good stuff. Using her keen sense of observation and her innate writing skills, she kept a detailed log of what she observed and wrote her own version of the events, as if she were writing stories for the press. Eventually, she asked for an appointment with the top executive. She arrived elegantly dressed. With confidence and poise, she presented her observations and her stories, then asked for, and got, a shot at the job. Three months later she was promoted to head of the PR department at Paramount and started traveling all over the world.

VOLUNTEER YOUR TIME AND ENERGY ✒ You do not have to live in an ashram to have an ecstatic work experience, nor do you have to give up your career to be of service. Hughes Goodwin is a financial counselor who works with people to articulate their life goals and plan their financial futures. He directs a financial investment company that manages millions of dollars. One of his tasks is to manage people's savings, and he always asks them this basic question: "What do you want out of your life?" What Goodwin wanted out of his own life was to be of service to others, and his volunteer work has been a great source of spiritual nourishment. Every year, he and his family take on a special project.

> One year I went down to Nicaragua with my family—
> my wife, and my eleven-year-old son and fourteen-
> year-old daughter—and we helped them build schools
> for their villages. I realized down there how wealthy I

was compared to these people who had few material possessions, and that I would be okay if I had nothing because I was happy within myself as I was. Money wasn't who I was, and my life wasn't about pursuing money for money's sake. I had to have a higher purpose.

MONEY AND ABUNDANCE ❧ Our anti-ecstatic consumer culture wants us to desire more and more while feeling we never have enough. As a consequence, many people feel that working for money is the sole *raison d'être* of working. Hughes Goodwin says, "It's important to understand what money is and isn't. It is a tool that can do tremendous good, but it also can destroy people. It does not buy any of the things that are truly valuable: love, true relationships, and the respect of others."

Money is often used to control relationships. Part of working with money is demystifying it, taking the power out of it and giving it back to ourselves. The best way to do that is to discuss finances openly. Goodwin and his family have created a ritual to do just this:

> We have regular family meetings every week to discuss family affairs. The meeting begins with creating a circle, lighting a candle, and each member of the family—me, my wife, and my two kids—says something nice about the other. Then we have an open discussion about money. We touch on earnings and spendings, purchases for the house, improvements on the house. It is an open forum to discuss anything. Together, we decide to which charity we are going to give money and how much. This way it's not just dad or mom deciding, it is all of us. Then we move on to vacations. We talk about where we'd like to go, and we tell the kids how much it is going to cost. When the family takes a trip, we have the kids keep a running total of all of our expenses. That way they know the airfare, the gas, the car rental, the food, hotels, everything, so they can learn how much "having fun" really costs.

Goodwin started on a shoestring budget. He's now a millionaire. What's the secret? I asked him. "If you want abundance, give first. And this means giving to yourself as well as to others." Goodwin adds, "You become financially successful when you feel that you are making a contribution to the world. Then you will throw your soul and your spirit into the work and you will be successful." He offers the following simple, yet powerful, advice on what it takes to work ecstatically and create abundance:

- Love the work you do.
- Let the work express who you are.
- Be the best you can be.
- Learn to give back to your community and to charity first; cultivate the concept of tithing.
- Pay yourself second.
- Be frugal: live beneath your means and save a percentage of everything that you make for your whole lifetime.

THE ELEMENTS OF EMPOWERMENT

Success relies on your power to know who you are and what you want from your third *chakra,* the source of the power within you. When that radiant sun rises to shine forth into the world, you are revealed to yourself and others as the magnificent being you have been all along. To keep the inner fire stoked, practice these five keys to empowerment.

- Know what you want. My experience with people has shown me that we *always* know what we want, but we often do not allow ourselves to *trust* that we do know or we fear committing to what we want.
- Share what you know. Sharing our insights, the wisdom we have gained from experience, connects us to others and allows us to process our own understanding at a deeper level. Group work offers invaluable support and feedback.
- Face your resistances. We must embrace our shadows by making a list of the objections, fears, and doubts that arise in the face of our commitments ("It's too hard," "My partner won't like it").
- Take action. Fear appears in the shadows of indecision, but it disappears in the light of action. We should

take real steps toward our goal, no matter how small. We can use the affirmations in the *Chakra* Map or the invocation that begins this chapter to help us stay on track.

๛ Be patient. The journey of a thousand miles begins with one step, but there are a lot of steps. If we take them one by one, we can allow ourselves to enjoy each step rather than racing toward the finish line.

We are the sum of all we have done and how we have lived. And whether our efforts are widely acclaimed, or hardly noticed, they still shine in the world through us. Near the end of his life, Mahatma Gandhi was on a train when a reporter on the platform by his window called out to him, "Gandhi, do you have a message for the world?" Gandhi called through the window as the train pulled away, "My life is my message!" The same holds true for us all. To know this, and then to live it, gives us power.

THE CHAKRA TALK

When you do the *Chakra* Talk (page 138) with your third *chakra,* invoke the voice of your power. The following examples from my students show the range of voices that may come from the solar center.

JENNY ๛ I am radiating energy, vibration, essence. Powerful, yet peaceful. Balanced. Strong.

JOHN ๛ I am determination beyond logic. A place of commitment and integrity, where there is a home. A place to radiate from, to join the universe. I bring John to the edge where I feel no boundaries.

MARIANNE ๛ I am the original expression of my power. I am a wave rising out of the sea, catching the light to shine in my own way. I am the bright sun. I am creation made manifest in the world. I give light to all *chakras* below and above. I am will and determination. I am the life force made manifest. I am the warrior. I know how to hold my warrior stick. I know how to stomp my feet.

SUSAN ∼ I am a bright, powerful center. I take apart the things of the world and put them back together.

FRANNIE ∼ I am a spearhead. I protect Frannie. I am competitive and I feel tough. I give Frannie strength for her empathy.

LEONA ∼ I am a volcano. Often Leona keeps me tight and holds me in because she's afraid of my power. I am strong in my masculinity. See me, hear me. I go out in the world. Yes, I will do what I want to do.

A RITUAL OF EMPOWERMENT

A lesson we must learn in our third chakra *is how not to give our power away. When our third* chakra *is weak, we are not grounded in our own identity and strength, and we tend to give our power away by seeking approval instead of acting from our own clarity and integrity. We do this because our point of reference, our perception of our own identity, is still located outside ourselves. Thus we seek our identity by trying to please others, to be loved, to get approval. Shamans describe how, when we come from this place of insecurity, we unconsciously send energy lines that bind us to another person or circumstance. We become "hooked" to others energetically, thereby losing ourselves and our power.*

PURPOSE
∼ To learn how to come back to your own center at any moment.
∼ To be able to deal powerfully and confidently with a new situation.
∼ To feel strong and centered before you speak or perform in public.

- To heal quickly, after someone you love has passed away.
- To reclaim your energy when you feel you have given it away to others.
- To prepare for a difficult separation.

PREPARATION

- You can do this ritual on your own, or with another person sitting face to face with you. If the person is absent or has passed away, just imagine that he or she is there, sitting with you.
- Set aside fifteen to twenty minutes (I recommend mornings, before the workday begins) during which you will not be disturbed or interrupted. It is important, once you begin this ritual, to complete it, so that your energy does not stay locked in one *chakra*. If you are interrupted return to where you were and finish the ritual.
- If you are in a relationship, do this exercise every once in a while. You will feel that you can relate more freely and playfully together.
- If you need to forgive someone who hurt you, broke your heart, interrupted you, or did not listen to you, do this ritual once a day until you feel free of the hurt.
- Have a bottle of essential oil of mint next to you to clarify the energy of your aura.
- Create your sacred space: just a simple moment of lighting a candle and a stick of incense. Clear the space by ringing a bell or playing a CD of gongs for a few minutes.

PRACTICE

- Sit comfortably and start with a Heart Salutation (page 75). If you are imagining a partner sitting in front of you, do the Heart Salutation with that person in your imagination. If you are doing the ritual with a partner who is physically present, start with a Melting Hug and a Heart Salutation. Sit opposite each other comfortably and relax, taking a few deep breaths. Skip the next two steps and continue.
- Close your eyes and take a few deep breaths. Still with your eyes closed, focus on a person with whom or a situation in which you feel that you have some unfinished business (the sadness of an unresolved separation, a sudden departure, someone at work with whom you feel uncomfortable, and so on).

ॐ Now, in your mind's eye, tell that person that you want to complete the situation between you and that it's important to clarify and complete your connection.

ॐ Rest the palm of your left hand on your solar plexus, and the palm of your right hand on top of the back of your left hand, so that you hands are resting gently against each other. Visualize a cord of energy stretching from your solar plexus to that person's solar plexus—from your power center to that person's power center. Remember your connection with that person, see the different situations during which you had difficulties.

ॐ Now, with a strong inhalation, raise both hands (still in the same position) above your head.

ॐ Immediately, on the exhalation, bring both hands strongly down in a single sweep, like a guillotine or sharp sword, and cut that cord. *Swooosh!*

ॐ And now, with your right hand, gently push the energy toward the other person and say, "I give you back your power."

ॐ Bring your hand back to your solar plexus and say, "I take my power back." As you touch your solar plexus, inhale and visualize a spiral of energy going deep inside your body. Taking a deep breath, feel that strength coming back to you.

ॐ Continue in this way, repeating all the above steps, for each *chakra*. Moving your hands to your chest, visualize the cord of energy that goes from your heart center to his or her heart center, and repeat the cord-cutting step for this *chakra:* inhaling deeply, bringing your hands up, exhaling strongly, cutting the cord, giving back his or her power, and taking your own. Do this for your throat, your third eye, and your crown, then go to your belly, and finally to your sex center.

ॐ To feel your wholeness, the fullness of your energy field, complete the ritual by cleansing the auric field around your body. Put a few drops of essential oil of mint in the palms of your hands and rub them together. Breathing deeply, gently move your hands across the crown of your head, your forehead, throat, heart, solar plexus, belly and sexual center, and end by touching the ground.

ॐ Now rest quietly for a moment, and feel that you are reconnected with yourself, whole, complete, mended. Feel the peace and the silence.

ॐ End with a Heart Salutation.

⌇ Don't worry if you are doing this "exactly." If you understand the purpose, you will find your own way of doing it. Do make sure to cut swiftly and energetically, and declare, "I give you back your power and I take my power back" loud and clear.

⌇ If you do this ritual with a partner, avoid talking about the process afterward. Just separate and go about your business for some hours.

⌇ If you do this with a deceased person, you may want to ask him or her inwardly if he or she agrees to do this meditation. If you receive the impression that he or she is resistant, explain the purpose in a loving, positive sense.

⌇ The most common misunderstanding here is to think that you are cutting away all connection with a person. *You are not!* Only when you have your energy back can you truly be friends. Remember: Power is focused energy. Start with yourself! Only then can you freely choose how you want to be connected. You can keep on loving each other without losing energy or giving it away unconsciously.

⌇ Many strong emotions may come up during this process. Let them come! Let yourself feel them, express them, cry them. And then continue on to the next *chakra* until you have completed all of them.

⌇ You may want to start at the sexual center and move up to the crown, rather than start at the solar plexus. Follow your own guidance.

⌇ Try this for three to seven days and feel the difference!

CHAPTER ELEVEN

THE FOURTH CHAKRA:
THE PULSE OF LIFE

THE FOURTH TANTRIC KEY:
WE ARE ONE

I am golden, I am love. I have seen many forms,
many storms, heartaches, heartbreaks, laughter and
joy. And I still don't know how deep I can be. I
hold silence and I hold songs. I leave no footprints
in time. I can move through space and connect with
other hearts.

            ❧ The Voice of the Fourth *Chakra,*
                     from a *Chakra* Talk

THE CHAKRA MAP

ECSTASY ❧ The ecstasy of love and surrender.
IMAGES ❧ Shiva and Shakti in a Tantric embrace; two
lovers merging and melting in an embrace.

PHYSICAL LOCATION ⧉ The center of the chest, breasts, shoulders, arms, and hands.

BODY PARTS ⧉ The lungs, heart, and circulatory system.

POWER ⧉ Patience, trust, surrender.

ENDOCRINE GLANDS ⧉ Thymus gland, which is the Taoist House of Heart.

MAIN FUNCTIONS ⧉ Healing and completion: becoming whole; finding common ground with your beloved; and experiencing the sacred marriage between your energy and consciousness, your inner woman and your inner man, and your anima and your animus.

ESSENCE ⧉ Love, forgiveness, surrender.

FEARS ⧉ Commitment: of trusting, of receiving, of not being lovable.

MASCULINE POWER ⧉ Magnetism, the power to inspire and penetrate, protector and benefactor, detachment from passions, peacefulness, inner happiness.

FEMININE POWER ⧉ Purity, innocence, attractiveness, devotion that attracts the power of the life force upward from sex to Spirit and tempers the fire of power.

OPEN AND RELAXED ⧉ "I let go and I forgive," "I receive you as myself," "I accept you as you are," "I care," "I trust you," "I feel safe," "My heart is at peace."

BLOCKED OR CONTRACTED ⧉ "You hurt me and I can't let go," "I am alone," "Nobody loves me," "I am abandoned," "I am disappointed," "Prove to me that you love me."

Positive qualities ⧉ Nurturing: protecting like the mother, doing what's best. Compassion: the ability to feel what the other person feels. Forgiveness: the ability to let go of hurts or wounds; loving beyond conditions and reasons. Loyalty, innocence, transmutation of lust and power into love and surrender. Connection: a feeling of oneness with the God/Goddess, being generous because you know that we are all interconnected and that what you give comes back.

Negative patterns ⧉ Protecting the wounded heart: defensive, jealous, afraid to love and be disappointed, fear of closeness and intimacy, cynical about love, disregards others, sarcastic, undermining, seduces to buy love. Self-abnegation: feels unworthy to receive; do-gooder; fear of taking risks, of expressing what you really feel, of confronting someone you are angry with; overpleasing; difficulty saying no, needy.

THE CHALLENGE ⮞ Forgive and let go; heal the wound and move on; giving is receiving.

HEALING AFFIRMATIONS ⮞ "I am lovable," "I am loved," "I am grateful," "I love you as you are," "We are one," "I give love and I receive love."

QUESTIONS FOR GUIDANCE ⮞ "How does my heart feel right now?" "Can I let go of this, right now?" "Is this attractive to me?" "Can I open myself to trust?"

ARCHETYPES ⮞ Christ (as protector). Love: Vishnu and Laksmi, Aphrodite, Isis, Eros. Union: from marriage to partnership; from union to fusion; from sharing to merging.

THE ESSENCE OF THE FOURTH CHAKRA

All activities should be done with [the] intention
. . . to awaken the heart.

⮞ Pema Chödrön

In the *chakras* below the heart we learn passion, connection, balance, and power; we experience desire and learn to survive in the world. But in the fourth *chakra,* the Pulse of Life, we enter a new dimension. Here our lower three *chakras* are unified, infused with Spirit, and our love and surrender connect us with others and the world.

We are born in innocence, with an open heart. But inevitably our heart is wounded, and it begins to close. Paradoxically, many of us first encounter life's strangeness and receive wounds to the heart through those who love us first: our parents. Our contact with them defines the future patterns of all our relationships. With them we first enact the positive and negative forms of relationship: love, nurturing, friendship, seduction, anger, manipulation, and even betrayal and rejection.

As we grow older and the issues and aspects of love become more complex and impenetrable, we begin to defend our heart to protect ourselves. We fear the vulnerability of the heart. We fear being hurt, used, and abandoned. We fear giving freely; the price seems too great. Because when we love, we give those we love the power to touch us at our core. We become delicate, transparent, as vulnerable as in childhood.

THE HEART IS THE BRIDGE
BETWEEN THE CHAKRAS

Most of our conflicts in love and sex have their source in the division between our genitals and our heart, our first and fourth *chakras.* In our first two *chakras,* we desire wonderful feelings, pleasurable sensations, streaming passions that never end. When we approach our heart from our sexual center or our belly center, we can mistake lust and need for love. Then, when lust inevitably fades or need is unsatisfied, we wonder where our love has gone. The healing delights of sex are wonderful, but love based only in pleasure is a fragile flower. Have you ever spent a night of great sexual passion, only to wake up in the morning beside a stranger? SkyDancing Tantra teaches that in the heart, we learn the difference between *falling* in love, a biological narcotic rush, and *rising* in love, a state of deep clarity and conscious bliss.

If we are bound to concerns of personal power in the solar center, we may barter love for admiration or security. Confusing love with power, we may assume the right to direct the love story, to impose our will on our beloved, to try to get what we feel we are owed.

When our ego-mind rules our heart, seeking control, love vanishes. Our heart requires freedom to love. The ego-mind is full of divisions, interpretations, and complex agendas for molding love and life itself into secure, pre-established forms. It has its own code of survival. Hide! Don't be vulnerable! Give with one hand and take with the other! Let's make a deal!

Kaveesha, a Tantric mystic, founder and director of the Osho Academy in Sedona, Arizona, says:

> We don't want to give up all the dramas of those first three *chakras*—we fear our lover will leave, we are tired

of being stepped on, we are engaged in power struggles. Yet going into the heart requires a tremendous leap. Everyone desires a merging, harmonious, intelligent relationship. But as long as you feel you must change or blame the other, or change yourself for the other, it's a losing situation. You can't stay in your drama *and* bring the heart in. You can't just do affirmations and exercises and expect everything to be fine. The heart is in another dimension beyond all that.

When we respond from the heart, we say yes to ourself; and others find us attractive. When we approach life with a defensive heart, we seek love yet cannot receive it. We won't find it in a guru, or through Tantra, or by dreaming of rock stars or movie goddesses. They cannot give us the love we need to find in ourselves first, in our own hearts.

AN OPEN HEART ❧ Until our fourth *chakra* opens, we think others must change for us to be happy or that we must change to make them happy. But this illusion *is* unhappiness. We cannot change others, but we can change our relationship to any situation. Remember a time when you responded from your heart in a difficult situation? Perhaps your lover was ready to leave you, and you cried but let go because you knew in your heart the relationship was over. Or perhaps, struggling with an uncomfortable work situation, you ignored your mind, which told you to stay for the money, and made the decision to leave because you felt in your heart it was best.

The heart teaches us integrity, to not compromise with our truth, to join power with love, and love with respect. Choosing what appears difficult at first, often turns out best later on; difficult demands can press us beyond our limitations into new freedom; we learn to be our authentic selves no matter what the circumstances.

ROMANCE, FANTASY, AND LOVE ❧ The mind fantasizes endlessly and romance fuels our sexual passion. But our passion cannot last unless it matures into devotion. When betrayal bursts the golden bubble of our romantic illusions, our heart must learn the art of forgiving and moving beyond appearances. The only cure for betrayal is forgiveness. The art of forgiveness is the key to the innocent heart.

FORGIVENESS ❧ In this world of duality, of energies in conflict, there is no love without hate, no shadow without light, no pleasure without pain, and no trust without disappointment. Only in our heart can we embrace and resolve the paradoxes that bewilder our mind.

In every moment we have a choice: to contract our heart in fear, or expand it in love. Christ, betrayed by his disciple and crucified, said from the Cross, "Father, why have you forsaken me?" This was the agony of betrayal. But he also said, "Father, forgive them" and "Thy will be done." This was the transcendence of the agony of betrayal by an awakened heart, where even death at the hands of a loved one became a doorway to resurrection. When we make the choice to forgive in the face of personal pain, to transcend the temptation to cling to anger and hurt, the heart expands. This is not easy, yet it is crucial to our growth.

Forgiveness is not something we "should" or "ought to" do. It is simply a step to be taken when we are ready to leave behind rage, sorrow, bitterness, and other painful feelings. The following meditation is designed to heal a heart that carries the burden of such heavy and painful emotions. It is simple in form, but if you practice it over time you will begin to feel a sense of lightness and peace.

❧ Begin with the Heart Salutation (page 75). Then take several deep breaths, relax your muscles, and bring your mind to rest.

❧ In your mind's eye, see the person with whom you have a negative connection. Honestly examine your part in this relationship. If you have ever hurt or betrayed him or her, intentionally or unintentionally, acknowledge it to yourself. Then allow yourself to remember how he or she has hurt or betrayed you. Simply acknowledge the feelings that arise. This is the pain you are healing.

❧ Now put your hands over your heart. Find the place

in your heart that suffers all this and that truly desires to
let it go. Feel and be in this place for a few moments.

∾ If you have hurt or betrayed this person, take responsibility for your part in the drama, for any pain you
may have caused, however large or small. Inwardly offer
the person sincere apologies.

∾ Now feel the pain this person has caused you, and
the resulting rage, bitterness, or any disturbing emotions
that you wish to release.

∾ Feel and express inwardly to this person your wish
to forgive and let go until you can feel the burden of
these emotions lift and your heart feels lighter.

∾ End with a Heart Salutation.

Remember, when we forgive others, it does not mean that
whatever he or she did to us was right or justifiable. We are simply choosing to release him or her and the painful emotions that
bind us to that person and move on.

KEEPING LOVE ALIVE

When we are in love, we fall in love with life. We become creative, alive, enthusiastic with expanded possibilities. We are flying! We are SkyDancers! Love inspires us to co-create a life that
is like a work of art. Love inspires us to seduce, serve, enchant,
challenge, surprise, and delight—not just in the bedroom, but in
every moment. Love is Tantra, weaving together all the qualities,
energies, and gifts of lovers in a collaborative union.

Love is an art that requires wide-open eyes, and a conscious
choice to look again and again, to learn from the worst as well
as the best in ourself and others.

Love involves contradictions: union and solitude, intimacy
and mystery, commitment and detachment. It is good to cultivate solitude as well as closeness, to touch while being silent, to
rest and breathe together, to allow the other in your heart to become more mysterious year by year. Lovers practice love as an
art in the face of paradox. Lovers draw apart and return again,
attracted by renewed longing and desire. Lovers see the potential for enchantment in every moment. Their love re-enchants
the world.

Yet such magic is often challenged. We have all known those

moments when we open our heart to another and are engulfed in strong emotions. Devotion gives way to impatience, joy turns into fear, desire into jealousy. Tantra teaches that strong emotions can be our allies. Emotions are energy in motion. Sometimes we need to explode, to release and express our hurt. In love, we can express our anger and pain and be transformed, without losing love.

When difficult feelings arise, create (with your partner or alone) a sacred and safe space where you can express your emotions freely. Sit opposite each other. Put a pile of pillows between you. That pile represents all your anger, your troubles, possibly your partner. I call it the "Wounded Heap."

Be as total as you can. Give yourself to this process. Your partner can practice compassionate listening, not identifying with your feelings ("He or she has all this pain," "It is my fault," "I am bad," and so on). Your partner is a witness.

Call on the support of the fifth *chakra,* your voice; and the third *chakra,* your power. Breathing deeply, focus on the frustrations you hold in your chest, heart, or belly; then let loose, hit the pillows with all your might and with the deeply felt sound of those emotions—open-mouthed moans, deep growls (do not use words). While you give a voice to your heart, use your body to move; let your arms and hands match the power of your sounds. Shout your rage, weep your longing. Stay with this as long as you need. Then slow down, and end with a few long sighs. Close with a Heart Salutation and a hug.

This is a crucial step toward healing emotional and sexual wounds, wounds of the heart. Through such practices, you and your lover will progressively learn to accept each other as you are, to feel your emotions as energy patterns that do not need to be judged, but accepted and released. The key here is not to make the other wrong. Even when you communicate in words, avoid saying, "You did" or "It is your fault if." Instead, use "I feel" and stay within your own experience. And the healing will go even deeper if it concludes with tender care and sensual pleasure.

Another approach is to make a concrete representation of your love for each other. My friends Gabriella and Dom feel that spiritual growth is the most important aspect of their relationship. Together, they created a collage representing their relationship, as a continual reminder of their commitment to each other. "Our collage has a waterfall, angels, and in the center, a picture of a couple embracing in the nude," Gabriella told me. "And behind them is a tiger. It's a powerful visual reminder to both of us of our coming together."

Annie and Dave have another ritual:

> About once a week, we have an evening devoted to pleasure. We feed each other sensuous foods—ice cream, papaya, chocolate mousse. Then we have a candlelit bubble bath together and share a ritual with dance and massage. We always begin by sitting in front of our meditation altar to invoke the spirit. We say to each other, "I honor you as a divine aspect of myself." When we honor each other in this way, we see each other as messengers of the gods, as divine incarnations, and our relationship becomes a sacred marriage.

The question in relationships is this: What does it mean to be open to another human being, to be truthful, take risks, and go deeper? Allow yourself to look and ask in every moment: Am I being true to myself? Am I being true to the relationship? Does our relationship have depth and fullness? Does what I am doing deepen our relationship or dilute it?

PAYING ATTENTION When we see the one we love through the eyes of the heart we are deeply attentive. Attention is choice. We choose what we pay attention to, and choosing one thing necessarily involves excluding something else. When we focus on our beloved to the exclusion of others, he or she becomes the center of our world. It is a risky investment.

When you stop paying attention through the heart, small events can bring up hidden hurts. Your partner leaves a mess on the kitchen counter. You react. Suddenly you find yourselves in an old argument. Intuitively, you know you are not really arguing about the counter. Next time you find yourself arguing over small potatoes, try this simple exercise:

> Instead of taking your anger and the obvious issue at face value and going off down the same old path, stop.
> Feel into your anger, feel the power and effect of this emotion in your body/mind.

✎ Now, examine other areas of your relationship until you find a deeper issue that resonates with that anger. Maybe you feel a lack of attention from your partner, feel criticized, undervalued or betrayed? Did your father behave in a similar way with your mother? Did their marriage break up?

Many real-life issues attach themselves to unimportant things like messy counters. Yet little arguments are rarely about little things. Make a practice of discovering the issues that lie beneath what seems obvious. In resolving the real issues directly with your partner, energy is released and renewal is possible.

SURRENDER ✎ Surrender is essential to an open heart. Many people mistakenly equate surrender with loss of free will or personal power. But surrender means "to melt into that which is higher." It means to honor and welcome your highest potential.

We do not surrender by making a deal with God or by giving up our power, but by embracing what *is*. Our love is the great leap of the heart; and we call its fullness surrender. It is a leap in faith, despite our fears, into the innocence of new beginnings. And by risking our heart and opening to love, we taste essential freedom and joy.

Our great challenge is to balance our heart's surrender with our mundane needs, obligations, and ambitions. Although these threaten the intimacy of lovers and disturb the delicate web of relationships, they are the very obstacles and tests beyond which love must grow to survive. Love is our greatest teacher. It calls us to surrender beyond our limits and fixed ideas into the uncharted freedom of the awakened heart: the door to God and Goddess, to all that is unnamable and indescribable. When our heart opens and our love becomes surrender, we can love in all ways, in all dimensions, beyond our conditioning and our fears. Then our pain will teach us wisdom. Then we have come home.

Surrender is the *way* of freedom. It connects us to our Source and allows us to blossom as ecstatic beings. It doesn't take years of therapy or complex spiritual practices. You can surrender where you are. Right here. Right now. How? We begin by letting go of our attachment to being *right;* by trusting that life is on our side, by accepting what *is* as a teaching. My friend

Duncan Campbell, an attorney and talk-show host, was impressed by his experience of surrender on a visit to India.

I began to see—in the stores, on the street—that the Indians moved at a slower pace. After a while, I fell into that rhythm too. I began to let go of my need to *do* something, to make things happen, to pack things into a schedule. I decided to simply surrender to the moment, to see what life would bring me instead of trying to fit life into my mold. I began to relax and allow the space for something to take place that might surprise me. And as I did that, each day I would get a sort of "confirmatory miracle"—something I wanted to accomplish *would* get accomplished. Usually it was three or four or five days later, and in a way that was so much better for me and for my original intention. After a while I began to do this as a conscious practice—to wait for the message to emerge from the environment and be responsive to it.

When we feel deep into the center of our heart and accept what is there, we find a space without boundaries, where nothing needs to be resolved, explained, or changed. At first we may feel sadness or grief or fear. But if we are willing to accept what we feel, our relationship to these feelings begins to change and a longing awakens: to live in the world with an open heart, undefended against life, to be there for our friends when they are in trouble.

This new longing is poignant, tender, even sad, yet it contains an immense potential. As Pema Chödrön says in *Start Where You Are,* our wounds actually "give us the chance to work on patience and kindness." This is how we transform all "that messy stuff that we usually push away" and reconnect with our soft heart, our clarity, and our ability to open farther.

When we can embrace who we are *as* we are, we become curious about life, full of wonder and delight. We realize that we can love and surrender to this moment exactly as it is. If it's great. If it's painful. If it's lousy. Whether or not it fits our picture. When we accept this moment as it is and learn what it has to teach us, we are free. There is nothing special that we need, no particular state to achieve, no picture to hold onto, no agenda to impose on the world. When we are present in this moment with an open heart, we begin to appreciate ourselves and welcome each other. We fall in love with life.

The Chakra Talk

When you do the *Chakra* Talk (page 138) with your fourth *chakra,* you will hear the voice of your heart, your innocence, your emotions. The following examples from my students express the range of voices and images you may experience when you let your heart speak its truth.

DEANNA ☙ I can be very tender. I can be very strong. I beat with the pulse of life. I can whisper like the winds. I am the mystery, I am the poem.

NICHOLAS ☙ I have seen many storms, relationships, heartaches, heartbreaks, laughter, and joy. And I still don't know how deep I can be. I hold silence, and I hold the songs. I am love. I leave no footprints in time. I can move through space and connect instantaneously with family and friends, with other hearts. I am your home.

EDDY ☙ I nourish your solar plexus with my love. I connect through to your hands to give healing and expression. I connect with your voice to sing and communicate.

DICK ☙ I can cry, I can nurture your feelings with the water of life. I can be compassion. I am the color of the Caribbean, a cool heart flowing with understanding, part of a bigger beat through rhythm and nature.

DAVID ☙ I was encased in ice so thick that David was not even aware how hidden away and almost lifeless I was. I was finally able to communicate with the rest of David that it was a matter of life and death to blast away and dissolve the ice palace in which I have been trapped. At times I watched as David was in despair at being able to feel or connect, and all I could do was wait for other opportunities to be uncovered, for the ice armor to be chipped away. Now, finally, I am free to step out in the light and the celebration and the joy.

ARIELLE ⮞ I'm vibration, I'm bliss, I'm movement, I'm the activator of ecstasy. . . . I'm a healer, I vibrate through your whole being. I connect, I'm a connector. I fill space with energy.

RITUAL: THE ART OF ECSTATIC UNION— A SACRED MARRIAGE

Here is a celebration of the heart in a Ritual of Union with your beloved. It is offered as a support for your inspiration, so that you can move beyond what is traditional to create a unique form adapted to your wishes and the needs of the moment.

The Ritual of Union is a new way to declare your love, through your beloved, to all your friends and your community. It can be full of humor, poetry, and caring, with a Tantric flavor! As the mistress of ceremony on the path of SkyDancing Tantra, it has been my joy to create many marriage ceremonies in many countries. They are universal—independent of creed, race, religion, or sexual preference—and can be enjoyed by all who are ready to celebrate.

This nontraditional ritual does not affirm an engagement till death do you part. Rather, it is intended to inspire you to create a feast that affirms your connection with your beloved. With some modification, you can use it to celebrate the beginning of a creative partnership, the affirmation of a deep friendship, or a recommitment between lovers or husbands and wives who wish to renew their vows. If such a ceremony seems too powerful or too unusual for your older relatives, consider having a traditional ceremony for them and holding this celebration separately for your community of close friends.

This is not a ritual for a formal legal marriage, although it could be. Hence I have called the partners in this ritual "Chosen Lady" and the "Chosen Lord." You can choose any name that seems appropriate to you: Shakti (the Goddess) and Shiva (the God), Great Mistress and Great Master, or Aphrodite and Dionysus, the goddess and god of love. You may enjoy calling the bride and groom by their real names, and by these archetypal names during the celebration.

PREPARATION

🙦 Designing the ceremony is a wonderful way of bringing your community of friends together. Gather with your partner and your friends to determine what the goal and the phases of the ritual should be. For instance, celebrate love in creative ways, through dance, song, poetry, and gift sharing. Make a list of the steps.

🙦 Following the suggestions in Chapters 5 and 6, make a list of all the props, music, food, and types of space you will need; delegate the job of gathering these elements to several friends. Select a Guardian of the Ceremony to keep track of how the process unfolds. If this is to be a legal marriage, this person can be the priest, minister, justice of the peace. Select people to be the guardians of time, sound, space, and ritual objects.

🙦 Prepare the sacred space for the ceremony in advance, following the guidelines in Chapter 6. If your ceremony is indoors, you will need a large room with couches and pillows arranged around the edges. This allows the older people to sit comfortably, while the younger ones can sit on pillows on the floor.

🙦 Arrange a beautiful center for the room with flowers, silks, and two pillows facing each other, where the pair will sit.

🙦 Have on hand two silk blindfolds and seven votive candles.

🙦 If you are holding the ceremony outside, prepare a space in the center for a small fire and have the fire ready to be lit.

PRACTICE

🙦 A marriage ritual can be intimidating. It is good for the couple to each have time on his or her own, to relax with friends of the same gender. Here you can just be who you are and be appreciated. This time apart allows the partners to feel individually empowered before they go through the ceremony together. If possible, let the men and women gather in separate rooms, away from each other.

Empowerment of the Chosen Lady

👁 The women join hands and form a circle around the Chosen Lady. They can choose to create a dancing circle, turning around the Chosen Lady, singing and dancing for her. Or each woman in turn can give her a hug and a wish, or express appreciation for who she is, what she has accomplished.

👁 Then the women can share with her short stories of wisdom about their experience of being in a committed relationship. They can share poems about the enlightenment of woman. This poem from *Music of the Soul* by Sidi Shaykh Muhammad is one of my favorites. It praises Laila, who is the Shakti of the Sufi tradition:

> *There is no sleeping when you see the face of Laila.*
> *She fills the world,*
> *And yet all the world is but a scent from Her fragrance.*
> *She says . . .*
> *"I live in everything,*
> *But I return to be one.*
> *I want you to be like me,*
> *To be one, to be Laila,*
> *In everything, in every moment, in every face."*

👁 Finally, the Chosen Lady's mother or best friend puts a garland of flowers around her neck, embraces her, and says, "Welcome! Love has chosen you today. You are the Chosen One. May this knowing of yourself as the lover who gives love and the beloved who receives love always remain in your heart."

Empowerment of the Chosen Lord

👁 The men create a similar process for the Chosen Lord, forming a circle around him. Together, they can dance, sing, and praise his male qualities: strength, power, courage, and so on; they enact playfully a warrior dance to the accompaniment of drumming; or each man can offer the Chosen Lord a gift symbolizing an aspect of his power. For instance, one friend gives him a lychee fruit, tender and juicy, which he puts in his mouth. While he sucks it succulently, the giver could say, "May this gift awaken your sensual delights!" Another friend could give him a white silk scarf, saying, "I put this scarf around your neck to protect your spirit."

꙳ Finally, his father or best friend greets him with a hug, puts a garland of flowers around his neck, and says, "Welcome! Love has chosen you today. You are the Chosen One. May this knowing of yourself as the lover who gives love and the beloved who receives love always remain in your heart."

The Meeting

꙳ Now the group of men blindfold the Chosen Lord and the group of women blindfold the Chosen Lady, and they lead the couple to the ceremonial space. The two partners stand facing each other across the room, with the central decorations between them. The group of men and women form a circle around them.

꙳ The Guardian of the Ceremony says, "The time has come, beloveds, for you to discover each other through the eyes of the heart. As you relax your face, touch your heart, touch your eyes. Discover each other afresh, as if you had never seen each other, with the eyes of the heart, the eyes of innocence, as if for the first time."

꙳ The Guardian of the Ceremony lights the seven votive candles and asks the couple to remove their blindfolds. Now they gaze at each other. Fully present. Then they observe the people, the space. . . . They walk toward each other, hold hands above the flames, and look in each other's eyes.

꙳ The Guardian of the Ceremony throws rice above them, to symbolize everyone's offering to the earth, and gratefulness for the fruits of the earth. As the grains fall on the flames and on their heads, the guardian says, "May the God and Goddess of love bring blessings, fertility, and abundance to your union."

Marking the Entry into Union

꙳ Now the pair stand facing each other, holding hands, ready to mark the entry into their sacred union. He sits on a chair. A basin filled with scented water is brought with a white towel.

꙳ She kneels and gently washes his feet and wipes them. Then she is seated, and he does the same to her. They hug each other.

꙳ The Guardian of the Ceremony says, "And now you are ready to walk the path of love and Spirit together."

Calling the Blessings

❧ Now, slowly, the couple moves to stand next to each other, holding hands. Slowly, they start walking step by conscious step around the fire. While they walk the first step, the group forming a circle around them sings or hums a gentle sound, such as "Aaaah" or "Oooommm," from their hearts.

❧ With the first step, the Chosen Lord says, "Beloved, I am the Earth that carries you, the Home that protects you, the Heart you belong to. I choose to love you equally, through the highs and lows of our life together."

❧ With the second step, the Chosen Lady looks into his eyes and says, "Oh, Great One, I am the water that quenches your thirst, the womb to hold your seed. I choose to love you so that you may feel strong, healthy, and creative."

❧ With the third step, he looks into her eyes and says, "Beloved, my love surrounds you with brilliance and grace. When you receive it, let it expand to others and shower them with joy."

❧ With the fourth step, she looks into his eyes and says, "Oh Great One, I open my heart to you. Teach me to surrender to the way of devotion. I am your Earth, you are my Heaven, I am in you and you are in me."

❧ With the fifth step, he looks into her eyes and says, "Beloved, in you my soul dances with delight and inspiration. You are the song, I am the singer. May we create together truth and abundance."

❧ With the sixth step, she looks at him and says, "You are the light, I am the vision, you are the path, I am the guide. May we understand each other with compassion and insight."

❧ With the seventh step, they say together, "Your Spirit and my Spirit are one."

Tying the Ring

❧ They now exchange the rings. The Guardian of the Ceremony says, "These rings symbolize the never-ending nature of giving and receiving love. Now exchange the rings."

❧ The Chosen Lord puts the ring around his Chosen Lady's ring finger and says, "I take you to be my partner in life. With this ring I join our two lives as one. Let our journey together begin." And the Chosen Lady puts the ring on her Chosen Lord's finger and says the same.

≪. Now the Guardian of the Ceremony says, "I now declare you joined as Partners for Life" (or "husband and wife," or "merged as one" or whatever the right words are for you). And the couple exchanges a kiss.*

The Showering of the Gifts

≪. The couple sit on the two pillows, face to face, with the seven candles all around them. For the next fifteen minutes, while soft music is playing, friends bring gifts of all sorts: sensual foods, such as sugared ginger, lychee fruits, figs, and papaya, to feed them; bells and Tibetan singing bowls to ring around their heads and bodies; a bowl filled with water in which a red rose is floating; a Chinese silver ball holding a bell-like chime inside; or a flower.†

≪. The pair takes each gift and offers it to the other with a blessing or a wish.

≪. End with a hug.

The General Celebration

≪. The meal begins with a toast to the pair by each of their parents, who express what they appreciate and love about their child and their child's chosen partner. If the parents are not present, let the elders in the group represent that function and give the toast. Here is a beautiful toast that can be given by a chosen person: "Thank you for opening our hearts, for allowing your family and your community to join our hearts as one in this beautiful celebration of your love. May your union be blessed."

≪. Together, the assembly of friends and family honor all present with a Heart Salutation (page 75) and the celebration concludes with food, drink, dance, and the joyful celebration of love.

POINTERS

≪. Feel free to shorten or adapt this ritual to your needs.

---

* This ritual is applicable to same-sex as well as heterosexual couples. Please feel free to change and create this ceremony to meet your own special needs.

† See the ritual of Awakening the Senses in *The Art of Sexual Ecstasy* for more details of this part of the ritual.

≈ The bride and bridegroom may prefer to have the Guardian of the Ceremony read them the Calling of the Blessings as they step around the center and the fire.

≈ Make sure you have a Guardian of the Time, so that each step of the ritual does not take longer than planned.

CHAPTER TWELVE

≈≈≈≈≈≈≈≈≈≈≈≈≈≈≈≈≈≈≈≈≈≈≈≈≈≈≈≈≈≈≈

THE FIFTH CHAKRA:
THE SONG OF THE SOUL

THE FIFTH TANTRIC KEY:
YOU ARE THE CREATOR AND THE CREATION

*I am the messenger. I give resonance, form, richness
to your energy. I speak the dream. I am the place
through which dark truths come. I speak the sweet
whispers of the heart. I sing your song.*

The Voice of the Fifth *Chakra,*
from a *Chakra* Talk

THE CHAKRA MAP

ECSTASY ❧ The ecstasy of inspiration.
IMAGES ❧ An angel flying in the sky (a SkyDancer)
blowing a trumpet; the Lord Krishna playing the flute and
charming all, a shooting star (a great wish or idea), a lightning bolt (sudden inspiration).
PHYSICAL LOCATION ❧ The throat and neck.

BODY PARTS ⊷ Throat, vocal cords, ears, mouth, teeth, jaw, neck vertebrae.

ENDOCRINE GLANDS ⊷ Thyroid, which is the Taoist House of Growth.

MAIN FUNCTIONS ⊷ To create, communicate, and discriminate; to give voice to the heart.

ESSENCE ⊷ Resonance.

FEARS ⊷ Of authority, to trust one's talent, of trusting in the God/Goddess's protection, of choosing freely, of not being creative, of not having the willpower and discipline to succeed, of telling the truth, of not conforming.

MASCULINE POWER ⊷ To speak out, tell it like it is, communicate your vision, ask for what you want, define and respect boundaries, generate enthusiasm, spread the word, express your talent (dance, painting, writing, speaking, acting, etc.); the will and discipline to learn and to create.

FEMININE POWER ⊷ Looking within to receive inspiration, listening to your inner guidance, finding your own voice (as a speaker or a writer); creative improvisation (in dance, singing, and other arts), clairaudience (communication without words), revelation through dreams, prayer.

OPEN AND RELAXED ⊷ "I open myself to receive spontaneous inspiration," "I am playful and welcome spirit every moment," "I have a one-pointed commitment to create and manifest my unique talent," "I tell my truth: Truth is erotic," "I feel what I say and I say what I feel," "I am in harmony with my environment."

BLOCKED OR CONTRACTED ⊷ "Show me how it works," "I can't do this without you," "I'll say what you want to hear so you'll love me," "I must control my feelings," "I want guidance, but don't give me bad news," "I want to be ecstatic, but I don't want to change."

Positive qualities ⊷ Ability to tune into the pulse of another or an event, feeling the resonance with a person or situation (the ability to tune into him or her, valuing inspiration), the ability to breathe Spirit (dynamic guidance and information) into our life; the natural impulse to purify the body/mind (diet, meditation, etc.), to attune to subtler levels of perception, to hear the silence between the words and/or the sounds.

Negative patterns ❧ Shy, can't express feelings, incapable of confrontation, would rather be polite than express one's truth, self-critical, judges and blames self and other, tendency to be unreliable; false promises, confused; plays dumb; indecisive (can't decide between the head and the heart), acts helpless, no goals, anxious, nervous chatter.

THE CHALLENGE ❧ To remember: those who know don't speak; those who speak don't know. Listen to the silence between your words, that's when the God/Goddess speaks to you.

HEALING AFFIRMATIONS ❧ "I listen to my heart and express what I feel," "I am in tune with existence," "I feel vibrant and alive," "I create beauty," "I sing the song of my soul," "I am in tune with Spirit," "I make the choice to love my voice."

QUESTIONS FOR GUIDANCE ❧ "What can I learn from this?" "Am I in harmony with this person or situation? If not, what is the dissonance?" "What am I avoiding?" "Do I have the willpower and the discipline to do this?" "Am I kidding myself, or is this my truth?"

ARCHETYPES ❧ Hermes/Mercury (presides over communication and coordination between different dimensions of reality), Saraswati (patroness of the arts), Shiva (the great teacher or guru), Shakti "Shakini."

THE ESSENCE OF THE FIFTH CHAKRA

My teacher used to say, "The voice is the only instrument made by God. All the other instruments are made by man."

❧ Shabda Khan

How does the passion of sex, the flow of love, the sharing of power actually *sound?* Our throat center—our voice of truth, the song of our soul—is the abode of inspiration, the gate that opens to join heart and mind, sex and Spirit.

Through the first four *chakras,* our consciousness discovers how to be present here, on this earth, in this body, with self, with others. Now our consciousness expands beyond the boundaries of skin and bones to more subtle and invisible rhythms.

In the throat center we give a color, a song, a voice to our energy. We translate our physical reality into words, sounds, and new creations. We grow and expand through sound; we taste new possibilities, we celebrate the sacred and chant the names of the God and Goddess.

Our creative drive expresses our hunger to awaken. In Jon Marc Hammer's *The Jeshua Letters,* Jeshua says,

> There is nothing,
> absolutely nothing
> you can create
> that is not an expression
> of your longing to awaken.

We can approach the art of communicating in one of two ways. Either with a utilitarian approach, merely expressing information needed to get the job done. Or with a deeper approach, becoming aware of how we say things, the tone of voice, the silence between words, the feelings we express.

THE POWER OF VOICE

We have treasures hidden inside ourselves. When we remain at the utilitarian level, we are like a person who keeps a precious Stradivarius violin stored in the attic. An open throat *chakra* is the door to the wonders of self-manifestation and creativity. And the blocks and difficulties encountered here are teachers on our way to self-empowerment and success in the world.

Mary, for example, grew up with a father who was a powerful lawyer. Whenever something important had to be discussed between them—her grades at school, decisions about her holidays, her education, her difficulties in life—she would be called to her father's imposing law office. He sat behind his desk, an intimidating patriarchal figure in a large armchair. She sat in the client's chair looking up at him across the broad mahogany desk. Whenever she tried to present her point of view, her father would interrupt with a discourse. She could hardly complete a sentence. Her words, she said, seemed unimportant to a man accustomed to engaging in verbal combat to win his case. As a result, over the years, her throat became blocked. Mary developed an acute speech defect. She could not speak in front of others without rushing to the end of her sentence in a nervous, tense, high-pitched voice. The very act of speaking brought up old fears of being interrupted; painful feelings of being overwhelmed, unheard, unloved, unseen, and unappreciated.

In her late twenties, Mary became a successful writer and was called to speak in public. It was a disaster. Unconsciously convinced that no one was interested in what she had to say, she shouted very loudly and spoke very fast, leaving no space between her words. She left her audiences overwhelmed and exhausted. This grew so painful for Mary that she began speech and sound therapy. She was taught to shout any sounds as loud as she could for thirty minutes per session; to speak so slowly that she left long pauses between words; to lower her voice tone so it resonated from her belly. Voice work became a deeply healing therapy which she pursued diligently for years. She now speaks five languages fluently and teaches and speaks throughout the world. And the most common compliments she receives are, "You are such an inspirational speaker!" and, "You have such a wonderful voice!"

Many of us have felt our voices stifled as we grew up. Sound therapist Don Campbell, author of *The Mozart Effect,* says that we are trained from early childhood to suppress and flatten our natural self-expression—vocal and physical—and thus our creativity. The effects of this chronic self-suppression contribute to heart disease, migraines, substance abuse, depression, and numerous other stress-related illnesses. In fact, many therapists now advocate and practice voice therapies, using singing, and chanting words, notes, and tones to express and release long-repressed emotions.

TELLING OUR TRUTH

Truth is erotic. When we speak our truth, we become bold, exciting, attractive. We are empowered. By stifling our truth, we stifle our creativity. We become trapped in relationships and circumstances in which *not* speaking the truth is the price of admission. It requires courage and commitment to speak our truth. In doing so, we take a risk. The risk to be authentic.

Every time we part our lips is an opportunity to express the mystery of life, of love. Communication is important in all relationships, especially during lovemaking. When a man tells a woman in bed what he likes about her body, how beautiful she looks, of his love for her, it gives her confidence. And a woman can do the same for her lover. Expressing your pleasure audibly during lovemaking—with abandon; with words and moans and sighs; and even with wild, primal noises—opens the heart, pleasures the mind, and allows passion to flow.

Simple or special moments and occasions present us with opportunities to practice the joy of creative communication: going out on a romantic date; teaching or playing with our children; singing; acting; telling stories; public speaking or teaching; letter, journal or creative writing; composing or performing music; even resolving personal conflicts and disagreements with family, friends, and co-workers. Let your voice be your instrument of truthful and moving expression!

TELLING YOUR TRUTH

PURPOSE
To clear unfinished business with the people in your life.

PREPARATION
- Allow a half an hour of time when you will not be disturbed.
- Have a paper and pen at hand.
- Be alone in the room with no noise and no music.

PRACTICE
- Begin with the Heart Salutation (page 75)
- Make a list of three people (your partner, parents, children, friends, co-workers) in your current life with whom you may

have unfinished business. Perhaps shyness prevented you from expressing your true feelings or you have unexpressed anger toward them.

🙞 Next to each person's name, write a simple summary of what it is you did not express clearly. For example: "You said you loved me, but you never call anymore. I'm always the one who does the calling. I'd like to clear this up." "You wanted me to be available for a meeting, so I reserved the time. Then you forgot to tell me the meeting was canceled. I don't feel respected."

🙞 Now put your paper and pencil away, sit back and relax, close your eyes, take a few deep breaths, and begin to focus within.

🙞 With your inner eye, see the first person on your list. Speak her name, see her face, feel her now. Notice how you feel in your body. Keep breathing. See yourself standing or sitting straight in front of her.

🙞 Now use your voice to tell the person sincerely, from your heart, what has bothered you and what you need from her to reestablish an easy and open-hearted connection. Speak in the *I* form in present tense; and use simple, short sentences. For example: to the person who canceled the meeting without telling you: I don't feel respected. I know you have a lot to do, but so do I. I propose we have a ten-minute meeting at four o'clock today to make sure we can coordinate our schedules."

🙞 Keep speaking in this way until you reach a resolution inside yourself. You will know that has happened when you feel relaxed inside and at ease with the person.

🙞 See yourself saying good-bye, shaking hands, or hugging. End the exercise with a Heart Salutation.

🙞 Focus on the next person on your list and proceed in the same way.

POINTERS

🙞 Allow yourself to move around, make gestures, shout, and scream if you need to. Releasing pent-up frustrations in this way is healthy and will leave you feeling lighter.

🙞 Put a few pillows on the floor and let them represent the person you are communicating with. When you are expressing your anger at the person, at the same time hit the pillow with large, expansive arm and body movements. Release a big sound from your throat every time you hit the pillow.

☙ If you prefer a quieter approach, sit in meditation, review your connection to the person, and listen to your internal dialogue with her. See if you can set up a real-life situation when you can complete the exchange face to face.

FINDING YOUR AUTHENTIC VOICE

Music can teach us about speaking the truth.

My friend Ariel Kalma, an accomplished musician and composer, told me:

> For me, music is the expression of the truth in the fifth *chakra*. One of my teachers said every note has a meaning; when you play, you weave notes together to make sentences, to create musical conversations. The word *expression* means "coming out of." If truth is coming out of me when I play, I feel in tune. If not, I feel off key. And when my voice is tuned and my being is tuned to truth, truth comes through. Playing music is like speaking the truth. Either you are or you are not in tune. You may be off by a hair or a whole note. Learning to be truthful is learning to say what you mean. Not halfway, or half a tone down. Speaking the truth is like playing a note just right.

BECOMING AWARE OF YOUR WORDS ☙ To the degree that we express our truth, we are in tune. Each situation in life calls for a certain attitude, a certain voice. At times, the voice we use is not our own. For example, as parents we may use a deep, pompous voice with our children to express our authority, when what is called for is a gentle voice that expresses love and concern. Or we use a contracted, high-pitched, whiny voice with our partner that reflects an old relationship with a parent, when what is called for is our true, resonant voice that expresses our inner needs.

Words have the power to wound or heal. We are often unaware of how our words sound to others. To find out, try this simple exercise. For one day, carry a small notebook. Observe the way you speak to others, and jot down what you notice:

> How much time did I spend today in negative or critical speech (about others, myself, my work, and so on)?
>
> How do people respond to my words? Notice how their bodies respond: Do they shrink away? Expand? Relax? Tense up?
>
> How do I feel about my own conversation? Do I feel energized, replenished, depleted?

During the next day, engage in a very specific awareness exercise. Avoid any automatic responses when you speak. Make a commitment to speak *only* respectfully and truthfully. Acknowledge each person you speak to in a positive and supportive way. Observe the effects.

> Is it hard for me to praise others? Do people lighten up when I do praise them? Do I, and they, feel energized?
>
> Do I see how my words and the way I choose to use my voice can uplift others or cast them down?
>
> Can I see that my voice is a creative spiritual instrument of remarkable power?

CREATING SUCCESSFUL COMMUNICATION Teaching people about love and sexual communication I developed these steps to ensure successful communication in a variety of situations.

> Assume the other person has good intentions and that he is doing the best he can.
>
> Practice the Golden Rule of communication: Speak to others the way you want them to speak to you.
>
> Begin by expressing appreciation so the other will feel received and heard.

& Before you speak, be clear about your purpose. Then, be specific and express the facts.

& Share your truth from the heart, without blame.

& Say five or six sentences at most, then be silent. Let your words sink in. Now listen. Breathe deeply and slowly. Welcome the person, the moment, in your heart.

& Remember, this person, this situation, this moment are your teachers. Stay open. Be present and listen.

SPEAKING IN PUBLIC WITHOUT FEAR *&* When you speak in public, imagine the conference room is a room in your house. You got up, washed your face, brushed your teeth, got dressed, and now you are walking into the living room to hang out with your friends. Speak as you would to your friends. When you enter the room and face people, keep the following points in mind.

Use the Qualities of All Your Chakras *&* The path of SkyDancing Tantra teaches that when we prepare to speak in public, it is helpful to remember all our *chakras,* as if speaking their energies, using their qualities:

& *Speaking from your crown:* Begin and end with silence. While you speak, take the time to remember Spirit, and listen to the silence between your words.

& *Speaking from your third eye:* Express a vision. Guide people to connect with that center, close their eyes, and look within.

& *Speaking from your throat:* Let your voice enjoy and express its melodious nature. Speak in different voices— tender, authoritative, gliding, singing. . . . Play with your voice.

& *Speaking from your heart:* Talk to people as if they were your lover. Emphasize places of "common ground." Make yourself available to answer questions as a friend.

& *Speaking from your belly:* Move about, let your body show itself, make spontaneous gestures that support your discourse. Have fun! It's a dance. The more you

move, the more you will create a sense of ease and flow for everyone.

 ◆ *Speaking from your sex:* Turn people on. Seduce them with your words. Be sexy, daring, and funny.

ACTIVE LISTENING

Listening, being present in the moment, is the key. When you sing, Shabda Khan, says, you have to be listening every moment. It's a balance of power and beauty, expression and emptiness. If you are not empty enough to listen, what can you hear and what can you express?

LISTENING TO SILENCE ◆ It is said that the silence between notes gives music its beauty; and that great actors know how to make their silences as powerful as any spoken dialogue. Our silences can be creative acts. We can be dynamically silent, and let our spirit manifest without words. This silence is presence. And when our *chakras* are aligned with another's, our energies merge in soul-to-soul communion, where words are unnecessary and silence communicates all.

Ariel Kalma describes such an experience, which occurred when he met Ama, who became his wife:

> I saw this gorgeous lady with a beautiful red hibiscus flower behind her ear. I looked at her, she looked at me, and time stopped. We did not say one word. The whole world around us disappeared. Her partner left, the noise disappeared, only silence was there. I took her hand and took her to a secret place in an empty room downstairs. We just held each other in that place and did not talk for one hour. Any sound or word that came into my consciousness had no meaning; the meeting of our eyes, our hearts, our beings, our mutual silence, was stronger than words could express.

THE VOICE OF YOUR SILENT MIND ◆ In our inner silence, we can hear our true voice. This happened to my friend Terry, a writer. A few years ago Terry experienced a crippling writer's block. Worse, he felt he had nothing left to express. Finally, he went on a shamanic journey to find his voice. Guided by a shaman, he met his spirit guide: a female black panther.

> Her mission, the panther said, was to guide me through my inner chaos to a chamber of silence, where I would be able to hear my true voice. But when we arrived in the chamber and I tried to listen, I found that this inner voice was a barely audible whisper. I had to strain hard to hear it. The least noise or disturbance outside would interrupt the process, and I would lose my connection with the voice.

Every time he approached the silence, it vanished. Whenever he thought he had finally found it, some new interruption intruded and he lost it again. His writer's block continued.

> Finally I gave up. It was a warm, gorgeous night and I decided to sit under the stars. I leaned against an oak tree in meditation, and asked for help. Instantly, the black panther came into my mind and said, "Follow me."
> She led me down a dark, narrow corridor into a womblike room of total silence. I let go. I relaxed. I did nothing. And as I sat there, I suddenly contracted in absolute terror. I thought, What if I dissolve and die? The panther said, "Fear of death. Let it go."
> "How?"
> "Just be here. Don't do anything at all."
> And my fear left the room with death.
> Then I heard a faint whisper, like a distant stream. I strained to hear better, and the whisper disappeared. It was my inner voice. It wanted to tell me something. But every time I *tried* to hear it, it disappeared. It was incredibly frustrating. Then I noticed that my straining actually prevented the voice of my own Spirit from entering my conscious awareness. I had to let go even of the desire to receive, yet be available for whatever wanted to be manifested—*or not manifested.*

Then Terry let go. He looked at the stars. He felt the strength of the tree supporting his spine. And great delight arose in him. The delight of being alive. Of simply being there. Like the tree and the stars. He let himself fall deep into a centered place of stillness where everything was just as it was. Where life was sufficient. And he understood equanimity. It didn't matter what he got or didn't get. Just being in itself was enough. "At that moment," he told me, "the whisper came back. I just waited, welcoming. And the voice said, 'When the mind is quiet, the Guest comes uninvited.' I haven't had any trouble writing since then."

In the act of creation, we hear the voice of the Spirit. When we trust, this voice sings the song of our soul. Such inspiration comes when our heart is in a state of tranquility.

LAUGHTER

Laughter is like having an orgasm in your throat. The spirit of Tantra shines best through laughter. When we laugh, we cannot take ourself seriously. When we laugh, we *only* laugh: we can't think, we can hardly move. Laughter can release tremendous energy and clear energy blocks. Research has shown that laughter can even heal disease, emotional as well as physical.

Have you ever heard the story of Hotei, the laughing Buddha? His entire teaching consisted of laughter. Wherever he traveled he would stand in the middle of town and start laughing, a big belly laughter that shook his entire being. His laughter was so real, so infectious, that soon everyone around him would begin laughing in response, until entire villages were overwhelmed by laughter.

THE CHAKRA TALK

When you do the *Chakra* Talk (page 138) with your fifth *chakra,* listen to the message of your true voice. The following examples from my students will give you an idea of the range of voices and images you may experience.

> CARLA ∾ I'm your voice. I'm afraid to be loud, to be full and expansive and demanding. I think nobody wants to hear me. When I speak, I'm not sure if it is me that comes through, or if I'm just a parrot speaking in other people's voices.

KARIM ᗰ I am the door to the body and the mind. I am the one who speaks for the spirits and who makes friends with the body. I am the throat. I take the energy that is all around, assimilate it, and give it a voice.

ELEANOR ᗰ I am the one who asks the question, "Who am I?"

BETTE ᗰ I am your guide. I speak your truth. You have a unique talent to contribute, and it is my task to find out what that is, and to create it.

GEORGE ᗰ I team up with the belly. With the support of the belly my voice is grounded in your bones. Then, when my voice speaks the truth, your body dances and your heart sings.

ADRIANA ᗰ I am the sounding board of your soul. The gateway of your breath. I am speech. I am laughter. I am silence. I invoke the Spirit into the body and create new forms. I am the funnel of the flow. I am the poet. I am the singer. I sing the song of your soul.

RITUAL: THE SONG OF ECSTASY

When we speak falsely, use our voice to please, or cajole, or bully, or manipulate, our throat center becomes tense and contracted. But when we allow the integrated voice of body, heart, mind, and Spirit to emerge, we can move mountains. For thousands of years, in many parts of the world, music and singing have been used as a spiritual practice.

Just as the resonance of one high, operatic note can break a crystal glass, and the right words can open a mind or a heart, the right sound can open your chakras. The word chakra means "vortex, center of resonance." If we direct a sound that resonates into the center of a chakra, it can open like a flower. Every mystery school from ancient times to the present uses sound for these purposes.

You can tune your chakras just as you can tune a musical instru-

ment. We have all experienced how pure and melodious notes emanate from a well-tuned instrument and how discordant, unpleasant notes emanate from an instrument that is poorly tuned. The same happens with our chakras. You can tune them by singing or chanting your sounds.

When you tune a chakra, you increase the range of its energy field. In so doing, you expand your charisma, your presence, and your ability to touch and inspire others through your speech. The Song of Ecstasy ritual does this.

PURPOSE

❧ To bring lightness, joy, emotional release, and spontaneous creativity into your life.

❧ To free yourself from performance anxiety.

❧ To clear your inner channels to allow more energy and inspiration to flow through you.

❧ To encourage and develop spontaneity and trust in your artistic and creative abilities.

PREPARATION

❧ Set aside about half an hour for this ritual if you do it alone or with your partner. If you do it in a group, set aside forty-five minutes. Feel free to adapt, expand, or shorten the process according to the needs of the moment.

❧ Create a "singing stick": a tree branch that you polish or decorate with colored threads and beads, a crystal wand, or a stone that is easy to hold in your hands.

❧ Create a sacred space. You will alternate between standing and sitting, so have some comfortable chairs or pillows available.

❧ Have one blindfold for each person.

PRACTICE

Gibberish Meditation

❧ Begin with the Heart Salutation (page 75).

❧ Stand up, stay relaxed, with knees slightly bent and eyes closed (use a blindfold if you wish). Think of something that has bothered you lately, or that you feel uncomfortable about, or some unfinished business you have with someone. Imagine that you are in the situation right now.

❧ Begin to make a monotonous sound, such as *"La, la, la,"*

and let the mind gradually bring forth new sounds. Continue until unfamiliar wordlike sounds arise. These sounds or words should not be in any language that you know: just nonsense words, unconscious sounds.

∾ When you begin to enjoy it and get the knack of it, expand your range, moving your tongue and mouth to produce sounds that seem like words from an unknown language but really express what you are feeling. Be as if you were in an animated discussion, proving your point, gesturing with your arms, hands, neck, and head. Imagine the response of the people you are communicating with. Act out the sounds and feelings you would have and how you would respond to them. Have fun, let it all out. Keep going for ten minutes.

∾ When you have said all you have to say, remain totally silent and still. Enjoy that moment. Listen to the silence between the sounds around you; feel that you are the center of soundless sound, as you try to hear your heartbeat, your inner sound. Silence.

Singsong Sharing

∾ Now take your blindfold off. If you are in a group, sit down in the circle. If you are with a partner, sit on your pillows or chairs face to face. Look around and appreciate what you see.

∾ Begin to pass the Singing Stick around the circle (or to your partner). Each time you hold the stick, close your eyes, look within, feel what you want to communicate to the group, to the other person, to yourself.

∾ Imagine you are a magician of song and magic sounds. Take a deep breath and open your mouth and throat wide. Pushing out from your belly, begin to sing a nonsense song—make it up, improvise. Go up and down the scale, vocalize, go to growling or animal sounds and back to notes. Sing notes that are long and thin, deep and resonant, high and crystalline. Play with this for three to five minutes, putting all your attention and energy in it. Remember, this is a dialogue. Look at the others as you sing; you are showing them who you are through your voice. You are communicating your message to them.

∾ When you are finished, pass the singing stick around to the next person. And they now start their song.

🍃 When everyone has had a turn, put the stick in the center and take a moment to close your eyes and let all these songs resonate inside your heart. Enjoy this moment.

Chakra *Tuning*

🍃 Alone or with others, lay your hands on your sexual center.

🍃 Close your eyes, take a deep breath, and let a sound emerge from your sexual center, a deep root sound, an earth sound. You could try *aum* (pronounced in three syllables: *aa, oo, mm,* or as *Ooo Mmm*).

🍃 Play with the sound. Send it through your belly, down into your pelvis, your sexual center. Imagine that part of your body is singing, resonating, responding, vibrating with that sound. Try different sounds for a minute or two.

🍃 Now rest your hands on your belly center, at the navel, and take a deep breath in the belly. On the exhalation, begin to make a sound that resonates in the belly. Try with your mouth open, then with your mouth closed. Try *Ooo Mmm* again.

🍃 Imagine the sound vibrating in the belly, and let your belly respond and sing for a minute or two.

🍃 Now continue upward in the same way for your solar plexus, heart, throat, third eye, and crown *chakras.*

🍃 End with a silent moment, relaxing. Note how your *chakras* now feel aligned and connected, how your mind feels clear and peaceful and how you can hear the "soundless sound" of your inner silence. Yourself, as the silent center of all sounds, the Source whence all sounds end and begin.

🍃 End with a Heart Salutation and a Melting Hug.

POINTERS

🍃 If you are familiar with voice work, this will seem easy to you. If you have never practiced exercising sound and voice, you might feel strange or shy. You may find that it is easier to do this with a group of friends first, where everyone can be silly and have fun, and then move into it alone later.

🍃 Remember your "growing edge." Even if this seems weird at first, take yourself beyond your normal limits. It is only by trying the unfamiliar that you discover unexpected creative impulses and inspiration and heal old shyness or feelings of helplessness.

You can easily do only one part of this ritual. Try doing only the Gibberish Meditation for ten of fifteen minutes; or just the Singsong Sharing for twenty minutes; or just the *Chakra* Tuning for ten minutes.

You can add spontaneous stretching or dance movements to the Gibberish Meditation and the *Chakra* Tuning. Be playful and crazy about it, do not judge yourself about being silly or ridiculous, just play with innocence, like a clown: improvise!

CHAPTER THIRTEEN

The Sixth Chakra:
The Full Moon

The Sixth Tantric Key:
Look Within—You Are the Light

I am the age of wisdom. I am the sight at the center
of wisdom, a ray of knowledge, an arrow of
connection with what is deepest in universe and self.
Center of grace and elegance. The lightness of being.
I am the goddess, shaman, mystery of life and
death. The vibrant connection with the unknown.

                    ▸ The Voice of the Sixth *Chakra,*
                                 from a *Chakra* Talk

THE CHAKRA MAP

ECSTASY ▸ The ecstasy of insight.
IMAGES ▸ The full moon illuminating the way on a dark road. The cooling light of the full moon shining on the wa-

ters of the ocean, a circle, a young maiden wearing a flowing white robe.

PHYSICAL LOCATION ◈ The forehead, between the eyebrows.

BODY PARTS ◈ The brain, the neurologic system, the eyes and nose.

ENDOCRINE GLANDS ◈ The pituitary, which is the Taoist House of Intelligence.

MAIN FUNCTIONS ◈ Detachment and witnessing, insight that frees and the vision that gives direction, uniting understanding and intuitive guidance to perceive the higher spiritual or symbolic meaning of situations, seeing energy as light, rising beyond problems to get the global vision, the greater picture.

FEARS ◈ Of confronting demons, of hearing unpleasant truths, of the future, of trusting your intuition.

ESSENCE ◈ Seeing beyond.

MASCULINE POWER ◈ Justice and fairness: discriminating by seeing both sides. One-pointedness: seeing things clearly and dispassionately. Discipline: in life, in spiritual practice, mastery over passions. Detachment: witnessing what is so.

FEMININE POWER ◈ Honoring and understanding the voice of the heart: listening attentively to others and understanding them, accepting your own shortcomings compassionately; willingness to change and grow.

OPEN AND RELAXED ◈ "I know the answer," "I see the way," "I can see reality beyond fear or emotional attachments," "I separate truth from illusion," "I see the greater meaning," "I understand the symbolic meaning of a situation," "I see the energy of everything around me."

BLOCKED OR CONTRACTED ◈ "I don't see the point," "I don't get it," "I don't know where I am going," "What you see is what you get," "Life has no greater purpose."

Positive qualities ◈ Focus: being in the moment, paying attention, holding a clear vision of your intention in any situation and being guided by it. Inner focus: listening to the heart; receiving guidance in the form of visions, images, or intuitive voices. Imaginative, creative. Transformative: transforming the passions (anger, greed, and so on) to access the spiritual dimension. All-seeing: evaluating all aspects of a situation before responding, perceiving the common ground that connects disparate thoughts or situations, having the overview.

Negative patterns 🙠 Perfectionist: bogged down by details, can't see the big picture. Rigid belief system: stubborn, resistant, having fixed opinions about how things should be, living by the book, wanting things to remain the same, attached to illusions. Indecisive: letting others evaluate and decide what's right, confused and without a clear life direction. Alone in the universe: not connected to higher guidance, paranoid tendencies, worrying about the future, missing the point. Always asking questions because one is afraid of not understanding, difficulty in seeing anything that is not obvious, self-pity, the martyr syndrome.

THE CHALLENGE 🙠 Look within while you act without.

HEALING AFFIRMATIONS 🙠 "I choose to grow up and wake up," "I let go of struggle," "I see the light at the end of the tunnel," "I hear the voice of Spirit," "I create a clear vision of my life's purpose," "I choose what makes me grow," "I look, I see, I listen, I hear."

QUESTIONS FOR GUIDANCE 🙠 "Am I clear?" "Do I feel right in this situation, with this person?" "Is this good for my growth?" "Who is choosing here?" "What is the intention behind this choice?" "Do I see the consequence of this choice?" "Who am I beyond the judgments and the choices?"

ARCHETYPES 🙠 The hermit, the sage, the holy man, the holy woman, the spiritual teacher; Shiva and Shakti merged into one being, half-male and half-female.

THE ESSENCE OF THE SIXTH CHAKRA

If therefore thine eye be single, thy whole body shall
be full of light.

<9. *Matthew 6:22*

The sixth *chakra* is a full moon whose face is ever-changing:
sometimes clear and bright, sometimes obscured by clouds of
thinking and emotion. It is a place of clarity and vision, chaos
and illusion. It is the mind in which something is always occurring, whether we notice or not.

Our thoughts chatter on and on. Images appear in endless
succession, seducing our attention. It often seems these thoughts
and images *are* our mind. Yet all our thoughts and visions and
mental creations occur in a space without boundaries: our Sky
Mind. There the clouds of our moods, thoughts, beliefs, and perceptions come and go, like changing weather, but the sky remains,
containing all. This permanent, unchangeable background is the
clear consciousness of the Sky Mind. It is the true nature of
"mind at large," which is spacious and ever available to us.

I call our awareness of this dimensionless space the "Witness."
The Witness experiences life directly, beyond thinking and imagining, unaffected by what happens, simply observing what is.

The question of the sixth *chakra* is, How can we become the
Witness, who is free like the eagle flying high over the landscape, its sharp eyes focused on every detail, as well as the big
picture? Will we dwell in Sky Mind as the Witness who is free?
Or will we remain distracted by what the Buddhists call Monkey Mind, the nonstop chatter of our undisciplined mental
processes? Will we have clarity or confusion? Vision or illusion?

When our third eye opens, the Witness looks out. And in
that clear seeing, we attain contentment. For we know that we
are not "born in sin," rejected by some God who threw our
forebears out of the Garden of Eden. The misery, the shame, the
guilt of this predicament has to be seen for what it is: a cosmic
joke. The moment our third eye opens, we are free of that myth.
Great relief and joy fills our being as we awaken to the inherent

perfection of our eternal nature. Our open third eye pierces the veils that obscure our essential purity. But this awakening takes intense focus and a profound desire to wake up. And perhaps something more.

A Zen story tells of a monk who meditated for years, yet could not reach enlightenment. In despair, he approached the abbot who told him to try for one more year. The year passed, and enlightenment did not arrive. Again the monk went to the abbot, who told him to meditate for one more month. At the end of that month, in the same condition he had been in a year before, the monk went yet again to the abbot, who said, "If you are not enlightened in three days, you had better kill yourself." On the second day, the monk achieved enlightenment.

Sometimes more time is not what we need at all. And when all our time has finally run out, the answer often comes. Our awakening in this *chakra* happens when we become conscious of *being*, rather than remain unconsciously identified with the content and activity of our minds. Like the Zen abbot, it helps to remove the illusion of future time, and come face to face with our moment of truth, which is always *this* moment. We can never be free, awake, or happy in the future. Only *now*. Yet we must somehow trick our mind that clings to illusions of future everything. What if we only had one month to live? Would we still think our happiness, our awakening to ecstasy, lay years in the future? We might drop a few illusions rather quickly and like the eagle flying free, see the exquisite pattern formed by all the seemingly disparate threads of our existence.

THE NATURE OF INTELLIGENCE

For many people who seek a higher consciousness, the mind seems to be the enemy, a source of anxiety, troubles, and distractions. Yet the mind is extremely useful in our everyday living, and intelligence is only one aspect of the mind. But what do we mean by intelligence?

Intelligence allows us to weave many perceptions into one clear vision or understanding; to expand our perspective, explore new possibilities; to assess, distinguish, compare, and choose. Intelligence is the art of weaving many options into one choice. This is how we evolve and change.

Free thinkers who follow their vision beyond the group

consensus, beyond the conventional taboos and teachings of their tribe, are often denigrated as eccentrics and misfits. Some return with new insights and revelations that enrich their culture and even change the course of history: Mohammed, Einstein, Picasso, Madame Curie, Gandhi are but a few among thousands of women and men whose courage and vision have made the world a better place. Intelligence is to risk thinking freely.

But intelligence is more than a thinking process. We have emotional intelligence, which enables us to feel and empathize. We have physical intelligence or coordination, which enables us to learn and perform simple and complex movements. All are essential for our balance and wholeness. All are aspects of what Rupert Sheldrake calls the "self-organizing intelligence of nature." This intelligence pervades the infinitely complex and flawlessly functioning universes; it animates all existence, from subatomic particles to the synchronized orbits of galaxies. And it is what we discover when our thoughts vanish and we enter our Sky Mind as the Witness of our own nature.

When our third eye opens, we awaken to this intelligence, a detachment and direct observation that brings clarity and perspective, the vision of our place and purpose within the big picture. As a friend once told me, "When I am caught up in the storm in my teacup, I remember that my life on earth is only a drop in the ocean of existence. This helps me to wake up and see the forest instead of the trees and connect with the peace beyond the storm."

Yet the clarity and vision of our Witness is not just otherworldly, but also very much "this-worldly." It moves us to put our wisdom and insight into action, to incarnate our truths in person. For even wisdom becomes delusion if we do not integrate it into our lives in concrete ways. Even the insight that "we are all one" is no deeper than a fortune cookie if we cannot get along with others or hold down a job or take care of our bodies. And our greatest visions are useless if we do not harness ourselves to their power and bring them to fruition.

THE SONG OF THE SOUL OPENS THE THIRD EYE
One summer I was teaching the Love and Ecstasy Training at the Omega Institute in Rhinebeck, New York. As I passed the concert hall on the way to my room, I saw a group of musicians

rehearsing. I walked in, and saw my friend, the virtuoso composer Michael Harrison, playing piano on stage. He was giving a concert that evening with the great flutist Paul Horn.

Michael invited me to play tamboura (a drone instrument used as a background accompaniment to Indian music) at the concert. That evening, I was honored to participate in a most exquisite performance. Accompanied by a group of talented musicians, Michael and Paul improvised perfect harmonies and rhythms. Then each played solo. Michael also sang Indian *ragas* (classical vocal music) while I played the tamboura.

After the concert, Michael and I walked out together. The moon was full. A warm summer breeze blew across the glowing fields. Michael held his tamboura wrapped in a blanket. We went down to the beach by the lake, and sat in silence, legs crossed, the tamboura between us. Silver moonlight rippled on the water. The stars shimmered, bright and sharp, in a cloudless sky. The concert had opened our hearts.

Gently, Michael began to play the tamboura and sing, inviting me to sing with him. At first I was shy. I loved Indian music and the way the human voice can slide up and down the scales. But he was a great singer, and I a beginner. His eyes were glowing. It was such a tender invitation. How could I resist?

Spontaneously, we turned toward each other and shared a Heart Salutation. Our foreheads met and our third eyes touched and seemed to fuse, as a powerful magnetic current passed between them. With our foreheads resting against each other, we began to sing. I became pure listening, an empty vessel, totally receptive, merging with Michael's voice, my ears so sensitive I could hear the silence between the notes. My attention had never been so focused. I followed every intonation of his voice, gliding along the notes, seeking the sound in the same places in my body that resonated with his sound: the belly, the throat, the heart . . . slow and fast . . . all the way up to my third eye. I almost knew which note would be next, and where in my body it would resonate. I felt as if I had become a living flute. My voice blended with his voice, carried by each note, singing the song of the soul in an eternal moment.

We were completely attuned. Heart to heart. Eye to eye. Soul to soul. In timeless communion. In this awakening of our sixth *chakra,* our entwined voices rose up in song through our throats like the serpent of the life force, to penetrate our third eyes.

At last we fell silent, our souls shining like beams through our third eyes, connecting us to one another and to the whole universe. And there was only silence and bliss.

VISUALIZATION

The ability to think in pictures, to project images of what we intend to create, are abilities of our third eye. Ancient mystics said that the pituitary gland allowed us to see the inner light, to transform energy in visions. Since ancient times men and women have rendered their spiritual visions through art as a way of anchoring them in *this* world.

Our third eye is the window between the inner spiritual world and the outer, apparently ordinary, world. Mike and Nancy Samuels say in *Seeing with the Mind's Eye,* "A person who holds a sacred image in her mind experiences the effects produced by the specific energy of that image, effects which extend to the world around her."

VISUALIZING THE DEITY The highly developed system of Tantra teaches us to visualize forms, colors, objects, and deities as a way to transform our consciousness. We contemplate internally an image of divinity—a Buddha, a Tara, a Dakini—through creative imagination. The next step is to identify with the divinity, to become him or her in spirit, and finally to merge in a transforming union.

By *visualizing a deity,* an image that represents an already existing energy within us, we invoke this quality in ourselves. Then we can share it and help to awaken it in others. These Tantric deities represent the aspect in each of us of pure energy and beauty, pure consciousness or Spirit: our awakened selves. When we call our partners by such names, we are saying, I honor who he or she truly is: a being of infinite creative potential.

VISUAL MANIFESTATION What we see behind our eyes is what we manifest. If we hold in our mind a clear vision of what we wish to accomplish and feel it as alive and real, we create in our mind and body a deep connection to our vision as a living reality. This is the power of the third eye. It connects us by subtle strands of energy to that which we seek to create, and draws us to it. We have hitched our wagon to a star. Michael Harrison says,

> I use visualization and affirmations constantly in my life. If I want to record an album, I imagine and feel that the album is already complete. I see a record-release party with all my friends and the people from the record label. I give thanks for it *as if it had already happened*. I do this process at the end of my morning meditation, when I'm the most relaxed, clear, and energetic. And at times during the day, I close my eyes, relax, and visualize what I want to achieve or manifest.

THE POWER OF VISUALIZATION ❧ The following Zen story illustrates third eye visioning in action. A master craftsman in ancient China was commissioned by the emperor to make a cabinet for the emperor's bedroom in the Imperial Palace. The craftsman, a Zen monk, told the emperor he would not be able to begin the work for five days. The monk was seen by the emperor's spies simply sitting, apparently doing nothing for the entire time. Then, when five days had passed, the monk got up. Within three days, he had made the most extraordinary cabinet anyone had ever seen. The emperor was so pleased and so curious that he had the monk brought before him and asked what he had been doing the five days before he had begun his work.

"All the first day," said the monk, "I spent releasing every thought of fear of failure, of dread of punishment if my work should displease the emperor. All the second day, I spent releasing every thought of inadequacy, and every belief that I might lack the skill to produce a cabinet worthy of the emperor. All the third day, I spent releasing every hope and desire for fame, glory, and reward if I should produce a cabinet that would please the emperor. All the fourth day, I spent releasing the pride that might arise in me if I should succeed in my task and earn the praise of the emperor. And all the fifth day, I spent beholding in my mind the clear vision of that cabinet which I knew even an emperor would desire, which now stands before you."

HOW WE PREVENT OURSELVES FROM SEEING
Emanuel Swedenborg, the great mystic, said that the individual

is the space of free will between heaven and hell. Tantric practices of prayer, mantra, and remembrance of divine beings, images, and teachings are based on this insight. What we hold in our mind shapes our character and decides, in every moment, whether we live in heaven or in hell.

The most common thing that prevents us from seeing the big picture is our own negative thoughts, our internalized voices. "You can't do that!" "Don't even try, it will never work!" Where do we acquire these inner prophets of doom? A friend of mine explained it this way: "My father was a critic. He believed the best way to educate me was to berate me for what I had not done right. Now my father's voice has become my inner critic. . . . And I am always watching out for what might go wrong instead of appreciating how lucky I truly am."

My critical mind, my ego, has also developed the tendency to be "Life's Security Guard." It watches life unfold with the slight suspicion that things are not right as they are. It must keep its watchful eye on everything or things will surely get out of hand. Its paranoia, however mild, is rarely disappointed. This person does the wrong thing, that plan fails, and even traffic lights and astrological transits synchronize themselves to interfere with its most important plans. It is hard when the deposed ruler of the universe has taken up residence in your mind!

Like most inner critics, mine cuts both ways. If no one else is good enough, neither am I. It prefers that I spend as much time as possible examining with a magnifying glass the gaping flaws in my personality, and measuring with a yardstick the distance between my present state of evolution and Ultimate Perfection Itself, which is where it constantly assures me I should be by now.

REMEMBER YOURSELF ᔤ In the cloudy gloom of my inner critic's negativity, the clarity of my Witness and the inherent joy of being alive disappear like gray pigeons in the fog. It helps to remind myself that my inner critic is in reality one of my inner demons. And rather than argue or believe or fight with it, I can simply recognize it for what it is, face it directly, and disarm it with a deep breath, a smile, and a sense of humor.

That is the meaning of the admonition to "remember yourself": to remember that we already have everything we need within us. We do not have to match an ideal imposed on us by our parents, our teachers, or our church. The trap of idealism is that we feel bad if we do not achieve the unattainable, and we can be happy only when we're perfect.

EMBRACING YOUR DEMONS 🦂 We best defuse the power of our inner critic by facing and embracing it. This story of Tibetan saint Milarepa illustrates the point beautifully.

> One day Milarepa was doing practice in his cave. The local demons didn't like this at all, so they created a fearsome commotion in the cave. But instead of being either angry or fearful, Milarepa said, "Ah, I'm so glad you came. Let me serve you some tea, and after we have tea we can meditate together." When the demons heard this, they were deflated. They said to each other, "Our purpose is to scare. Once we can't scare him, we have no power." And so they left. Demons have no power when there is no fear.

I once knew an architect who used this power in his life when his financial resources dwindled. He wasn't getting any new commissions, and his creditors began to send him threatening letters. Finally, they began coming to his office demanding payment. Instead of refusing to see them, cowering in fear, or angrily defending himself, he treated them politely. No matter how abusive they were, he greeted each angry creditor with a smile, an offer of coffee, and a sincere apology for being behind in paying them. Then he would say, "Please tell me how we can work this out together!" No matter how angry they were when they came in, the creditors always left the office pacified!

Here is a practical exercise you can use to pacify your inner critic. For the first step:

> 🦂 Make a commitment to yourself that, during one day, you will observe and jot down each critical, self-bashing, or negative thought that appears in your mind.
> 🦂 Ask yourself, "Am I having these thoughts, or are these thoughts having me?"

🍂 What themes are recurring in this critical pattern? Work? Relationship? Your family? Yourself?

🍂 Notice how the thoughts affect the way you feel, act, respond to people. Does your energy drop when you mentally criticize, complain, or rage? Do you feel good about yourself when you have these thoughts? Why not?

🍂 When did this pattern start in your life? Did you have a parent or sibling who was critical? What words did they use? Did you feel victimized? Do these critical thoughts appear in you because you still feel the victim of incompetent people or unpleasant circumstances?

🍂 Check carefully how you create these situations.

🍂 How would you respond if you assumed that all of the situations have been created or initiated by you? What you said long ago, an assumption you made, a wrong motivation, and so on.

Now move on to step two.

🍂 When a critical thought appears, take note and say, "Next!" or "Stop!" and move on.

🍂 Get a pocket-sized clicker like the ones that golfers use to keep track of their strokes. Carry it around with you. Click it every time you catch yourself having a round of mental abuse. Tally your score. Is it ten, thirty, fifty clicks? You will see immediately how often you do it. Chances are you will feel very motivated to change that pattern.

CHOICE 🍂 Life is a process of discovering who we are as we choose our way from one imperfect moment to another. We are often bombarded by choices. Should we take this job or that? Marry this person or that? Go to school or travel the world?

When you become aware of turbulence inside your mind, when something is at stake and you must choose: stop. Find that place inside deeper than the chattering of your hopes and fears. Breathe, relax your body and mind. From a place of stillness, look within for the answer, in your third eye. Look to the guidance of your highest wisdom, your heart, your Witness. Ask yourself simple questions: What do I truly want? What am I afraid of? What will happen if I choose yes or no? Am I willing to accept the consequences of either choice? What is my heart's desire and my highest good? If you engage this inquiry and call for resolution with complete sincerity and great intention, clarity, insight will arise.

Intuitively, we already know the answers to most of our dilemmas. We simply need to go beyond the level of our internal dialogue to that place where the answers are simple and obvious. Getting there is the practice of the sixth *chakra,* the meditation of the Witness in Sky Mind.

Ama shared with me her personal story about choice.

My mother lives in a cottage behind our house. Yesterday morning, we happened to meet in the garden. She started to talk nonstop and I was still half asleep. I felt overwhelmed. In my mind, I realize I am becoming upset, angry. *Can't she be quiet in the morning? Why does she have to talk so much?* And there goes my inner critic, blaming, aggressive, complaining, inside my head. If I listen, I am ready to lash out. My words will hurt and cut like swords.

At this point I have a choice. I can listen to my thoughts and attack, or I can turn within, go to my heart, and realize what is happening in this moment: nonacceptance. I don't accept her as she is. I am bothered. Then I can choose. I either accept her right now, and *be available for a moment* or I can tell her, "I am sorry, I need quiet," and then go away without lashing out at her. I can find my own truth in the moment and choose which way I go. Becoming aware of my inner dialogue gives me a choice. I can connect with my heart and tell my truth in a way that respects the other.

One's truth, and how we respond to the world, changes moment by moment. SkyDancing Tantra teaches us to be aware of what is, beyond judgment of "good" or "bad." Such awareness does not divide and reject. It is all-inclusive. It gives us the clarity and freedom to choose our truth, to be who we are.

The Chakra Talk

When you do the *Chakra* Talk (page 138) with your sixth *chakra*, you will hear the voice of your third eye, your flying eagle, your window of clarity. The following examples from my students will give you an idea of the range of voices and images you may experience.

SANDRA ❧ I am a clear white light burning in the center. I work in symbols, and words are difficult for me. I ask for permission to show my symbols. I ask for permission to allow those symbols to be received. They are there, covered by dust, noise, sickness. The light burns bright, but cannot be seen for the smothering of dust, sickness.

VALERIE ❧ I'm shut down. Slammed shut. Total blackness. I can't see through the doorway. Chaos keeps me from seeing through.

DAVID ❧ I am old. I am completely and unutterably still. I can see the energies, the pulses of the universe, the Void. I am huge. I am a speck. Complete silence. I am beyond the cares of the body. I am he who gives dreams a voice.

THERESE ❧ Center of visions for you and many. I speak my truths fast and furiously. Deeper knowledge of the self. Deeper connection of the Divine. Remembrance of the divine within you. You connect to many places, many dimensions. It is all energy. Go deep. Dwell in me. Meditate in this center. Pathways and truths here to be held. All here.

RAE ❧ I am the age of wisdom. I am the ray of insight at the center of your wisdom. I connect you to the vastness of the universe and the depth of yourself. I am the center of grace and elegance. I am the lightness of being. Your vibrant connection with the unknown. Your guide and your dream.

APRIL ❧ Fear not your visions. They are meant to stimulate love to flow.

RITUAL: GENERATING CLARITY AND INSIGHT

This ritual will help you experience the sixth tantric key: Look within, you are the light.

Focus, attention, concentration, expansion, and completion: these powers, developed through the third eye, open the door to our ability to be creative in the world. In everyday life we tend to get exhausted by the constant demands made on us. At the root of it is the need to pay attention, and the fact that the world is constantly drawing us outward. This can be very depleting and is a major cause of stress. Why? Because we are giving out energy, but it does not come back to us in the same way.

These are the three keys to personal success in life: the ability to take on the power of the Witness, the power of insight, and the power of acceptance. This ritual is presented in three parts. You can do them independently of each other, or one after the other.

RITUAL ONE: THE WITNESS

PURPOSE
❧ To see yourself as the Source from which all things emanate and to which all things return.
❧ To master attention and concentration, and anchor these abilities in yourself so that they are accessible at all times.
❧ To remain connected to yourself as the source of all your actions and perceptions at all times.
❧ To develop the talent of witnessing: seeing without being attached or identified to what you see.
❧ To allow your intelligence the inner space to be creative.
❧ To learn the secret of staying relaxed in every situation.
❧ To know your consciousness is limitless.

PREPARATION

∾ Set aside thirty minutes to one hour of undisturbed time.

∾ Create a simple, uncluttered sacred space.

∾ Prepare a white candle on a plate or candle holder in front of you. Make sure you have matches or a lighter.

∾ Sit on a chair or a pillow.

∾ Have your journal close by to take notes at the end.

∾ You can do this alone, with a partner, or in a group.

PRACTICE

∾ Begin with a Heart Salutation (page 75).

∾ Close your eyes and breathe deeply and quietly. Be silent.

∾ Consciously, release tension in the muscles around your eyes, jaw, mouth, until your whole face is relaxed.

∾ Imagine also you are relaxing the muscles around your eyes inside your head, so that your automatic eye movements slow down.

∾ Now gently focus behind your closed eyelids, into the center of your head. Enjoy the darkness there. Send your breath there. If you find agitation or many thoughts or images there, just watch your breathing and continue to look within, beyond the chatter. Breathe deeply.

∾ Now bring your awareness to the third eye. Behind your closed eyes, focus on a point just between your eyebrows. The focus should not be an effort, just a relaxed looking. Continue to be aware of your breathing.

∾ Stay in that dark space inside. You are looking at your inner being, witnessing what is there. This is the consciousness resting in itself, the source of your being. That which can be observed, your thoughts, is not you. But that which cannot be observed is the Witness, your real self.

∾ After a while, you may notice a magnetic attraction pulling your energy toward the third eye, your inner center of attention. It is effortless, not a doing, more a watching, a resting at your higher center. This attention is *presence*.

∾ Continue this practice for ten minutes every day.

∾ After one week, begin to integrate this practice in your daily life. Look at people and things from that center, from your third eye. Notice, when you do this, how you are able to see something with your eyes, but at the same time to see yourself seeing. There is a part of you that is not involved directly with the object of your experience. That part is the Witness.

✿ Now gradually develop this awareness: You are in touch with yourself, centered in your third eye, while you are looking and interacting with people and things outside of yourself.

POINTERS

✿ This practice is very subtle. Its powerful effects develop over time. Eventually, it will give you the ability to stay attentive during long periods, to focus on things without being tired. You become more productive with less effort.

✿ At first, it may seem that when you close your eyes to look within, only whirling thoughts and impressions invade your consciousness. Notice how you can let them do their thing while you continue unperturbed to focus from within on the center between your eyebrows.

✿ Eventually, your third eye opens and you begin to have "insight," the ability, through seeing within, to combine outer perception with inner perception. *Insight* means that you can receive intuitive information, from invisible sources: inner guides, your higher self, the God or Goddess. This can guide you through life and help you avoid numerous pitfalls, rash decisions, not being clear about what you do or why, falling under other people's influence, and so on.

RITUAL TWO: THE POWER OF INSIGHT

Ideally, you would practice ritual one for a week and then you would include rituals two and three in a single session.

PURPOSE

✿ To expand your awareness and energy to the whole context of the situation, seeing not just with your ego-mind or your specialist's eye, but seeing with the mind at large, taking in the whole situation.

✿ To place yourself in the right context and hence to make the right decisions without allowing others to step over your boundaries.

PREPARATION

ᴥ Same as for ritual one.

ᴥ This exercise is best done at night, in the dark.

PRACTICE

ᴥ Light the candle and begin to look at the flame, breathing without effort.

ᴥ Look directly into the flame and observe its form. See that it becomes a rainbow of colors you may not have seen there before. You are giving it your full attention and discovering the unseen colors and forms of energy.

ᴥ Now relax your gaze and expand it, softly, from the flame to the space *around* the flame. See the shimmering rainbow colors, the bluish hue of the light expanding around the flame. See how the aura of the light expands.

ᴥ Now close your eyes and see the shimmering light, the aura inside your third eye.

POINTERS

ᴥ Begin to apply this skill to people. Look into them. Then relax your gaze and look at the space around them, at their aura, the emanation of their energy. After some practice, you will begin to develop your innate ability to read people's energies, to understand what they are feeling even without words.

RITUAL THREE: COMPLETION, THE POWER OF ACCEPTANCE

PURPOSE

ᴥ To become the other and remain yourself.

ᴥ To receive energy as well as give it in any moment, thus completing the circle and staying charged energetically.

ᴥ To accept what you receive while remaining centered in yourself.

PREPARATION

ᴥ Same as for ritual one.

ᴥ Do this with a partner.

~ Sit across from your partner. Look into each other's eyes. Breathe quietly.

~ Now focus on your partner's left eye, looking in, as you did with the candle flame. This is the receptive eye. Breathe quietly.

~ Now unfocus your gaze and look at your partner's whole face. Relax the eyes. Don't focus.

~ Now look at the whole person, resting your gaze on your partner and expanding it gradually to take in the surroundings.

~ Feel as if you were looking through the third eye. See if you can perceive the subtle energy emanating from the person as you perceived the energy emanating from the flame of the candle.

~ Do not stare with a fixed gaze. Relax the muscles around the eyes; let your gaze just rest on the space around your partner.

~ Now allow yourself to receive the gaze of your partner. Feel the energy that is sent to you. Imagine you are surrounded by it and bathe in it. Allow yourself to feel replenished by it.

~ Feel that you simply receive this energy and you are empowered by your partner's attention. Remain receptive, receiving, not emissive and sending.

~ Finally, enjoy this new twist: Imagine you are sitting in your partner's position, looking at yourself. Energy is emanating toward *you*. Now, back into your own position, energy returns to you. You are receiving what you were giving. The cycle is complete.

~ Enjoy perceiving people and the world through this awareness of giving and receiving, creating a circle of completion.

~ Close your eyes now, and rest in your inner tranquility.

POINTERS

~ In this ritual you are completing the circle of energy. You are not just giving your power and attention *to* someone, you are receiving it *at the same time.* In this way yin and yang are balanced in your third eye.

~ Practice this ritual of completion for a week. Sense how it helps you stay whole, no longer allowing your energy to be depleted, even during intense meetings at work. Feel how you now have the option to feel constantly recharged, as you welcome and receive back the energy you give to others.

_ヽ_ At first you might feel shy or uncomfortable to be looked at by someone else. You may be afraid of being judged, you may think about your appearance, and so on. To move beyond that, go back to the lesson of ritual two: insight. With a relaxed, unfocused gaze, see what is around the person. This will diffuse the anxiety of receiving energy, the anxiety of losing control.

_ヽ_ You can practice this exercise with anything that has life energy. For example, look at a rose. Feel that the rose is looking at you and sending you energy and fragrance (it is!). If you are in nature, do this with a tree.

_ヽ_ When touching your lover, feel how he or she is sending you energy back when he or she touches you. Receive it to complete the circle of giving and receiving.

CHAPTER FOURTEEN

The Seventh Chakra: The Open Sky

The Seventh Tantric Key: Go Beyond—You Are Free!

*I welcome the one who was never born and who
will never die.*

> ❧ The Voice of the Seventh *Chakra,*
> from a *Chakra* Talk

THE CHAKRA MAP

ECSTASY ❧ The ecstasy of awakening or spaciousness.
IMAGES ❧ The Holy Grail, a golden bowl receiving a stream of light, a thousand-petaled lotus, white light shining like a halo above your head, an aura of light illuminating a yogi/yogini's body during meditation.
PHYSICAL LOCATION ❧ The crown of the head.
BODY PARTS ❧ The cerebral cortex.
ENDOCRINE GLANDS ❧ The pineal gland, which is the Taoist House of Spirit.

MAIN FUNCTIONS ☙ Gateway to the divine Spirit, spiritual insight.

FEARS ☙ Of losing one's sense of identity, of feeling different, of being alone.

ESSENCE ☙ Transcendence: knower, knowing, and known dissolve into one state beyond distinction.

MASCULINE POWER ☙ Radiance, illumination, going beyond preoccupations with physical or emotional issues and dwelling in the dimension of infinity; feeling the ineffable and subtle presence of the soul.*

FEMININE POWER ☙ Dwelling in the state of *samadhi,* or perfect peace and stillness; contemplation of an intimate relation with the divine; grace; devotion to a spiritual teacher or spiritual path.*

OPEN AND RELAXED ☙ "I receive infinite amounts of energy," "Everything is possible," "I have, deep within me, the blueprint for harmony, balance, and perfection," "This moment is all there is, this moment is perfect."

BLOCKED OR CONTRACTED ☙ "I feel discontented, incomplete, unfulfilled, without a clear direction," "I am afraid to surrender to divine will," "I am afraid of going mad, losing my direction, the sense of who I am," "Nothing makes sense anymore."

Positive qualities ☙ Able to live in the moment: capacity to be fully present, seeking the divine connection in all things, ability to see each person as a teacher, each situation as an opportunity to wake up and shake hands with Spirit. Generous and adventurous: willing to help and to heal, generosity of Spirit and of pocket.

Negative patterns ☙ Empty: wanders through life spiritually homeless, uncertain, like an empty shell without a soul; vague; despairing. Rigidity: uses fixed spiritual beliefs and ideas dogmatically to protect inner fear, self-righteous, know-it-all, spiritual elitist, narrow belief system, derides spirituality as irrational hocus-pocus.

---

* At this level, there is no more gender distinction. The separation between what is feminine and what is masculine is transcended when this *chakra* is open and free. When it isn't, the distinctions remain.

THE CHALLENGE ❧ Your perfection exists beyond struggle.

HEALING AFFIRMATIONS ❧ "I let go of that which binds me," "Peace is my home," "I know that ecstasy is always available," "God happens anytime, anywhere."

QUESTIONS FOR GUIDANCE ❧ "Is God/Goddess here now?" "Can I feel the divine connection?" "Does this situation, person, fulfill my higher purpose, or my evolution?" "Can I take the leap?" "Who is left when I am not a man and I am not a woman?" "Who may I serve?" "How can I help?"

ARCHETYPES ❧ The alchemist, master of fusion and transmutation; the union of Shiva (pure consciousness or Spirit) and Shakti (pure energy of life) in *ecstasy;* the spiritual teacher, guide, wise man, wise woman, the guru within, your higher self, divine guidance becoming manifest.

The Essence of the Seventh Chakra

All our ideas of some future heaven are illusions
that prevent our awakening now, in this moment.

❧ Margot Anand

Waking up can be painful. It takes courage and hard work, change and growth, moving from the familiar into the unknown. It means challenging and re-evaluating *everything:* how we live, think, relate to people, earn money, and spend our time. Waking up begins with a sense of boredom, dissatisfaction, pain, and a yearning for change, for more and deeper meaning in our lives.

We have all experienced EveryDay Ecstasy, our true nature, those simple, joyous moments that come in the midst of our ordinary life. But growing up in this anti-ecstatic culture, we are taught to be ashamed of our bodies, to approach life through our minds, to build defenses around our hearts. We are taught that our very humanness, the life and world around us, are the enemies of Spirit, rather than its ground. And the resulting sense of anxiety and separation slows the natural flow of our joy to a trickle.

But my assertion, based in ancient Tantric wisdom, is that our bodies, lives, and circumstances do not stand between us and EveryDay Ecstasy. They are the *prima materia,* the humble vessels of a living joy. And when we accept this, when we relax, surrender, and get out of our own way, our consciousness expands and rises, and ecstasy becomes the natural expression of our being, the heartbeat of our Spirit pulsing through us.

The art of SkyDancing Tantra teaches that our true nature is revealed not by renouncing the joys and pleasures of ordinary and sensual life but by immersing ourselves in them with such acute awareness that the bliss of our natural state becomes obvious in our own experience. We can find it in our jobs, our houses, our kitchens, our partners, and our bedrooms. As Elwyn Chamberlain says in *Gates of Fire,* a brilliant Tantric novel, "What you don't know is the secret of the body. These muscles, these breasts, this womb, this lingam, they are all sacred gifts— all paths to heaven."

Tantra tells us we can master or purify only what we are willing to embrace directly in ourselves: our desires, our darkness, our passion, our pleasure, and our pain. Then we fall in love with life and find the bliss of our natural state reborn every moment. In the words of Miranda Shaw in *Passionate Enlightenment,* we "dive deep into the ocean of incarnation and harvest the pearls of enlightenment." In her book, she quotes an old Tantric Buddhist sutra:

> *Without meditating, without renouncing the world,*
> *Stay at home in the company of your mate.*
> *Perfect knowledge can be attained,*
> *While one is enjoying the pleasures of the senses.*

She goes on to tell how Manibhadra, housewife and Tantric yogini, became enlightened while doing housework. Carrying water from the well to her home, she stumbled and dropped the pot. And as it shattered and the water spilled out over the ground, the limiting boundaries of her ego mind shattered and she dissolved into the infinity of pure consciousness. Manibhadra shows us that awakening can happen unexpectedly and easily during our everyday life.

The message of Tantra is that we do not need to retire to a cave of asceticism and self-denial to find our inner freedom. We can find our bliss in the midst of our ordinary life. Awakenings come without warning. In a moment, we return to the pleasure of our natural state, to the utter delight of *being*. And we find ourself in a place we have always known: home. Everything is familiar, yet wonderfully new and indisputably right. It is as if, after a long absence, a time of struggle and uncertainty, we returned to a place of harmony and simplicity, where everything is as it should be—perhaps as it always was. Just one taste of this bliss, the mystics say, is worth a lifetime of struggle. And yet perhaps a lifetime of struggle is not required. Perhaps ecstasy, for all of us, is only a hair's breadth away.

In this book we have explored various definitions and implications of ecstatic states. We have defined Ecstatic Awakenings as the opening fireworks, the cork pulled out of the champagne bottle, a full-blown euphoria when the divine penetrates us in the midst of our existential doubts and aloneness. Yet such glorious moments are only reminders of our source and not the be-all and end-all of life.

We have also defined EveryDay Ecstasy as an equanimity of Spirit flowing through us, our capacity to stay connected to our Source in the midst of ordinary life. EveryDay Ecstasy can be cultivated and become a part of our everyday lives in the ongoing process of our transformation.

The journey from energy to ecstasy, from unconsciousness to awakening, is the greatest journey there is. When energy flows unobstructed through the body, we experience pleasure. When pleasure is accepted in trust, it flows into the heart and becomes delight. When that energy rises into a mind freed of negative thoughts, consciousness is awakened in the forms of light, clarity, spaciousness, and expanded sensory perceptions. Energy streams through the body with the force of great pleasure. And we begin to smell, hear, see, taste, and touch things in a more deeply sensual way.

And as our seventh *chakra* opens, our personal egoic life

merges with the impersonal life of awakened consciousness and we realize the radiance of our own timeless nature.

We transcend the illusions of duality, the activity of our ego-mind, and realize our nature as Spirit. And we know beyond the shadow of a doubt that the ground of our ecstasy is not in some far off realm of bliss, but here in this life we are living now. And our path becomes as wide as the whole world.

The idea that "I am one with all that is," may seem far-fetched, even frightening. Yet there is wisdom in the fear of our loss of ego and in the fear of delusion. There is a fine line between delusion and enlightenment. And we need strength and wisdom to ground and embody the powerful current of this "Light" in our lives. For to simply say "I am God" is not the actual realization of our divine self-nature. Thomas Jefferson's words "The price of freedom is eternal vigilance" are true at every level.

THE DARK NIGHT OF THE SOUL

At times, we wander in the dark, tried and tested, lost and confused, wondering, "Where is the light? Is it even real? And what must I do to find it?"

As we move deeper into this forest of unknowns, we encounter the "dark night of the soul," when all our familiar attachments and consolations lose their meaning, when the past is disintegrating and the future is unknown and we are left on a dark plain of longing. My friend Raz Engrassi, the director of the Hoffman Quadrinity Institute, says of this dark night, "Often when we are suffering, we think we are a million miles away from God. We think that God has abandoned us."

Yet such suffering brings us face to face with who we are and what we have made of ourselves. And we can pass through this dark night by recognizing that our suffering, however painful, has a purpose: our own awakening. When we seek the meaning hidden within it, our suffering can become a wake-up call, a path to the divine rather than a path of separation.

The path to the light leads through the darkness, through the valley of the shadow of death. Hopelessly lost, we have nothing to guide us but faith. To live in the world by faith is to walk a razor's edge. Yet faith makes even our mistakes and their, at times, painful consequences sacred teachings. How we use our experience is everything. This is how traumatic events shatter some people and transform others.

We suffer when we attempt to impose our conditions, our agendas on life, choosing, manipulating, rejecting, demanding, and complaining, doing everything except being present to what is. Better to let the universe be what it is, and to accept our place in it. As my friend Paul Lowe says, "Life as it is, is exactly the way it is supposed to be for you in this very moment. *This is it!* Wherever you are, *this is your life.* And if you embrace it exactly as it is, then it will become whatever it is meant to be next, without your needing to control, change or manipulate it. You will accept and live each moment as it is." This is what it means to be awake, and to live by faith. We can awaken in *any* moment.

It is also useful to remember that "what we resist, persists"; that the ego is not our enemy. When we make it our enemy, we give it our power and use it against ourselves, like a ventriloquist tormented by his or her own dummy. Our ego is a natural phenomenon, like weather. We can study its patterns and learn how it functions and not be caught unconscious in its many snares.

If we demonized bad weather the way we are encouraged to demonize our ego, we would rightly be called superstitious. Lamenting and obsessing over our terrible ego and carrying out elaborate plans to annihilate it, is itself an act of "ego masturbation." Why not simply take it into account, in a natural way, while serving a useful purpose in the world? Fear and guilt meditations on our ego inflate it to absurd proportions. So let us treat our ego like the weather and go about our business as divine beings, absorbed in the miracle of life itself.

MEDITATION

Many people think meditation is enforced concentration, another form of doing, a willful effort directed toward a specific goal. But true meditation is simply the state of conscious being, of enjoying our own nature. It cannot be made to happen. It can only be experienced. It is there when we surrender all effort, when we notice our own nature before fear and struggle and desire arise. It is there as our original state, before we impose anything on it. It is there when we cease to drive it away by our very efforts of seeking it.

True meditation is the simple state of being what we always are: not doing anything to it, or about it; not thinking, not seeking, not grasping or holding on; not meditating; not even celebrating the apparent discovery of our own nature. When we worry that nothing is happening, it disappears. When we feel we must do something, it is gone. But when we understand that this nondoing of being has no reason or goal or purpose, that it is simply what we are, our own nature, our center, the most precious thing we never lost and need never seek again, then we will know the purest delight and joy of simply *being*. In truth, we cannot *know* what *is* at all. We can only *be* what is. This very state itself is true meditation.

This meditation is our Sky Mind. It is always there, behind every state of emotion, confusion, joy, and pain. Our Sky Mind in Buddhism is called "the view."

As teacher Nagpa Rinpoche says, "We experience our enlightened state because it sparkles through continuously. If it did not sparkle through, we would not be able to come out of confusion. We can do so, because the enlightened state is there anyway, it is our very nature." We distract ourselves from our own enlightenment. But, as Nagpa Rimpoche says, it sparkles through, because *that is its nature.* Seeking nothingness is perhaps one more way of distracting ourselves from that which sparkles through everything.

The sparkling life force is not mere formless energy: it is unaccountably intelligent, beyond genius. This self-organizing, universal intelligence inheres in all things. The precisely choreographed orbits of planets, galaxies, and solar systems; the intricate subatomic dances of molecules and atoms; the cycles and order in nature; the universal nature of DNA all reveal the workings of an incomprehensibly vast intelligence.

Life knows where it is going. It does not stop to explain itself. But it is always teaching us as it unfolds in infinitely complex patterns and inexplicable synchronicities. And we are swept along whether we struggle against or swim with its irresistible current. Our minds and bodies are a unique part of this living stream. We are ourselves complex, finely tuned biochemical creations animated and lived by this vast intelligence, whose genius is imprinted in our very cells, whose appearance is ever-changing, whose nature is eternally the same.

WHAT IS ENLIGHTENMENT?

Paul Lowe, author of *The Experiment Is Over*, says of enlightenment, "It is beyond normal experience because it is not an experience. Thinking is a barrier to it. The thought of what 'it' is, is a barrier to it. It is not a knowing." Lowe notes that when you are present to life,

> whatever is appropriate will be clear for you in that moment. Where to go, who to be with, and what to do. When you are in the stream of life, *you are life*. In this very moment is the experience of freedom. . . .

In this state, our ego becomes transparent. We feel one in Spirit with those around us. And our joy, no longer dependent on outer events, wells up from within us, from our own hearts. Recognizing the perfection of what is, we no longer seek to manipulate our inner or outer experience. We are no longer in conflict. We are on our true path in the world, and life is on our side. In such ecstatic moments we are unique and singular, yet one with all.

We are free, moment to moment, in the face of whatever arises. We are no longer slaves to or enemies of desire, fear, anger, and all the humdrum demands of living. Life becomes a blessing rather than a problem to be solved. Our ego, with its endless thoughts and plans, does not control us. We are free to choose, not what life bring us but how we live what comes. We feel connected to a Source vaster than any definition, word, or concept. When we see that life arises moment to moment, that is how we live it. Each moment is an invitation to swim in the water, dance in the wind, delight in the sun. We let go of the I that wants to understand, control, and choose everything. We let go of our self-importance. We are present without any conditions or demands. We embrace our moments fully. We are truly alive. And we go on simply living.

SIMPLE TRUTHS ஒ We can experience ecstasy anywhere, anytime, every day. My friend Harold Dull, a therapist and founder of the Watsu bodywork technique, shared with me this experience of ecstatic awakening:

I was out in the hills, gazing at a calm pool, when I felt a kind of "call" to climb up this small mountain. As I climbed, I felt as if I was being "drawn" up the hill, and as I neared the top, a state of awe came over me, a kind of incredulity and joy. It was very powerful. When I came to the very top I saw a ring of trees. They were bright with light in all their leaves, and shining. At that moment I felt a divine presence. It was so powerful that I fell to my knees. Then the presence was beside me, lifting me to my feet. It seemed to be holding me up. I started walking, guided by this presence beside me. I felt strongly the thought, "This is God beside me." Then the presence led me along a ridge, then down into a gully, down a stream bed. Halfway down I came to a place where the path split in two directions. One was rough going, full of brambles. The other was clear, an easy path. I asked the presence, "Which way?" And I heard the words, "Whichever way you go, I am with you." In that moment, I became completely ecstatic. This was the truth! I took the easy path down and sat by a stream. I saw children playing in the water, and the trees were shining in the sun. And I just sat watching it all, feeling so blessed. I felt myself sitting in the hand of God. It was a state of pure joy. I looked down and saw my own upturned hands and felt in the center of my own palms that "hand of God" feeling. For months afterward, if I just sat still and looked down at the center of my hands, I'd remember and feel everything being "in the hand of God."

JOY IS A SPIRITUAL PRACTICE ➳ What is really happening when we cultivate what brings us joy? Joy, from a Tantric perspective, is the ultimate form of prayer. It *is* a spiritual practice. It is a living affirmation of our inherent perfection, our "God-Self." When we are *in joy,* in that moment we are *in love.* We are that through which the creator is creating. We are complete. We are "with Source."

Perhaps our joy, our freedom, is like the moment of laughter when *we* disappear and there is only the experience of humor and delight. Joy and laughter may be forms of enlightenment, involuntary moments when we are fully present, possessed and shaken by the humor of reality; free of all pain, sorrow, and dilemma; free of hope and fear, past and future.

While writing this book, I spent time with many mystics and teachers who have spent decades practicing various disciplines of awakening. And each, from his or her own traditions and realizations, confirmed the insights which I first encountered in Tantra. They are simple, human principles:

- Embrace your sexuality.
- Embrace your body.
- Find your power, your flow, and your balance.
- Love and have compassion for yourself and others.
- Trust and surrender to life.
- Be authentic, express your truth, sing your song, and follow your vision.
- And finally, surrender to life, which *is* your Source.

In this regard, the following words are worth repeating: Life arises moment to moment, and that is the truest way to live it. Respond to each moment as an invitation from life to *you*. Let go of the need to control, to choose, to understand. Embrace your moments fully.

Be alive. This is it!

THE CHAKRA TALK

When you do the *Chakra* Talk (page 138) with your seventh *chakra,* you will invoke the voice of your Spirit, your connection with the Source. The following examples from my students will give you an idea of the range of voices and images you may experience. At the seventh level we are beyond words, and the *chakra* talk reflects this. At this level, many people are completely silent and meditative and cannot utter a word.

> MARIANNE ⁊ I am the empty vessel at the crown. I am the queen and the servant. I serve all, I see all, for I don't need to say anything or show anything. I simply am . . . I don't want anything. I am going nowhere.

JONATHAN ❧ In me is all space, I am empty, I am no body, I don't know anything. And that feels okay. It feels empty and blissful here.

KATHY ❧ I am she who was never born and who will never die.

MARGOT ❧ Silence is the answer. There is nothing that can be said here. Just gratitude and receiving blessings.

RITUAL: THE EMPTY SKY

In the Vijnana Bhairava Tantra, in which Shiva teaches Shakti the ways of enlightenment, Shiva says, "In summer, when you see the entire sky endlessly clear, enter such clarity." The following ritual gives us the way to know and "enter such clarity" and enjoy the nature of Sky Mind. You can carry this experience with you through all moments of your life. Then you will discover how to enjoy life as it is with clarity and ease. You will know directly the experience of all-encompassing awareness.

PURPOSE
❧ To experience the nature of Sky Mind.
❧ To discover how to access this expanded state of consciousness.
❧ To learn how to carry this awareness with you in every moment.

PREPARATION
❧ Choose a beautiful sunny day, with a cloudless sky, and go to a beautiful spot in nature where you will not be disturbed.
❧ Take a blanket to lie on.
❧ Set aside about thirty to forty minutes.

PRACTICE
❧ Find a comfortable spot, spread your blanket, and begin with the Heart Salutation (page 75).

∽ Lie down, take a deep breath, exhale fully, and relax as completely as you can.

∽ As you breathe deeply, with every exhalation relax your face, the muscles around your eyes, your jaw.

∽ Make sure you do not need to squint because of the sun, but can keep your eyes open, yet relaxed.

∽ Now contemplate the vastness of the sky. Simply look at it with a relaxed gaze, not focusing on anything in particular. Gently, relax into the endless blue space.

∽ With every inhalation, feel yourself taking the vastness of the sky into your being. With every exhalation, feel yourself bathed in this vastness.

∽ Watch when your thoughts pull you away from this contemplation—"The sky is so blue, it's so beautiful, I don't look at the sky enough." Let those thoughts go, don't follow them. Come back to your breath, your contemplation. Relax your gaze, feel the vastness, feel as if you were merging with it.

∽ Gaze at the sky as if you were trying to find the boundaries of this vast space. Go deeper into it. Allow yourself to be bathed, permeated by the vastness.

∽ When you feel that the boundaries between your consciousness and the sky are melting away, merge with the sky, close your eyes, and feel the spaciousness within. Behind your closed eyes, you are this vast sky. See and feel the vastness inside.

∽ Allow yourself to be bathed, cleansed by this vast all-encompassing space of the sky within you and around you.

∽ As you practice, notice the silence, the gap between the thoughts, notice the mind dropping away. Enjoy the peace and the clarity.

POINTERS

∽ When thoughts appear, be aware of the background, the vastness of the sky. Do not pay attention to the thoughts, let them go.

∽ The sky is like the space in which your thoughts move. When you do not pay attention to the thoughts, but look at the space inside and outside, you discover the spaciousness of your Sky Mind.

∽ Be aware, from now on, of the Sky Mind in your daily life. Remember that it is the clear consciousness that contains the thoughts but is not the thoughts. Notice, day by day, the silence between the thoughts.

🔊 You are the witness that observes what happens yet is not identified with it.

🔊 Gradually, allow yourself to dwell in the Sky Mind in all moments of your life: as you make love, cook, or work.

MAKE A COMMITMENT TO ECSTASY

It's in every one of us. I just remembered.
It's like I've been sleeping for years.
I'm not awake as I can be. But my seeing's better.
I can see, through the tears.
I've been realizing that I've bought this ticket,
and watching only half of the show.

And there are scenery and lights, and a cast of
    thousands,
who all know what I know.
And it's good that it's so.
It's in every one of us, to be wise.
Find your heart, open up both your eyes.
We can all know everything, without ever knowing
    why.
It's in every one of us, by and by.

                                    ❧ David Pomeranz

Now that we have traveled together through all the *chakras* and
explored the path of EveryDay Ecstasy, I would like to leave you
with a few ways to integrate this information even more con-

cretely into your life and into your relationships with family and friends.

Remember that an ecstatic life is something you can create through daily practice. There are skills you will need to develop and conditions you will need to create to bring ecstasy into your daily life.

CREATE AN ECSTATIC LIFE

What if you began each day from a state of creative awareness, with a clear vision of what you want and how it can be achieved? For example, when you want to create a perfect dinner party for good friends, you begin with a vision of a warm gathering filled with intimate friendship, laughter, and good food. You begin, first imaginatively, then actually, to feel and create the atmosphere—you choose a menu, the lighting, the dishes you will use, the music or games you will play. You feel the enjoyment of the evening itself as you prepare for it and anticipate it throughout the day. Below is a ritual for starting your day with clarity, by opening all your centers.

A RITUAL FOR BEGINNING THE DAY

PURPOSE
🌦 To remind yourself that each day represents a brand new opportunity to taste the sacredness of life; a chance to be nurtured by the mystery; a chance to relate lovingly, happily, and even with laughter to everyone around you.

PREPARATION
🌦 Have on hand a candle, incense, and matches.
🌦 Prepare a good sound system with slow, meditative music. (Be sure to pick music that will not interfere with your thoughts and that will not run out before the ritual is completed.)
🌦 Sit on a comfortable pillow.

🍃 Wake up fifteen minutes earlier to allow yourself the time to perform this ritual without feeling rushed.

PRACTICE

🍃 As you wake up, open your eyes slowly, and close them. Then open them again, this time with awareness. Take a few slow, deep breaths and remind yourself that you wanted to get up early this morning to perform this ritual.

🍃 Get up, put on a robe (make sure you're warm and comfortable), and stretch slowly or shake your body loose from the night's sleep.

🍃 Light a candle and stick of incense to begin creating your sacred space.

🍃 Play your music.

🍃 Sit on your meditation pillow, in a comfortable position. If you are doing this ritual with a partner, sit opposite each other, holding hands.

🍃 Relax for a few moments, eyes closed, watching the movement of your breath. When you feel calm and quiet, go on to the next step.

🍃 Begin to focus gently and effortlessly on the day ahead, breathing slowly and deeply. Go through the day, envisioning each moment. See if one difficult challenge presents itself (for instance, you have too much to do today and not enough time to do it, or your child is home sick from school). Look at the thoughts as you would look at a passing landscape through a car window. Let the thoughts come and go.

🍃 Pay attention to your body. How does your body react to these thoughts? Do you feel any tight spots? A constriction in your chest, stomach cramps, heart palpitations, a simple tensing of the muscles of your jaw and neck? Zoom in on the part of your day's vision that is causing your body pain. This is what you will transform in the ritual. (If you find more than one painful area, take them one at a time. Don't try to do too much at once.)

🍃 Keep breathing calmly and deeply. Create a mental picture of the difficult moment that you're dreading in your day to come. (We'll use the example of a stressful project at work, one you have to work on with difficult people.) Now release the image, let it travel through your *chakras,* allowing the energy of each *chakra* to transform it.

The Root of Creation

☙ Let your awareness dwell in the first *chakra,* in your genitals. Relax your genital muscles into the earth and allow them to feel vibrant, ready, grounded. Here is where you will generate the vision.

☙ See the difficult situation existing inside your first *chakra,* let it resonate, and begin the transformation.

☙ Say (to yourself or out loud), "There is enough time, money, trust, love, understanding to heal this situation."

☙ Envision the scene filled with a sense of abundance and resolution. Feel that this is already true, that it has happened. You should not feel pressure to *make* it happen. When you have this vision firmly in mind, go on to the next *chakra.*

The Flowing Stream

☙ Let your awareness dwell in your navel area. Breathe into your belly and soften the muscles.

☙ See the difficult situation existing inside your second *chakra,* and surround it with a sea of fluidity and flexibility.

☙ Say to yourself, "I am open to change."

☙ See yourself enjoying the flow of conversation. See everyone finding the place of flexibility in the situation, being open to changing opinions and positions, adapting effortlessly to the currents of energy that your vision carries. When you have an image of the situation transformed by openness and possibility, go on to the next *chakra.*

The Radiant Sun

☙ Let your awareness dwell in your solar plexus. Breathe into your solar plexus, feel it expanding, relaxed, and powerful.

☙ See the difficult situation existing inside your third *chakra,* and infuse it with energy and power.

☙ Say to yourself, "I have all the energy I need to complete this project."

☙ See yourself and all the people in your image feeling alive and on purpose. You make correct choices, you are innovative and responsible. Your authority is respected. When you have an image of the situation transformed through positive action, go on to the next *chakra*.

The Pulse of Life

&. Let your awareness dwell in the center of your chest, in your heart area. Open your chest, relaxing the muscles that surround your heart. Feel your heart opening to receive.

&. See the difficult situation existing inside your fourth *chakra*, and surround the image and everyone in it with love and acceptance.

&. Say to yourself, "I am ready to create a common ground." Don't dwell on successes or failures, or petty antagonism, but simply appreciate what everyone has done so far.

&. Let yourself see how much happier everyone is when they feel acknowledged, how much more motivated they are toward positive results. When you have an image of the situation transformed by love and acceptance, move on to the next *chakra*.

The Song of the Soul

&. Let your awareness dwell in your throat. Relax your throat, your jaw.

&. See the difficult situation existing inside your fifth *chakra*, and allow everyone in the vision to express their truth in a creative way.

&. Say to yourself, "I enjoy sharing my creative ideas and hearing others express theirs."

&. See the comical side of the situation. Exaggerate the image if you need to. See everyone dancing a jig around the office, diving off desks, flying paper airplanes over cubicle walls. See thought balloons coming out of their heads, filled with brilliant, witty, outrageous ideas. When your image is transformed by laughter and creative expression, go on to the next *chakra*.

The Full Moon

&. Let your awareness dwell in your third eye, the area between your eyebrows.

&. Feel the eye opening, taking in the scene with great objectivity. See the difficult situation existing inside your sixth *chakra*, and envision everyone in the scene feeling connected, integrated between body, mind, and Spirit.

❧ Say to yourself, "I act to realize my vision with intention and purpose. I am clear in my action and make the right choices."

❧ Now you see the big picture; you are no longer bogged down by details or identifying with criticism. You are witnessing the situation but are not lost in it. You have achieved a balance between understanding the context and listening to your intuitive guidance. Move on to the next *chakra*.

The Open Sky

❧ Let your awareness dwell in the top of your head. Relax the muscles of your scalp and allow this *chakra* to open, like a cup waiting to be filled. See the newly transformed situation existing as pure potential inside your seventh *chakra*.

❧ Say to yourself, "I am ready to receive what I need to heal this situation."

❧ See yourself linked with everyone in your image at a soul level. Your Spirits are connecting. You all have a role to play in this situation, and you all know exactly what needs to be done to move the project further. See all of you surrendering your ego needs ("I know better") to your greater purpose: harmony. You become one Spirit. You respect each other. All is well. When you have created this joyous image, let it go out of the top of your head and into the universe, knowing that it has already been accomplished. Move into your day with calm and certainty of success.

Completion

❧ Review your meditation. Have you created a joyous, harmonious day? Do you feel ready to move into your day with ease and confidence? If you're not quite ready, move through the *chakras* again to heal any remaining block.

❧ Take a moment to center yourself. Breathe calmly and deeply for a few more moments, and allow yourself to come back to the present moment. If you are working with a partner, wait for your partner to be ready and then share your visions with each other.

❧ You can adapt this meditation to your needs. If you have several difficult issues to deal with today, make a list and start at the beginning. Take the first: "Too much to do." Check your body's responses. Do you feel a tightness, a fear somewhere, related to that issue? Let's say it is in the solar plexus. Go there. Do the releasing in that *chakra,* then send out the vision from that *chakra* into the universe. Proceed in a similar way for the other issues, just relaxing and opening the *chakra* that needs it the most.

REMEMBER THESE SIMPLE TRUTHS

You can create each day of your life in this way, as a process of mastery and enjoyment, appreciating the inherent perfection of each moment in this apparently imperfect world. The ecstatic lifestyle doesn't call for putting on rose-colored glasses and insisting that *everything* is wonderful. It does call for expanding into your Sky Mind, seeing the big picture, and remembering a few simple truths. Every day, remember:

❧ You have come into this world to fulfill a unique purpose, role, or mission. Look for yours. And expect to be energized when you find it.

❧ Life doesn't have to be earned. It is already given. If you don't like the way yours is going, you can reclaim it and make changes.

❧ If your intention is clear, you can create magic. You do not have to be a victim. You can choose and act with power. You can do what you need to do. You can change what you need to change.

❧ Before starting any important project, or process, breathe deeply. Recall the positive and enlivening reasons that led to this step. Renew your commitment as often as necessary.

❧ Avoid sabotaging your goals and energy by mistakenly using your negative inner critic as a counselor.

❧ Love yourself, whatever you do. Have faith in who

you are now and in who you can become. And give
yourself credit for all that you have accomplished so far.

SEE EVERYTHING AS AN OPPORTUNITY
FOR AWAKENING

The Tantric approach recognizes that *everything* in life, every
moment, every experience, every situation, is an opportunity for
further awakening. This point of view makes all of life a matrix
for learning, healing, and growth. Here are some simple things
that you can do, even when things are difficult and stressful, to
change your *experience* by changing your *perspective*.

First, breathe deeply and relax. Stand back from the situation. Notice your judgments of "good" and "bad." Now see if
you can describe what is happening objectively, just as it is.
When you can see and objectively describe a situation without
judgment, then you can experience and relate to it objectively.
And what before seemed lousy or awful may now seem "inter-
esting," "fascinating," or even "amusing."

TAKE AN ECSTASY BREAK

Misery thrives on routine and predictability. Ecstasy loves new
scenery, surprise, and adventure. You don't have to change your
whole life all at once. But you can start where you are, in any
moment. Here are some simple ways to interrupt a dull routine
and bring a bit of freshness, and maybe adventure, into an otherwise predictable day.

TAKE FIVE ✿ Begin by taking a break from what you're doing, even if it's only five minutes. Go out of the office or the
house, breathe fresh air if you can find it, or take a walk around
the block or to a place you do not usually go. Take a few moments to go within, feel your breath, your body, your *chakras*.
Then notice your surroundings, the people, houses, or buildings
you see, the sky above. Listen, look, smell, feel. Remember that
this moment is real, pregnant with possibilities.

PLAN ECSTATIC BREAKS ✿ Now you can plan a longer
break. Schedule one day a week to go out in nature, even if you
can get only to a city park. If you can, plan a weekend trip to a
place you are excited about, that you would love to see. Perhaps

it is near a river or in the mountains or by the sea. Then, plan a longer and even more exciting trip, perhaps to a place you have always wanted to see. Maybe it is New York, San Francisco, Paris, Bali. Design the dream trip of a lifetime for yourself, with your lover or family. Notice how much energy and *joi de vivre* ("joy of life") this brings. Choose to live your dreams.

FIND AN ECSTATIC COMRADE ～ Choose a friend or partner as an ecstatic comrade. Agree to enhance each other's level of joy in life. For example, agree that after work on Monday one of you will pick up the other and take him or her on an adventure. It can be anything—a scenic drive out of town, tickets to a concert, an exotic meal. Whatever it is should be a surprise, something out of the ordinary rut, something that wakes you up from the predictable routine. Next time, reverse roles.

MAKE YOUR COMMITMENT TO ECSTASY NOW

Our true function as human beings is to connect life with Spirit and Spirit with life. And the miracle of it is that we may be the only creatures on this planet who are even capable of doing this. By choosing what is right and good for ourselves, our friends and families, our community, and our planet, we awaken from the anti-ecstatic conspiracy; we open the door to ecstasy.

When you understand what it means to be orgasmic in your everyday life, to live like a lover, you begin to ask yourself this basic question about everything you do: "Does this turn me on?" When you find yourself doing something, not because it turns you on, but for anti-ecstatic reasons—to meet your parents' expectations, out of social obligation or fear of criticism, to please your boss or impress your friends—stop: Remember that when you leave *yourself* out of situations in this way, there is no joy in them. By living for others, you miss out on your own life, the life you can have if you dare to choose it, the life that can bring you, *and those around you,* real pleasure, joy, and fulfillment. Make your commitment to ecstasy now.

PURPOSE

Here is a way to prepare yourself fully for success in the many actions of your daily life. You can use this process as preparation for making important choices, performing important tasks, or for discovering what is best or right for you in any situation. The more you practice this process, the easier and more effective it becomes.

PREPARATION

꙳ Before you make a move, take stock of the situation.

꙳ Do one of the Sky Mind exercises in this book as a way to clear yourself of distracting or troubling thoughts.

꙳ Connect with your inner Witness.

PRACTICE

꙳ Begin with a Heart Salutation (page 75).

꙳ Feel the energy of the situation you are dealing with, then ask for guidance from each *chakra,* as outlined below. (I have listed four questions below for each *chakra,* but you can formulate your own questions as they come to you.)

꙳ Listen to or feel each *chakra* for the responses.

The Root of Creation

꙳ Does this turn me on?

꙳ Am I getting what I need?

꙳ Does this feel safe?

꙳ Do I feel connected (to my body, this project, this person, and so on)?

The Flowing Stream

꙳ What is my gut feeling here?

꙳ Does this feel comfortable?

꙳ Do I feel in balance or off balance here?

꙳ If I knew exactly what the right move is, what would it be?

The Radiant Sun

- Do I respect myself here?
- Am I gaining or losing power in this situation?
- How do I stand my ground here?
- Can I afford to do this?

The Pulse of Life

- Is this (person, project) attractive or desirable to me?
- Am I taking care of myself?
- Is this good for me? For the other(s)?
- Is love happening here?

The Song of the Soul

- Is this the truth? On my part? On the other's part?
- Is this the creative solution?
- Am I following my bliss here?
- Am I (or others) being authentic, speaking my (their) true feelings?

The Full Moon

- Do I know where this is leading?
- Is this clear for me? Do I really understand?
- Am I getting the whole picture?
- What is my inner guidance saying?

The Open Sky

- Is this furthering my spiritual evolution?
- Is this helping others, the world?
- Does this situation open me to light and Spirit?
- What does my higher self say in this matter?

POINTERS

- Notice when one *chakra* overpowers another (for example, your mind tells your heart how to behave) or when one *chakra* is not getting a voice at all. Act only after you have consulted and listened to all of your *chakras*.
- Though I have given four questions for each *chakra,* you may feel that one is enough.
- Keep a journal called Keys to Success, and trace the steps of

that journey over a three-month period. Enjoy noticing your progress in making clear decisions.

CREATE YOUR OWN CULTURE OF ECSTASY, YOUR OWN ECSTATIC SUPPORT GROUP

Gather with friends and weave your energies together with the intention of building community and supporting your mutual quest to live ecstatic lives and bring forth your highest potential. Meet, share, discuss, eat, and play together. Explore and experiment. Make it formal sometimes and informal other times. Building authentic bonds and deep intimacy is a step-by-step process. Be committed, creative, and daring.

The talking stick is a useful tool traditionally used by some American Indian groups. It is passed from person to person in a group and only the person holding it may speak. When he or she has spoken and been heard, the stick is passed along to whoever wishes to respond. This prevents those interruptions that commonly prevent groups from sinking down to deeper levels of communication. There are many creative forms of communication to explore, and you can make up your own.

Get together for an evening of creative expression. Read poetry and prose, things you and your friends have written, or things you have read that inspire you. Make a circle and have each person contribute one "gift." A song, a story, a poem, an insight. Get together for rituals or parties. Meet in your homes or in natural settings. Be offbeat. Have a moonlight picnic in a field or on the beach. Dance together, breathe together, sing, meditate, and share your truths. Relate to each other as ecstatic beings and create ecstatic spaces.

Make cooking a creative, communal affair that engages everyone, a time of ease, laughter, and nourishment for all. Let everyone add his or her own special flair to the evolving recipe.

Trade skills, barter, and exchange with each other, build something together. These are powerful ways to build community. Here are some basic ingredients of ecstatic support groups:

- An exceptional welcome for everyone.
- Regular meetings, a clear structure, and a commitment from the group to stay in the structure. Or an agreement for informality if this is desired.
- Long, enjoyable meals prepared with everyone's love and served in beautiful settings.
- A commitment to ecstasy.
- Keeping a sense of humor or a commitment not to let the gathering degenerate into chronic seriousness.
- Play.
- A commitment to sharing your truth, and accepting others in their truth.
- Enjoying each other's differences.
- Exploring and experimenting with inner male and female. For example, you could have a gathering in which the men in the group play the "feminine" roles, doing the cooking and serving, and the women play the "masculine" roles, taking authority for discussions and decisions that night.
- Create a sacred space for your group (see Chapter 5) in which an agreement of total acceptance is made, all may act from innocence, with no judgments or expectations.

Remember, it takes a strong intention to create community in our society. But if you do this, you will notice changes in yourself and others. The little sacrifices and inconveniences we make to establish real community are simply the rubbing away of our rough edges, the edges that stand in the way of our relationships with others. When you practice community in the ongoing gathering of your new tribe, you learn to communicate more freely, to listen more deeply from the heart, to be more relaxed with others and within yourself. You feel more nurtured and less threatened by others. You realize you are not alone in your life. You discover more clearly who you are.

This kind of gathering is the most basic and ancient form of community, as old as the first fire made by humans, around which they must have sat in gratitude and awe. We can do the same today. We can gather together, and discover and build community anew with each other.

RESOURCES FOR ECSTATIC MOMENTS

MUSIC

Margot Anand has created a music compilation recording to accompany *The Art of Everyday Ecstasy*. Featuring music from her workshops, it will guide you to your own experience of everyday ecstasy. *Music for Everyday Ecstasy*, a four-part journey in sound, is available from Spring Hill Music. To order, call (800) 427-7680.

Margot's CD *SkyDancing Tantra: A Call to Bliss* offers a blend of her own voice singing the sounds of the *chakras*, accompanied by synthesizer, saxophone, flute, and drums. It is intended for ecstatic moments. To order, call (415) 924-8306 or fax to (415) 924-8936.

AUDIOTAPES

The audiotape series *The Art of Sexual Magic* offers a wealth of rituals and visualizations developed and taught by Margot. To order, call Sounds True at (800) 333-9185. The audiotape *The Art of Sexual Ecstasy* has two of Margot's guided meditations from her book *The Art of Sexual Ecstasy* with musical accompaniment by Steven Halpern, one of today's foremost New Age musicians. To order, call Inner Peace Music at (415) 485-5321.

LECTURE TAPES

On Healing and Relationships, a panel discussion with Margot Anand, Harville Hendrix, and Brian Weiss. *The Seven Rhythms of Love* and *The Art of Living Ecstasy: SkyDancing Tantra,* workshops by Margot Anand. All three recorded by Sounds True at the Body & Soul Conference, Los Angeles, October 1996. To order call Sounds True at (800) 333-9185. "Achieving Ecstasy, Freeing Creativity," a workshop by Margot Anand. To order call Sound Horizons at (800) 524-8355.

BOOKS

The Art of Sexual Ecstasy and *The Art of Sexual Magic* by Margot Anand are available at major bookstores nationwide. To order from the publisher directly, contact Penguin Putnam Publishing at (800) 788-6262. To order by mail, write to Penguin Putnam Publishing, Book Orders, 200 Madison Avenue, New York, NY 10016.

PERSONAL RESOURCES

To connect with an ecstatic coach, an ecstatic support system, or to learn directly how to awaken your ecstatic self in every moment of your life, please contact the worldwide network of Sky-Dancing Institutes.

Margot Anand and the Certified SkyDancing Trainers offer a wide range of seminars, products, and educational programs.

Visit SkyDancing's Web site at www.skydancing.com

SDI USA. 524 San Anselmo Ave. Suite 133, San Anselmo, CA 94960. Tel: (800) 974-2584 or (415) 456-7310, Fax: (415) 456-9599, e-mail: SDIUSA@aol.com

SDI NEW YORK. Joan Lakin Associates, 175 West 12th Street, New York, NY. 10011. Tel: (212) 929-0096, Fax: (212) 242-7581

SDI SWITZERLAND. Aman Schroeter, Muehlegasse 33, 8001 Zurich, Switzerland. Tel/Fax: 011 411 261 0160

SDI FRANCOPHONE. Nital Brinkley, C.P. 233, 1066 Epalinges, Switzerland. Tel/Fax: 011 4121 784 2033, e-mail: nbrinkle-@worldcom.ch.

SDI ENGLAND. John Hawken, Lower Grumbla Farm, Newbridge, Penzance, Cornwall TR20 8QX, United Kingdom. Tel: 011 441 736 788304, Fax: 011 441 736 786260

SKYDANCING TANTRA FOR GAY AND HETEROSEXUAL PEOPLE. Institute for Meditation and Tantra, Armin Heining, Krausstrassel 5, 90443 Nuernberg, Germany. Tel: 0911 244 8616, Fax: 0911 244 8588, e-mail: Armin-Christoph. Heining@T-Online.de

SDI HOLLAND/BELGIUM. Renee Koopmans, Postbus 14, 6585 ZG Mook, Holland. Tel: 011 3124 6962890, Fax: 011 3124 6962830, e-mail: kursuspb@worldaccess.nl, Web site: new-agent.nl/koopmans

SDI CANADA. Robert and Lilana Baillod, BP 1154, Pointe Claire, Quebec, H9S 4H9 Canada. Tel: (514) 273-2434, Fax: (514) 273-0507

SDI GERMANY. Yatro Werner, Feichtstrasse 15, 81735 Munich, Germany. Tel: 011 4989 4365 1601, Fax: 011 4989 4365 1602

MORE RESOURCES

MICHAEL HARRISON. "In Flight" (Fortuna Records) and "From Ancient Worlds" (New Albion Records). Order CDs from Sound Spaces, (415) 383-1994.

ARIEL KALMA. "Gourmet Sax," "Flute for the Soul," and "Serenity." Order CDs from Nightingale Records, P.O. Box 30158, Tucson, AZ 85751.

PAUL RAMANA DAS AND MARILENA SILBEY. "Ecstatica 1", a soundtrack for lovers. Order from Living Ecstasy Institute, P.O. Box 613, Fairfax, CA 94978. Tel: (415) 499-1769, e-mail: yaluie@pacbell.net, Web site: www.hotstuffnyc.com/u-music

KAVEESHA. "Body Love," "Tantra: A Partnership in Meditation," and "The Channel of Understanding"(with Dhyan Yogi, M.D.). Order audiotapes from Osho's Mail Order, 1449 West Highway 89A, Sedona, AZ 86336. Tel: (520) 204-5628, fax: (520) 204-0043, e-mail: oshos@sedona.net

The vast wisdom of Osho is available in the form of books, audiotapes, and videotapes from **OSHO'S MAIL ORDER**, 1449 West Highway 89A, Sedona, AZ 86336, tel: (520) 204-5628, fax: (520) 204-0043, e-mail: oshos@sedona.net and from **OSHO VIHA MEDITATION CENTER**, distributor of all of Osho's discourses/teachings in the form of books, tapes, videos, and CDs: P.O. Box 352, Mill Valley, CA 94942. Tel: (415) 381-9861, fax: 381-6746, e-mail: oshoavi@aol.com

RAZ AND LISA INGRASEI. The Hoffman Quadrinity Process, taught at the Hoffman Institute, 223 San Anselmo Avenue, Ste. 4, San Anselmo, CA 94960. Tel: (415) 485-5220. Produces transformational levels of emotional freedom, compassion, and sprititual awakening for all participants.

HAROLD DULL. "Watsu, Freeing the Body in Water," "Bodywork Tantra," videos: "Watsu, I, II and III" and "Bodywork Tantra," available from Worldwide Aquatic Bodywork Association, Harbin Hot Springs, P.O. Box 889, Middletown, CA 95461. Tel: (707) 987-3801, fax (707) 987-9638.

ANNE CHANDLER. "Chakra Rock," Eagle's Quest Tai Chi Center, 147 Barnshed Lane, Guildford, CT 06437. Tel. (203) 457-9511.

TANTRA.COM. Tantric literature, products, videos, and CDs, Box 1818, Sebastopol, CA 95472. Tel: (800) 982-6872, fax: (707) 829-9542.

RAVEN RECORDS. (Gabrielle Roth's music) 744 Broad Street, Room 1815, Newark, NJ 07102. Tel: (201) 642-7942, fax: (201) 621-2185.

SOUNDS TRUE. P.O. Box 8010, Boulder, CO 80306. Tel: (800) 333-9185 or (303) 665-3151, fax: (303) 665-5292, e-mail: soundstrue@aol.com

BIBLIOGRAPHY

Achterberg, Jeanne, Ph.D.; Barbara Dossey, R.N., M.S., FAAN; and Kolkmeier, Leslie, R.N. Med. *Rituals of Healing: Using Imagery for Health and Wellness.* New York: Bantam Books, 1994.

Ackerman, Diane. *A Natural History of the Senses.* New York: Random House, 1990.

Adi Da, Samraj, Master. *See My Brightness Face to Face.* Middletown: The Dawn Horse Press, 1997.

Allione, Tsultrim. *Women of Wisdom.* London: Arkana, 1984.

Austen, Hallie Iglehart. *The Heart of the Goddess: Art, Myth and Meditations of the World's Sacred Feminine.* Berkeley: Wingbow Press, 1990.

Beck, Renee, and Metrick, Barbara Sydney. *The Art of Ritual.* Berkeley: Celestial Arts, 1990.

Blank, Joani. *Femalia.* San Francisco: Down There Press, 1993.

Bonheim, Jalaja. *The Serpent and the Wave: A Guide to Movement Meditation.* Berkeley: Celestial Arts, 1992.

Brauer, Alan P., M.D., and Brauer, Donna J. *The ESO Ecstasy Program.* New York: Warner Books, 1990.

Bruyere, Rosalyn L. *Wheels of Light.* New York: Simon & Schuster, 1989.

Bucke, Richard Maurice, M.D. *Cosmic Consciousness: A Study in the Evolution of the Human Mind.* Secaucus: Citadel Press, 1961.

Campbell, Don. *The Mozart Effect.* New York: Avon Books, 1997.

Camphausen, Rufus C. *The Yoni: Sacred Symbol of Female Creative Power.* Rochester: Inner Traditions, 1996.

Chang, Stephen T., M.D. *The Complete System of Self-Healing: Internal Exercises.* San Francisco: Tao Publishing, 1986.

Chödrön, Pema. *Start Where You Are: A Guide to Compassionate Living.* Boston: Shambhala, 1994.

Chopra, Deepak, M.D., *The Path to Love.* New York: Harmony Books, 1997.

_____. *Ageless Body, Timeless Mind.* New York: Harmony Books, 1993.

Cordes, Helen, and Walljasper, Jay. *Goodlife: Mastering the Art of Everyday Living.* Minneapolis: Utne Reader Books, 1997.

Csikszentmihalyi, Mihaly. *Flow, the Psychology of Optimal Experience.* Harper & Row: New York, 1990.

Dalai Lama, The, and Galen Rowel. *My Tibet.* Berkeley: University of California Press, 1990.

Douglas, Nik, and Slinger, Penny. *Sexual Secrets: The Alchemy of Ecstasy.* New York: Destiny Books, 1979.

Douglas, Nik. *Spiritual Sex.* New York: Pocket Books, 1997.

Dowman, Keith. *Sky Dancer: The Secret Life and Songs of the Lady Yeshe Tsogyel.* London: Routledge & Kegan Paul, 1984.

Dowman, Keith, and Sonam Paljor. *The Divine Madman: The Sublime Life and Songs of Drukpa Kunley.* London: Rider, 1980.

Driver, Tom, F. *The Magic of Ritual: Our Need for Liberating Rites that Transform Our Lives and Our Communities.* New York: Harper Collins, 1991.

Dull, Harold. *Watsu: Freeing the Body in Water.* Middletown: Harbin Springs Publishing, 1993.

Eisler, Riane. *The Chalice and the Blade: Our History, Our Future.* San Francisco: Harper & Row, 1987.

_____. *Sacred Pleasure: Sex, Myth, and the Politics of the Body—New Paths to Power and Love.* New York: HarperCollins, 1996.

Eisler, Riane, and Loye, David. *The Partnership Way: New Tools for Living and Learning, Healing Our Families, Our Communities and Our World.* New York: HarperCollins, 1990.

Fryba, Mirko. *The Art of Happiness: Teachings of Buddhist Psychology.* Boston: Shambhala, 1987.

Gadon, Elinor, W. *The Once and Future Goddess.* New York: Harper-Collins, 1989.

Gawain, Shakti. *Meditations: Creative Visualization and Meditation Exercises to Enrich Your Life.* San Rafael: New World Library, 1991.

Gershon, David, and Straub, Gail. *Empowerment: The Art of Creating Your Life as You Want It.* New York: Dell Publishing, 1989.

Griscom, Chris. *Ecstasy Is a New Frequency.* New York: Simon & Schuster, 1987.

Grof, Stanislav, M.D. *Beyond the Brain.* Albany: State University of New York Press, 1985.

Groff, Stanislav, M.D. with Bennett, Hal Zina. *The Holotrophic Mind: The Three Levels of Human Consciousness and How They Shape Our Lives.* New York: HarperSanFrancisco, 1990.

Grof, Stanislav, M.D., and Grof, Christina. *Spiritual Emergency: When Personal Transformation Becomes a Crisis.* Los Angeles: Jeremy Tarcher, Inc., 1989.

Hammer, Marc. *The Jeshua Letters: A Journey of Awakening.* Freeland: Kendra Press, 1994.

Harvey, Andrew. *The Way of Passion: A Celebration of Rumi*. Berkeley: Frog Ltd., 1994.

Heifetz, Ronald A., M.D. *Leadership Without Easy Answers*. Cambridge: Harvard University Press, 1994.

Hirschman, Jane R., and Munter, Carol H. *When Women Stop Hating Their Bodies*. New York: Random House, 1995.

Hoffman, Bob. *No One Is to Blame: Freedom from Compulsive Self-Defeating Behavior*. Oakland: Recycling Books, 1988.

Hope, Murry. *The Psychology of Ritual*. Longmead, GB: Element Books, 1988.

Johari, Harish. *Chakras: Energy Centers of Transformation*. Rochester: Destiny Books, 1987.

Johnson, Robert A. *Ecstasy: Understanding the Psychology of Joy*. New York: HarperCollins, 1987.

Joy, W. Brugh, M.D. *Joy's Way*. Los Angeles: J.P. Tarcher, 1979.

Judith, Anodea. *Wheels of Life: A User's Guide to the Chakra System*. St. Paul: Llewellyn Publications, 1996.

Judith, Anodea, and Vega, Selene. *The Sevenfold Journey: Reclaiming Mind, Body and Spirit Through the Chakras*. Freedom, CA: The Crossing Press, 1993.

Kabat-Zinn, Jon *Wherever You Go, There You Are: Mindfulness Meditation in Everyday Life*. New York: Hyperion, 1994.

Keen, Sam. *Hymns to an Unknown God: Awakening the Spirit in Everyday Life*. New York: Bantam Books, 1994.

Khan, Hazrat Inayat. *The Dance of the Soul: Sufi Sayings*. Delhi: Motilal Banarsidass Publishers, 1993.

_____. *The Mysticism of Music, Sound and Word: the Sufi Message*. Delhi: Motilal Banarsidass Publishers, 1988.

Khyentse, Dilgo. *Enlightened Courage*. Ithaca: Snow Lion Publications, 1993.

Kingston, Karen. *Creating Sacred Space With Feng Shui*. New York: Broadway Books, 1997.

Laski, Margharita. *Ecstasy in Secular and Religious Experience*. Los Angeles: Jeremy Tarcher, Inc., 1961.

Leonard, George. *Education and Ecstasy*. Berkeley: North Atlantic Books, 1968.

Leonard, George, and Murphy, Michael. *The Life We Are Given: A Long-Term Program for Realizing the Potential of Body, Mind, Heart and Soul*. New York: Putnam, 1995.

Leonard, Jim. *The Skill of Happiness: Creating Daily Ecstasy with Vivation*. Fond du Lac: Three Blue Herons Publishing, Inc., 1996.

Levy, Mark. *Technicians of Ecstasy*. Norfolk: Bramble Books, 1993.

Linn, Denise. *Sacred Space: Clearing and Enhancing the Energy of Your Home*. New York: Ballantine Books, 1995.

Macy, Joanna. *Despair and Personal Power in the Nuclear Age.* Philadelphia: New Society Publishers, 1983.

Maltz, Wendy, ed. *Passionate Hearts: The Poetry of Sexual Love.* Novato, CA: New World Library, 1996.

Milkman, Harvey, and Sunderwirth, Stanley. *Pathways to Pleasure: The Consciousness and Chemistry of Optimal Living.* New York: Lexington Books, 1993.

Mookerjee, Ajit, and Khanna, Madhu. *The Tantric Way.* England: Little, Brown and Company, 1977.

Moore, Thomas. *Care of the Soul: A Guide for Cultivating Depth and Sacredness in Everyday Life.* New York: HarperCollins, 1992.

_____. *The Re-Enchantment of Everyday Life.* New York: HarperCollins, 1996.

Moss, Richard, M.D. *The Second Miracle: Intimacy, Spirituality and Conscious Relationships.* Berkeley: Celestial Arts, 1995.

_____. *The I That Is We: Awakening to Higher Energies Through Unconditional Love.* Millbrae, CA: Celestial Arts, 1981.

Myss, Carolyn, Ph.D. *Anatomy of the Spirit.* New York, Harmony Books, 1996.

Nadeen, Satyam. *From Onions to Pearls: A Journal of Awakening and Deliverance.* Taos: New Freedom Press, 1996.

Naranjo, Claudio. *The End of Patriarchy and the Dawning of a Triune Society.* Oakland: Amber Lotus, 1994.

Naranjo, Claudio, and Ornstein, Robert E. *On the Psychology of Meditation.* New York: The Viking Press, 1971.

Nisker, Wes "Scoop." *Crazy Wisdom.* Berkeley: Ten Speed Press, 1990.

Norbu, Thinley. *White Sail: Crossing the Waves of Ocean Mind to the Serene Continent of the Triple Gems.* Boston: Shambhala, 1992.

Osborn, Diane K. *Reflections on the Art of Living: A Joseph Campbell Companion.* New York, HarperCollins, 1991.

Osborn, Carol. *Enough Is Enough: Simple Solutions for Complex People.* San Rafael: New World Library, 1992.

Osho. *The Book of the Secrets.* New York: Harper & Row, 1976.

_____. *Meditation: The Art of Ecstasy.* New York: Harper & Row, 1976.

_____. *Vigyan Bhairau Tantra.* Cologne: The Rebel Publishing House.

_____. *Meditation, the First and Last Freedom.* Koregaon Park: The Rebel Publishing House, 1988.

_____. *The Buddha: The Emptiness of the Heart.* Cologne: The Rebel Publishing House, 1989.

Pierrakos, John, M.D. *Core Energetics.* Mendocino: LifeRhythm, 1987.

Pierre, Rambach. *The Secret Message of Tantric Buddhism.* New York: Rizzoli, 1979.

Poonja, H.W.L. *Wake up and Roar.* Lucknow: Univeral Booksellers, 1992.

Redfield, James. *The Celestine Prophecy.* Hoover, CA: Satori Publishing, 1993.

Reilly, Patricia Lynn. *A God Who Looks Like Me: Discovering a Woman-Affirming Spirituality.* New York: Ballantine Books, 1995.

Resnick, Stella, Ph.D. *The Pleasure Zone.* Berkeley: Conari Press, 1997.

Rinpoche, Sogyal. *The Tibetan Book of Living and Dying.* New York: HarperCollins, 1992.

Rinpoche, Gyutrul. *The Secret Oral Teachings on Generating the Deity.* Taipei: SMC Publishing, Inc., 1992.

Robbins, Tom. *Jitterbug Perfume.* New York: Bantam Books, 1984.

Robertson, Ron. *The Birthplace.* Virginia Beach: Inkhorn, 1995.

Rock, William Pennel. *Performing Inside Out.* Acton: Between Two Worlds Press, 1990.

Roman, Sanaya. *Living With Joy: Keys to Personal Power and Spiritual Transformation.* Tiburon: H.J. Kramer, Inc., 1986.

Rossman, Martin L., M.D. *Healing Yourself: A Step-by-Step Program for Better Health Through Imagery.* New York: Walker and Company, 1987.

Roth, Gabrielle. *Maps to Ecstasy: Teachings of an Urban Shaman.* San Rafael: New World Library, 1989.

Rumi, Jelaluddin. *Love Is a Stranger.* Brattleboro, VT: Threshold Books, 1993.

_____. *Feeling the Shoulder of the Lion.* Putney, VT: Threshold Books, 1991.

Sangpo, Khetsun. *Tantric Practice in Nying-Ma.* Ithaca, NY: Snow Lion Publications, 1982.

Sannella, Lee, M.D. *The Kundalini Experience.* Lower Lake, CA: Integral Publishing, 1987.

Shaw, Miranda. *Passionate Enlightenment: Women in Tantric Buddhism.* Princeton: Princeton University Press, 1994.

Sheldrake, Rupert. *The Rebirth of Nature: The Greening of Science and God.* Rochester: Park Street Press, 1991.

Shiva, Shahram. T. *Rending the Veil: Literal and Poetic Translations of Rumi.* Prescott: Hohm Press, 1995.

Shulgin, Alexander, and Ann Shulgin. *Pihkal: A Chemical Love Story.* Berkeley: Transform Press, 1991.

Sidi, Shaykh Muhammad al-Jamal ar-Rifa'i as-Shadhili. *Music of the Soul: Sufi Teachings.* Santa Fe: Sidi Muhammad Press, 1994.

Simon, Sidney B. Dr., and Suzanne Simon. *Forgiveness: How to Make Peace with Your Past and Get on with Your Life.* New York: Warner Books, 1990.

Stone, Merlin. *When God Was a Woman.* San Diego: Harcourt Brace Jovanovich, 1976.

Suarez, Rick, Ph.D., Roger, C. Mills, Darlene Stewart, M.S. *Sanity, Insanity and Comon Sense: The Groundbreaking New Approach to Happiness.* New York: Fawcett Columbine, 1980.

Tsogyal, Lady. *Dakini Teachings.* Boston: Shambhala, 1990.

Wall, Vicky. *The Miracle of Colour Healing.* London: HarperCollins, 1990.

Walsch, Neale Donald. *Conversations with God.* Charlottesville: Hampton Roads Publishing Co., Inc., 1995.

Whitman, Walt. *Leaves of Grass.* New York: Rinehart & Co., 1959.

Williamson, Marianne. *A Woman's Worth.* New York: Ballantine Books, 1993.

INDEX

Choices, making, 253–54
Christ, 26, 76
Christ consciousness, 20
Clinton, Hillary Rodham, 43–44
Clothing and empowerment, 191
Coiled snake as symbol of first
    chakra, 152
Comfort, 18
Commitment to ecstasy, 276–88
    beginning the day, ritual for,
        277–82
    ecstasy breaks, taking, 283–84
    knowing what to do (a *chakra*
        consultation in daily life),
        285–87
    seeing everything as an
        opportunity for awakening, 283
    simple truths to remember,
        282–83
    support group, ecstatic, 287–88
Compulsions, 154
Conflict, willingness to engage in,
    189
Conscious relaxation, 178
Coordination, 247
Criticism, inner, 251–53
    exercise to pacify your, 252–53
Crown center, *see* Seventh *chakra*
Cultural creatives, 20–21
Curie, Madame, 247

Depression, 228
*Despair and Personal Power in the
    Nuclear Age* (Macy), 38
Dragon as symbol of first *chakra*, 152
Dull, Harold, 270–71

Ecstasy:
    anti-ecstatic conspiracy, 35–47
    of awakening and spaciousness, *see*
        Seventh *chakra*
    commitment to, *see* Commitment
        to ecstasy
    common experiences of, 19
    the dark side of, 25–27
    definitions of, 18–19, 20
    of flow, *see* Second *chakra*
    of insight, *see* Sixth *chakra*
    of inspiration, *see* Fifth *chakra*

of love and surrender, *see* Fourth
    chakra
of orgasm, *see* First *chakra*
personal descriptions of, 27–31
of power, *see* Third *chakra*
as transforming experience, 21–24
Ecstatic Awakenings, 11, 23, 266
Ecstatic partnership, 48–66
Ego, 270
Einstein, Albert, 36–37, 247
Eisler, Riane, 40
Elegance, 2
Elements, four, 123–24
Eliade, Mircea, 106
Ellis, Havelock, 42
Emotional intelligence, 247
Empowerment, *see* Power
End of Patriarchy, The (Naranjo), 39
Energy centers, *see* *Chakra* system;
    individual chakras
Energy-ecstasy connection, 67–85
Engrassi, Raz, 267
Environmental problems, 37
EveryDay Ecstasy, 85, 266
    the *chakras* and, *see* *Chakra* system;
        individual chakras
    commitment to, *see* Commitment
        to ecstasy
    cultivating, 266
    defined, 11, 85
    Ecstatic Awakenings distinguished
        from, 11
    exercise, 32–34
    Tantric keys to, 2
Experiment Is Over, The (Lowe), 270

Failure:
    facing, 188
    scapegoats for, 190
Faith, 267
Father figures, seeking, 190
Feminine side, *see* Inner female
Feng shui, 96
    personal, 191
Fifth *chakra*, 224–41
    blocked, effects of, 141
    Chakra Talk with, 236–37
    Chakra Tuning exercise to open
        and relax, 145

Money and work, 198–99
Monkey Mind, 245
Moss, Richard, 173
Movement and body esteem, 172
Mozart Effect, The (Campbell), 228
Music, 121–22, 231, 289
Music as element in creating a
ritual, 121–22

Naranjo, Claudio, 39
Nature and Other Mothers (Peterson),
97–98
Nature as sacred space, 93–95
New Age Journal, 192
Nudity, 172

Objects used in rituals, 122
Obsessions, 154
Omega Institute, 247
Open sky *chakra, see* Seventh *chakra*
Orgasm, 19, 70, 153–54
ecstasy of, *see* First *chakra*
in the seven *chakras*, 132–33
Osho, 8, 38, 194, 195, 196

Parents:
inner male and inner female
learned from, 50, 51
neglectful, 154
nonsexual physical affection
during child's puberty, 172
sexual development of children
and influence of, 150–51
wounds to the heart from, 207
Passionate Enlightenment (Shaw), 70,
265
Patriarchal God, 40, 41–42, 46, 245
Paul, 26
Performing Inside Out (Rock), 108
Peterson, Brenda, 97–98
Physical intelligence, 247
Picasso, Pablo, 247
Pituitary gland, 249
Pleasure, 18
balancing will and, 189–90
Pleasure Zone, The (Resnick), 18, 165
Power, 187–200
acting in accordance with your
values and, 188

balancing will and pleasure and,
189–90
confusing love with, 208
daring to risk and, 190
ecstasy of, *see* Third *chakra*
empowering others, 188–89
exercise for empowerment,
193–94
keys to empowerment, 188–89,
199–200
meeting life's challenges to
achieve, 186–87
practical empowerment, 191–93
responsibility and, 188, 190–91,
196–97
ritual of empowerment, 201–204
self-respect and, 187
work and, *see* Work
Practical empowerment, 191–93
Prana, 131
Prophet, The (Kahlil), 194
Psychological pain, 10–11
Puberty, 44–45, 51–52, 169–72
Pulse of Life, see Fourth *chakra*

Ray, Paul, 20
Relaxation, conscious, 178
Resnick, Stella, 18, 165
Resources for ecstatic moments,
289–93
Responsibility, taking, 188, 190–91,
196–97
Rimpoche, Nagpa, 269
Risk, daring to, 190
Rituals, 107–25
for beginning the day, 277–82
clearing your space, 98–99
compassionate, 111–13
completion, the power of
acceptance, 269–61
creating, 113–25
considering the participants,
115
ecstatic space, 119–21
energies and objects, 122
the four elements and, 123–24
general structure, 116
listening to your intuition
when, 114–15

as metaphor for life, 10, 70
obsessive behavior and, 154
religious and cultural repression
  of, 154
sexual development, 150–51
violence and, 42–44
Shakti and Shiva, myth of, 5–7, 132
Shaw, Miranda, 70, 265
Sheldrake, Rupert, 247
Shiva and Shakti, myth of, 5–7, 132
Silence:
  listening to, 234
  voice of your silent mind, 234–36
Sisgold, Steven, 44–45
Sixth *chakra*, 242–61
  awakening of, 247–49
  blocked, effects of, 141
  Chakra Talk with, 255–56
  Chakra Tuning exercise to open
    and relax, 145–46
  choice and, 253–54
  essence of, 245–46
  map of, 242–44
  nature of intelligence, 246–47
  preventing ourselves from seeing,
    inner criticism and, 250–53
  rituals for generating clarity and
    insight, 256–61
      completion, the power of
        acceptance, 259–61
      the power of insight, 258–59
      the witness, 256–58
  visualization, 249–50
SkyDancing Institutes, 9
SkyDancing Tantra: The Path to
  Bliss, 8–9
Sky Mind, 79, 245, 247, 254, 269
  defined, 20
Snake Time exercise, 174–75
Sogyel, Yeshe, 8
Solar plexus, *see* Third *chakra*
Song of Ecstasy, ritual of, 237–41
"Song of the Sky Loom," 93
Sounds, ritual, 121–22
Spaciousness, *chakra* of, *see* Seventh
  chakra
Spirit, 67, 68
  checking in with your, 82
  growth of your, 31–32

sexual energy and, 42
"Spiritual appearance," 191
Spiritual materialism, 84
Spoeri, Daniel, 101–102
Sri Yantra ceremony, 56–57
Start Where You Are (Chödrön), 215
Stress-related illnesses, 228
Structure of a ritual, 116
Substance abuse, 228
Suffering and awakening, 267–68
Support group, ecstatic, 287–88
Surrender, 214–16

Tantra:
  chakra system, *see* Chakra system
  essence of, 3–4
  mistaken beliefs about, 3
  origins of, 4–5
  as spiritual path to
    Enlightenment, 3
Tantra, The Supreme Understanding
  (Osho), 38
Tantras (scriptures), 7
Tantric Buddhism, 8
Tewa Pueblo Indians, 93
Theophan, the Recluse, 78
Thich Nhat Hanh, 94
Third *chakra*, 184–204
  blocked, effects of, 141
  Chakra Talk with, 200–201
  Chakra Tuning exercise to open
    and relax, 144–45
  essence of, 186–87
  map of, 184–86
  power and, *see* Power
  practicing a new skill to
    strengthen, 191–93
  ritual of empowerment, 201–204
Third eye center, *see* Sixth *chakra*
Throat center, *see* Fifth *chakra*
Timing of a ritual, 116
Trungpa, Chogyam, 84
Truthfulness, 228–29
  becoming aware of your words,
    231–32
  music and, 231
  telling your truth, 229–31

University of Munich, 10